Military Life

MILITARY LIFE

The Psychology of Serving in Peace and Combat

Volume 1: Military Performance

Edited by Thomas W. Britt, Carl Andrew Castro, and Amy B. Adler

JUL 0 7 2006

PRAEGER SECURITY INTERNATIONAL
Westport, Connecticut · London

Library of Congress Cataloging-in-Publication Data

Military life: the psychology of serving in peace and combat / edited
by Thomas W. Britt, Amy B. Adler, and Carl Andrew Castro.
  p. cm.
Includes bibliographical references and index.
ISBN 0-275-98300-5 ((set) : alk. paper)—ISBN 0-275-98301-3 ((v. 1) :
alk. paper)—ISBN 0-275-98302-1 ((v. 2) : alk. paper)—ISBN
0-275-98303-X ((v. 3) : alk. paper)—ISBN 0-275-98304-8 ((v. 4) :
alk. paper)
  1. Psychology, Military. 2. War—Psychological aspects. 3. Combat—
Psychological aspects. 4. Peace—Psychological aspects. 5. United
States—Army—Military life. 6. Combat disorders. 7. Post-traumatic
stress disorder. I. Britt, Thomas W., 1966– II. Adler, Amy B., 1963–
III. Castro, Carl Andrew.
  U22.3.M485 2006
  355.1'0973—dc22   2005017484

British Library Cataloguing in Publication Data is available.

Library of Congress Catalog Card Number: 2005017484
ISBN: 0–275–98300–5 (set)
  0–275–98301–3 (vol. 1)
  0–275–98302–1 (vol. 2)
  0–275–98303–X (vol. 3)
  0–275–98304–8 (vol. 4)

First published in 2006

Praeger Security International, 88 Post Road West, Westport, CT 06881
An imprint of Greenwood Publishing Group, Inc.
www.praeger.com

Printed in the United States of America

The paper used in this book complies with the
Permanent Paper Standard issued by the National
Information Standards Organization (Z39.48–1984).

10 9 8 7 6 5 4 3 2 1

In memory of my mother, Elizabeth ("Betty") Hannah Britt—TWB

To Colin, Corin, and Connor—CAC

To Gerald NMI Adler—ABA

CONTENTS

PREFACE

The psychological health and well-being of military personnel is important to the effectiveness of a nation's military, the adjustment of military families, and the integration of military personnel into the larger civilian community. A careful examination of the psychological issues confronting military personnel must necessarily be broad in scope and include a range of disciplines within psychology and the social sciences to provide a comprehensive assessment of the factors that affect the performance, health, and well-being of military personnel and their families. Such a multidisciplinary approach ensures researchers, military leaders, policy makers, and health care providers with a framework for understanding key factors relevant to modern military operations.

This four-volume set, *Military Life: The Psychology of Serving in Peace and Combat*, is organized around four defining fields of applied military psychology: military performance, operational stress, the military family, and military culture. Each volume begins with a riveting account of an individual's experience. These first-person accounts leave no doubt that the topics covered in this set are real, relevant, and deeply felt. The accounts are from the front line: the war and home front, as told by a veteran of Vietnam, the Gulf War, and Iraq; the precarious mental health of military personnel in a combat zone, as told by a military psychiatrist who served alongside Marines in combat; the anxiety and hope of military families on the front line of family separation, as told by an Army wife and mother of two service members turned military sociologist; and a psychologist with a front-row seat to observing the U.S. military's cultural shifts from Vietnam to the global war on terror. The stories told in these first-person accounts are stories of the authors' personal struggles with the challenges wrought by military conflict, incorporating the perspective that comes from their expertise, compassion, and humor. Three parts follow each of these first-person accounts. The chapters in each section are written by authorities selected for their knowledge in the field of military psychology, sociology, and other social sciences and shed light on the reality of life in the armed forces.

This set integrates the diverse influences on the well-being and performance of military personnel by developing separate volumes that address different facets of military psychology. By focusing on *Military Performance*, the first volume addresses the need to understand the determinants of how military personnel think, react, and behave on military operations. Several of the chapters in Volume 1 also have implications for the well-being of military personnel—such as the consequences of killing, how stress affects decision making, and how sleep loss affects operational effectiveness. Newly emerging issues in the armed forces are also discussed, including the role of terrorism, psychological operations, and advances in optimizing cognition on the battlefield. The impact of morale, the small military unit, and individual personality also provide insight into what influences the well-being and performance of military personnel.

The second volume in the set, *Operational Stress*, examines issues related to preparing military personnel to meet operational demands, details the psychological consequences of potentially traumatic events experienced on deployment, and reviews possible interventions that can support military personnel as they face such events. This volume includes descriptions of the experience of combat stress control teams on deployment, prisoners of war and the challenge of repatriation, the secular and spiritual role of military chaplains, the impact of military leaders, and the enduring role of small unit climate.

The third volume in the set takes an in-depth look at *The Military Family*. This comprehensive volume tackles the major stressors facing military families head on: family separation, family relocation, and dealing with the death of a service member. The particular issues confronting single parents, military children, and dual-military couples are also addressed. Another chapter addresses the balance between military work and family life. The problem of military family violence is the topic of the next chapter. A final chapter focuses on strategies for reducing military family conflict.

The fourth volume in the set, *Military Culture*, addresses the wider context of values, group diversity, and perceptions of the military, each of which has potential implications for the well-being and performance of military personnel. The role of values is explored in three chapters that address crosscultural values, the link between military values and performance, and the concept of courage. The next section explores specific groups within the military and the larger cultural trends that affect these groups: military reservists, women in the military, and the issue of gays serving in the armed forces. The final section of the volume examines how the military is perceived: the attitudes of service members about quality of life in the military, the role of the media in covering military operations, and the development of public attitudes toward the military and how these attitudes influence recruiting.

Producing this set required the effort and support of numerous people. In addition to thanking the authors for their outstanding chapters, we would like to thank Judy Pham, Hayley Brooks, Whitney Bryan, and Sarah Brink for their technical assistance in formatting the chapters. We would also like to thank Debbie Carvalko and the team at Praeger for providing valuable support and encouragement throughout the project. Finally, we appreciate the support provided by the Military Operational Medicine Directorate of the U.S. Army Medical Research and Materiel Command, Fort Detrick, Maryland. Note that the views expressed in this set are those of the authors and do not reflect the official policy or position of the Department of the Army, Department of Defense, or the U.S. Government.

We express our gratitude to the military personnel who have served their country in times of war and the families who have supported them. We hope this set in some small way can improve the lives of the next generation of service members and their families.

PART I

FIRST PERSON

CHAPTER 1

WHAT HAS BEFALLEN ME? THE PSYCHOLOGICAL AFTERMATH OF COMBAT

Spencer J. Campbell

The Journey Home

Nothing fixes a thing in memory, as the wish to forget it.

–Montaigne

When I was 29 years old, a decade after I'd left Vietnam, I started my educational pursuits at West Virginia State College. While talking with two of my classmates in the college cafeteria, the topic of the Vietnam War came up. I listened intently as my fellow students debated what they saw as the realities of war: what it would be like to kill someone, including women and children; what it would be like to see dead and severely mangled bodies; what it would be like to deal with someone trying to kill you; and what it would be like to return from a war and be considered a traitor for serving your country. I listened as they argued that given the human destruction that wars cause, no war could be called just or necessary.

I had stumbled upon two bright young men who were totally detached from what was absorbing my whole life and the lives of millions like me. Puzzled and somewhat excited that these bright young scholars were interested in the Vietnam War, I tried to explain to them what Vietnam was all about, at least from the perspective of someone who had been there. Then it gradually dawned on me how impossible my task really was. Even though I had experienced combat, I still had not yet fully processed my experiences in Vietnam. I became frightened as I realized that I did not know myself other than in a most superficial sense. Nor did I really know what the Vietnam War was all about. These realizations made me shiver. I felt keenly what philosopher Karl Jaspers calls the bottomlessness of the world. The image ran through my mind of these young men in their early teens sitting in front of the television watching the Vietnam War on the news with little or no understanding of what combat is like. As I thought about our discussion, I came to the conclusion that either my classmates' knowledge or my knowledge of the Vietnam War and the people who fought it was grotesquely inadequate. I left the cafeteria, twisted the throttle of my motorcycle and pulled onto the highway, my mind focused on the traffic, and once again my thoughts moved from the Vietnam War and focused on the here and now. As I shifted gears and increased my speed, however, the sound of the exhaust pipes and the vibration of my motorcycle reminded me of shooting an M60 caliber machine gun in combat, and strangely, I felt safe. It was a warm sunny evening, the sun was starting to slide behind the West Virginia mountains, the wind was in my face, the sound of my bike's pipes was music to my ears. Once again it was a great day to be alive, and Vietnam was in my past.

Yet when I arrived home, I could not get the discussion I had with my fellow classmates regarding the Vietnam War out of my mind. For the first time, I realized that I had developed false hopes that the objectives of the Vietnam War would be achieved. I saw that I had developed a false faith in my country. I remembered watching the news and observing the North Vietnamese enter Saigon in 1975 and capture the city. Yet only now was I flooded with emotion and understood for the first time how a Southern soldier from the Civil War must have felt in defeat. All my suffering and the suffering of millions like me had been for nothing. Did winning the battles and losing the war accomplish anything for me personally or for our nation? I understood that history would record the Vietnam War as a lost cause and few people, if any, would have an appreciation for the suffering and sacrifices of the soldiers who had served there.

Did my whirling thoughts result from the loss of my ability to hold on to my traditional perspective on Vietnam and war? I had served my country, done my duty. Yet the realization that the war had been for nothing shattered my view of how I had seen the war in Vietnam and my part in it, and I was now torn by internal conflict. I was amazed and embarrassed at my former simplemindedness and glad, despite everything, to finally be aware of it. I felt a rare sense of liberation from my discussion of war with these idealistic young men that was not present when I talked with my fellow Vietnam veterans about the war. I sat for hours and thought about Vietnam and me. From the discussion with my classmates, I developed a heightened self-awareness of my inability or unwillingness to process my combat experiences. Since that day, I have never again perceived myself as a victim of the Vietnam War.

The discussion with the two young nonveterans was so enlightening that for the first time I saw some simple and familiar things in a proper light. I realized that in my normal state I had been remote from the plainest and most simple truths. "It is quite in keeping with man's curious intellectual history," wrote Norman Angell, "that the simplest and most important questions are those he asks least often." The insights I developed from less than an hour of discussion with two young men changed the rest of my life. I no longer had the need to hold on to my naïve thoughts about war being just and necessary.

The passage of time put a new face on Vietnam and other life experiences. As I continued to gain insight about the impact of war on combat soldiers, I adapted to peacetime ways. As I became more able to emotionally process my combat experiences, I began to focus on becoming a mental health professional. While this transition was occurring in my life, it seemed scarcely credible that I had once felt curiously undressed without a pistol on my hip or a weapon in my hand. During this time in my life, I had trod softly on loose sod, unconsciously fearing booby traps designed to kill or maim the unwary soldier who stepped on them. As I attended graduate school with a new group of students that were only mildly interested in the Vietnam War, my memories of the war began to recede.

During my clinical social work internship at a Veterans Administration hospital, working with Vietnam veterans still struggling with the aftermath of the war, I came to believe that something was dreadfully wrong. When I realized how easily we forget those who suffered either in body and mind or who gave their lives before they understood their life's purpose, I wanted to rebel against the whole insane spectacle of human existence. I came to feel that, had I been a name on the Vietnam National Memorial, how little difference it would have made to anyone today. Then I began to ponder these questions: Are we, the survivors, changed at all in significant ways as a consequence of the Vietnam War? And if I am changed, how?

Answering only for myself, I must say, my life changed dramatically. Often in Vietnam I felt an utter dissociation from what had gone on before in my life: since my return from Vietnam in 1968, I have experienced an absence of continuity between those years and what I have become. As a clinical social worker and teacher, I strive to see my purpose and direction by combining my combat experiences with psychological theory of clinical practice. Yet to assimilate my intense war memories with the rest of my experience is sometimes difficult and even frightening. So why make the attempt? Why not continue to forget?

Those who have directly experienced combat and those who only write about it, watch it from a distance, or read about it, process the elements of war quite differently. Participants who do talk about their combat experiences are suspected of wanting to magnify their small egos. Many nonparticipants, on the other hand, want to read about war as fiction and so alter war so it is an art or entertainment, or view it simply as history. While books about war are admirable, they do not often make personal demands on the consumer to assimilate the emotional experience and build an emotional bridge across the abyss between peace and war. Consumers of war entertainment rarely ask why and what purpose war serves. Strangely, very few seem curious about the psychological and moral implications of man as warrior, husband, father, son, and citizen.

I am afraid to forget the sights, sounds, smells, and tastes of war. Time has taught me that life experiences we do not assimilate can rise up to haunt us in the present. Unless we remember and understand our past, we may become intellectual, emotional, and psychological refugees, in any sense, from our own country. Surely the menace of new wars and more frightful wars is not entirely unrelated to our failure to understand the wars we recently fought. If combat soldiers could gain some wisdom concerning what manner of men we are, and how war impacts who we are, and what we become as the result of our combat experience, then the experience of combat could have a more positive effect on our future.

I have come to the conclusion that it is exceedingly unlikely that I might ever be able to understand the why and wherefore of war. But my reflections do enable me to make sense of my own combat experiences. My deepest fear of my war years is that these happenings had no real purpose. Just as fate and chance enabled me to survive combat, my peacetime pursuits might well have little or no significance. This is a difficult conclusion that I am not willing to accept without a struggle. Indeed I cannot accept it at all except as a counsel of despair. At the end of every day in Vietnam, I examined the events of the day and attempted to determine if that day had significance for my future life, and if it didn't, then it could not possibly be worth the pain or cost of my experiencing it.

When I was in Vietnam, one of my fellow Marines predicted that I would be a lifer (professional 20-year Marine). To him, I had come to stand for the qualities of a Marine dedicated to the profession of war. At age nineteen, the idea both flattered me and insulted me, because I was seen as both a professional warrior and someone who followed all the rules. Yet as I reflected on my friend's observation of how he perceived me, I became impressed with its truth. I was becoming a proficient warrior, a thought which I would never have conceived on my own. As night fell over the northern mountains of South Vietnam, I sat alone in my foxhole and contemplated my friend's comments. At nineteen, I arrived at the conclusion that the worst that could be said about me was that I was becoming a Marine. Becoming a Marine meant to me that I was becoming a professional soldier, so used to combat that it had effected a deep change in my very nature.

The Demands of Combat

> Man has discovered death.
>
> —Yeats

In the mortal danger of daily combat, soldiers enter into a dazed condition that can best be described as physically exhausted and mentally drained. When in this state, they can be caught up in the fire of communal ecstasy (*esprit de corps*) and forget about the reality of death by losing their individuality and functioning with what I view as the ultimate commitment and application of professional soldiering.

When you observe soldiers who have fought continuous battles, the looks on their faces are frightening because their faces appear to be vacant and purposeless, devoid of all humanity. In this state, combat soldiers look as if they have pulled back the mystical curtain of immortality and stepped into the center of death and now have become controlled by a powerful, callous inhuman will. The mystery of death has been forever taken away from them because they have experienced it through its sights, sounds, smells, and tastes. For combat soldiers, meeting death no longer becomes an issue in life. Learning to experience the pleasures and emotions of life, however, can become a lifelong challenge.

The longer a soldier is in combat, the duller his mind becomes and the more he tires of war. In this physical, emotional, and spiritual condition, soldiers can begin to view death as a relief from what they are doing. Death can appear to weary combat soldiers as the rest and peaceful sleep they desire. I have observed exhausted combat soldiers sleeping while exposed to great danger. In Vietnam, I myself had moments where I viewed death as a kind of rest. With a few hours of rest, however, my thoughts were clear once again.

Combat is about fear and horror as well as boredom. For me, the fear of pain became a heavy burden to carry as I saw those around me being wounded, suffering, and dying. I believe that pain is something that is very real in our memories, but death is not. Most combat soldiers have witnessed enough gaping wounds and listened to the agonizing cries of the wounded often enough that they cannot consciously endure the thought of the same thing happening to them. I believe a soldier may only be dimly aware of dreading death, while he is very much aware of the fear of being painfully injured. Under these circumstances it has been my experience that fear dulls self-awareness as effectively as fatigue and routine, and both can have a lasting influence. Fear can even prey on a soldier's mind to the point where it makes him unfit for combat. Based on 20 months of combat in several theaters of war, my experience has been that the physical and psychological numbness combat soldiers experience is in fact directly related to the total environment of war.

After three months in Vietnam, I found it difficult to believe in any reality other than war. After six months in Vietnam, I often thought that when I returned to the United States I would like to go off and live like a hermit. It was difficult for me to face the prospect of returning home. I did not want to speak to anyone about my war years because I could not be as I was. I did not want to die, but I knew that I would never be able to live as I would have lived had I never gone to war. During my 395 days in Vietnam, my past had grown so distant and unreal that another way of life was hard to imagine. In Vietnam, I faced this realization about my life with piercing intensity.

After a battle, as we cleared the wounded and the dead from the battlefield, American, South Vietnamese, and Viet Cong, their bodies were scattered around in unusual and distorted postures. It was hard to imagine that they had been alive a few hours earlier. Witnessing tragic death is not human. Hardly anyone could look at the bodies without shuddering. Little imagination was required to see what death was like, for the eyes of those dead soldiers contained the image in painful clarity. The realities of combat I observed in Vietnam have been repeated on different battlefields and in every war. These experiences more often than not suffice to imprint on the minds of soldiers the indelible truth that death plays no favorites.

While in Vietnam, I felt the war was robbing me of any sense of identity and that I no longer possessed an ego or personal fate. I now know far better than I did then that there was another force much more determining of one's actions than simple need and desire. It was the emotional environment of warfare—more specifically, the atmosphere of violence. The threat to life and safety that the presence of the enemy created caused a consistent climate of emotional confusion set on a stage of violent actions and reactions. When you are at the front in a war shooting and killing, it is impossible to ignore, consciously or unconsciously, the fact that men are actively seeking to kill you in every way possible. Because of this reality, I immediately recognized that I was dependent on those around me. I also realized that my significance to those around me was based on the reality that I could use my weapon proficiently and thus was the means of security and survival for people I had never before met. This combination of danger and exposure is unequaled in forging links among people of unlike desire and temperament. These links are pragmatic and narrow but no less strong because of their accidental and general character.

Under these conditions, I found myself holding onto the memory of my civilian existence and stubbornly resisting the violence and irrational experiences going on around me. I wrote home to my parents and tried to hide the fact that I knew I was changing and could not return from the war as the same son that they had sent to war. For the first six months I convinced myself that Vietnam could not change me. Nevertheless, I eventually had to accept that once a soldier yields himself to the fortunes of war and has sought to kill and escape being killed and has survived, he is no longer what he was. The presence of others and the encompassing environment of threat and fear affect his moods and disposition. To survive, combat soldiers must surrender a measure of their personal will to the will of others and to a superior force. Most such men are transformed in some sense into fighters, whether they will it or not.

My combat experience taught me what it has always meant to be a soldier. Man, as a warrior, is only partly man, yet this experience is capable of transforming him as a person. When soldiers do not understand how and why their combat experiences have changed them, they are at risk of developing personality difficulties. Combat soldiers returning from war can repress their civilian habits of mind. When this occurs the soldier as fighter becomes a far different kind of person than he was as a coal miner, steelworker, mechanic, farmer, or clerk prior to combat.

Millions of men in our day—like the millions before them—have learned to live with the strange experiences of war. While the emotional environment of warfare has always been compelling, it has, in my opinion, drawn most of its participants from those who have been fascinated by the idea of war. From my combat experience I have learned that reasoning and reflection long after the war regarding one's actions and observations of war are part of that fascination. Before the fortuitous discussion with my fellow classmates, it was hard for me to think about war and to be alone with the thoughts of my combat experiences.

I believe that there are men who simply endure war, hating every moment. Though they may enjoy garrison life or military maneuvers, they experience nothing but distaste and horror for combat itself. I also have witnessed the reality that those who complain the most may not be immune to war's appeal. After 37 years of military service I have accepted the reality that soldiers complain as an inherited right and traditional duty, and few wish to admit to having a taste for war. Yet many men both hate and love combat. We know why we hate it. However, it is harder to know and harder to articulate why we love it. The newly experienced combat veteran may be eager to describe his emotions in combat, but it is the battle-hardened veterans for whom combat has offered the deeper appeals. For veterans from all wars, combat has been one of the greatest passages in their lives.

For those of us who have experienced war, what is its secret attraction? I believe it is the fear and exhilaration of war, as well as the camaraderie, that makes soldiers closer than brothers. Some combat veterans know one appeal of war and not the others, some experience all three, and of course, some may feel other appeals. These three are the realities of war for me. In my studies regarding the psychological impact of war, I have also found the three realities of my combat experience throughout the literature of war.

War is a spectacle—something to see—and its impact as such should never be underestimated. I believe that there is in all of us what the Bible calls "the lust of the eye." As human beings it is our nature to want to observe things. We do not want to miss something that is worth seeing. Our passion to witness events in most of us brings up our urge to participate in events that we are seeing. When you see people standing around looking at the scene of an accident on the interstate, you understand that the need to be a witness to catastrophic events is human nature. Our lust to be a witness to catastrophic events may in fact be a primal curiosity or impulse to observe the spectacular, the novel, and the unusual. As human beings we do not satisfy ourselves by observing the familiar, everyday things because they do not exhilarate us. Many a soldier has been drawn to military service to see what the confusion and murderous nature of war is like. This desire to experience war can be described as man's desire to escape the routines of civilian life and the restrictions of an unadventurous existence. We often become bored when our day-to-day existence does not provide us with the outlandish, exotic, and the strange. Although war has long periods of monotony and boredom, it also offers the opportunity to see other lands and other people.

Courage and Camaraderie

While trying to understand how courage worked in war, and how some men appeared to have it and others did not, I discovered that cowardice was in reality the other side of courage. To find courage in combat, cowardice is the vice and temptation that soldiers must overcome. Since I had no theoretical knowledge regarding the elusive psychology of courage and I had experienced fear, I focused on not giving in to my fears. I was committed to not failing those who depended on me. If fate gave me the opportunity to choose how I would die, then I was committed to making a difference for those who were with me. I did not want to be a coward or a hero. All I wanted was to have my misery and suffering make a difference, even if it was in only a small way. The only people I ever expected to acknowledge my existence were those with whom I served. I came to fully understand that life was a temporary gift, and when you die, you leave only what you have given to others.

The one genuine advantage I have found to combat is the experience of camaraderie that serving in a peacetime military can seldom offer. The feeling of acceptance and belonging with those you are serving with, I discovered, was the cementing force for our understanding of why we were fighting. Comradeship for me is the common goal that every individual is committed to, and this provides the motivation for combat soldiers to close with and destroy the enemy—that, and the simple desire to see the sun come up tomorrow.

While combat soldiers act in unison out of comradeship, they may also have other very different reasons for their actions. Their commitment to service can be based on keeping America free, their religious views, or a passionate political ideology. Yet combat taught me that these are only secondary goals. When days turn into months and months turn into years, soldiers begin experiencing psychological, emotional, and spiritual numbness. In this condition, you only fight for your fellow soldiers and to live another day. It's the loyalty to the group that is the essence of fighting morale. The commander who can preserve and strengthen group loyalty knows that all other psychological or physical factors are small in comparison. As a combat veteran, it is clear to me that feelings of loyalty are the result and not the cause of comradeship. Experience has taught me that soldiers may learn to be loyal out of fear or from national conviction even to those they dislike. However, such loyalty is rarely reliable with the great masses of men unless it has some cement in instinctive liking for their fellow soldiers and their feeling of belonging to the organization.

What Has Befallen Me?

Goodbye, darkness.

–William Manchester

Many years after the Vietnam War, I took one of my motorcycle trips to the mountains. I was caught in a rainstorm going up a hill on a small paved road I thought was in the middle of nowhere. The rain began to fall harder. As I approached the top of the hill, I saw a small country store. I parked my bike and entered. An elderly gentleman behind the counter said, "Welcome mister, you got here in time, the rain is startin' to fall harder." I purchased something to drink and we made small talk. I saw a picture of a young man in uniform and asked, "Who is that? The older gentleman replied, "It's me back in the big war." I replied, "I was in a war but it wasn't the big one. " For the next hour we shared war experiences. We discovered we had both been wounded. This man was remarkable. He had spent much more time in World War II than I had in Vietnam, but he appeared to be exceptionally at home in the world, as though he had sprung from nature herself and thought of himself as her authentic child. He appeared to be harmless, wise, and innocent. He dwelt here in the mountains, ready and willing to share a cup of coffee and chat with all who entered his establishment. After the rain stopped and I got on my bike to ride back down the mountain, I remembered a line I had read years earlier: "The little affairs of men here below are of great interest to God." Here was a man that war had not made sad or turned into a defeatist. His perspective about life had a kind of calmness. This man possessed and exemplified the kind of serenity I was searching for.

What had befallen me? My actions in the Vietnam War placed me in a state of intellectual, emotional, spiritual, and physical numbness. This process caused me to start rusting on the inside. Without internal peace there is no hope for a future, and a combat soldier's war will never end. How men process war focuses on man himself. War routinely reveals dimensions of human nature both above and below the acceptable standards for humanity. It is the struggle between these two dimensions that defines the man and the society.

PART II

HUMAN DIMENSIONS OF MILITARY OPERATIONS

CHAPTER 2

PSYCHOLOGICAL ASPECTS OF COMBAT

Robert K. Gifford

As American General John W. Vessey (1997, page xvii) wrote, "Peace is man's most fervent hope but war represents his surest experience." The experience of combat is often powerful and intense, yielding not only immediate psychological reactions, but also long-lasting effects that often shape the entire course of the participants' lives for years to come. Indeed, Hanson (2003) describes ways in which events that occur in battle have effects that extend beyond the lives of those who were there, and shape the thinking of families, friends, communities, and whole societies for decades and even centuries following the actual battle.

The essential purpose of warfare is to produce psychological and behavioral change, as von Clausewitz (1832/1982) pointed out many years ago. On both the tactical and strategic levels, most battles end when one side stops fighting, rather than with the annihilation of one side or another. Total destruction of an army or a population, while not unheard of, is not the norm. Wars end when the defeated side decides to fight no longer, not necessarily when the winning side wishes to declare victory. Thus, in this sense, war may be thought of as a primarily psychological event, with the killing, maiming, and destruction that occur in combat being means both to influence human behavior at the individual and group levels, and to force change in national policies and in the power relationship of nations or groups. Even the vast destructive power available with modern weapons has not changed that fact, as is shown by the debate over the use of precision-guided munitions versus less accurate, but more powerful weapons (Mandel, 2004), and

The views expressed in this chapter are those of the author and do not reflect the official policy or position of the U.S. Department of Defense or the U.S. Government.

the use of terminology such as "shock and awe" to describe the intent of an operational approach.

This chapter examines the psychological, social, and behavioral effects of combat and combat operations on those who have engaged in them. Much of what we know of the experience of combat is anecdotal or literary, since combat does not lend itself to careful scientific analysis. Western literature has a rich tradition of describing the experience of combat, going back at least as far as *The Iliad* and *The Odyssey*, and in more modern times, including memoirs from both world wars and Vietnam (e.g., Fussell, 1989; Graves, 1929/1968; Webb, 1978). While such accounts are highly individualistic, many suffer from biases of limited perspective and a desire for positive self-presentation, and certainly cannot qualify as scientific observation, they are the best accounts we have. Thus, they provide a starting point for examining the psychological effects of combat.

There are many different forms of combat, and thus there is no single psychological effect of combat. Instead, one finds many different experiences of combat, and many effects. The infantry soldier's experience is different from that of the pilot or aircrew member, the sailor, or the support soldier. All can be stressful, but the stresses may be very different. Of course, even within an occupational group, experiences will be different in terms of the type and level of intensity of combat experience. In any given operation, some support soldiers may see intense combat, while some infantry might see relatively little close fighting. So, in discussing the psychological effects of combat operations, we must remain aware that we are talking about a complex and varied phenomenon, not a single type of event or stressor.

Further, in addition to differences in experience based on military specialty or where one happens to be as the operation unfolds, cultural and historical factors will affect how people in different societies and in any given era experience war. Obviously, technological changes in how wars are fought—for example, the change from fighting with swords and spears to wars involving the use of long-range weapons, aircraft, and even weapons of mass destruction, have altered the experience of those who fight. Beyond that, there are variations over time and place in how societies view war in general, as well as any particular war, and these societal views of war can influence how combat affects participants. Hanson (2003, p. 213) notes that in Greece at the time of Socrates, the leading intellectuals and artists of society, including Socrates himself, were likely to serve as infantrymen and fight in the phalanx. War was seen as a natural state, and the concept of a "just war" centered on whether the war was conducted (a) according to the laws of the Greeks pertaining to treatment of prisoners, heralds, and civilians, and (b) in the true interests of the state. The moral question of killing the enemy in battle was not a particularly important issue.

In contrast to the culture of ancient Greece, or even our own more recent history (e.g., World War II), Shalev (2004) describes current Western societies as individual-oriented and risk-averse. Shalev further argues that this has implications for the psychological state of soldiers during and after combat. In societies such as the United States, where most people will not go into harm's way, the suffering, loss, and sacrifice of war are not shared by all, or even most. Shalev, citing his own research with

Israeli veterans of the war in Lebanon, points out that those who have served become a separate group within society, somewhat at odds with the rest of the culture, even if they have adjusted well on the whole. This group's experience is certainly very different from that of the ancient Greeks, who saw going to war as the normal thing for male citizens to do.

Despite the substantial differences in the experiences of soldiers at different times and in different places, one can look for commonalities of experience, while still noting that there is no one universal experience. The effects of combat operations on individuals are typically described in terms of negative psychological aftereffects. While this negative focus may oversimplify the experience of military operations, it is a good starting point for looking at the psychology of combat.

The Stress of Combat

In combat operations, soldiers are subject to many stressors, both from actual combat and from features of the deployment apart from direct combat. In its recent report from Operation Iraqi Freedom, the Army's Mental Health Advisory Team (MHAT) noted that combat stressors included: seeing destroyed homes and villages; seeing dead bodies or human remains; engaging in firefights or coming under small arms fire; engaging in hand-to-hand combat; being attacked or ambushed; personally knowing someone who was seriously injured or killed; being wounded or injured oneself; and being directly responsible for the death of an enemy combatant. The noncombat deployment stressors reported included uncertainty of redeployment date, length of the deployment, and lack of privacy or personal space (Department of the Army, 2004). The MHAT report found correlations between exposure to these stressors and various mental health problems measured by a mental health screen given as part of their survey. The report further demonstrated that some of the stressors resulted in real health issues with potential consequences, not just complaints from soldiers serving under difficult and dangerous conditions. For example, among combat stressors—being attacked or ambushed, engaging in a firefight, and duration in a hostile area—all were associated with screening positive for depression, anxiety, or posttraumatic stress. Among the deployment stressors, uncertain redeployment date was associated with screening positively for the same conditions.

The stress of intense combat, especially close combat or exposure to highly lethal weapons, has a particularly dramatic effect. As noted above, however, there are many other sources of stress in combat operations, some of which also occur in training, peacekeeping, or other noncombat deployments. For example, when not in actual combat, in many situations, soldiers will feel vulnerable to imminent attack and may have to cope with this stressor for months on end. Soldiers serving in combat typically also endure separation from family and friends, and may find, on returning from combat, that many things have changed at home in their absence. In addition, during their operational deployments, soldiers often will have endured exposure to environmental extremes, dehydration, nutritional deficits, sleep deprivation, primitive living conditions, and—in recent years, at least—exposure to toxic chemicals.

Occupational stressors similar to those found in civilian workplaces—for example, lack of a sense of purpose and low unit cohesion—can also affect soldiers in combat zones (Teague, McNally, & Litz, 2004). Because of these other sorts of stressors, operations that do not result in direct combat, such as peacekeeping operations, long training deployments, or disaster relief, may have some psychological effects similar to those experienced by soldiers in combat.

Combat Stress Reactions

Stress can lead to psychological breakdown in combat operations, and there is an extensive literature on combat stress reactions. Ingraham and Manning (1981) note that the appearance of psychiatric battle casualties in large numbers was first observed in the twentieth century. However, references to psychological reactions to war can be found in the Bible, the works of Homer (see Shay, 1994, 2002), and in Shakespeare's plays. Looking at more recent history, Hyams, Wignall, and Roswell (1996) reviewed English literature on war-related illnesses since 1863 and found similar clusters of symptoms among veterans of several wars from the American Civil War through the Persian Gulf War. Substantial numbers of veterans of each war exhibited syndromes that included both physiological and psychological symptoms. The physiological symptoms typically have had many causes, but were often associated with psychological stress, such as fatigue, sleep disturbance, headache, or impaired memory and concentration. These war syndromes have been given different names in different eras, but the reported symptoms appear to be similar. Thus, it appears that combat stress reactions and postwar syndromes have probably been with us for many years, even though, as Ingraham and Manning describe, factors such as the lethality of modern weapons and the rapid pace of maneuver may make modern combat even more likely to produce stress reactions.

The literature on combat stress focuses primarily on three main issues: the frequency of combat stress reactions, factors that increase the likelihood of combat stress reactions, and mitigating/protective factors. Combat stress reactions include both psychological breakdown during or shortly after combat and longer term effects such as posttraumatic stress disorder (PTSD) or reactions to combat experience that manifest themselves after combat is over, often after return from the combat zone.

Studies of psychological breakdown in battle give varying estimates of the prevalence of combat stress reactions, but all show that psychological breakdown is a significant source of casualties in war. In one study of American army forces in World War II, Glass (1973) reports combat stress reaction rates as ranging between 10 percent and 48 percent of wounded in action. Brill, Beebe, and Lowenstein (1953) report psychiatric combat stress reactions in 28.5 percent of the force in American combat divisions in World War II. Whether one takes the low estimate of 10 percent, the high estimate of 48 percent, or the middle number of 28.5 percent, it is clear that a substantial number of individuals exposed to prolonged combat suffered psychological reactions. It is probably not fruitful to attempt to develop a precise estimate of the prevalence of combat stress reactions, as different forces in different wars are likely to have varying rates. Further, as Noy (1991) notes, combat stress reaction estimates are confounded by lack of a common criterion for defining a stress casualty among the various studies, as well as by underestimation due to failure to include delayed reactions and combat stress reactions that appear in the statistics as other phenomena—for example, physical illnesses or discipline problems. For these reasons, any attempt to estimate a precise rate of combat stress reactions, or a range of rates linked to type of combat, is probably beyond the current state of the art.

The frequency of combat stress reactions rises with the duration and intensity of combat. However, just what duration of combat or level of intensity is required to produce unusually large numbers of combat stress reactions is hard to pin down. There is no set minimum level of exposure to combat, in terms of either duration or intensity, before combat stress reactions start to appear in substantial numbers. The U.S.'s experience in World War II and Korea suggested that 23 to 30 days in direct combat were required before a unit started showing large numbers of psychiatric casualties (Ingraham & Manning, 1981). However, in the Yom Kippur War of 1973, Israel encountered substantial numbers of combat stress reactions within 24 hours of intense combat, which Ingraham and Manning attributed to the lethality of modern weaponry and the high pace of warfare. Factors relating to the soldiers' sense of control also appear to play a role: rates are lower among a force that is winning, or holding the initiative in combat, than among a force that is retreating or facing imminent defeat. Being subjected to indirect fire, as from artillery or aircraft, also raises the rates (Belenky, Noy, & Solomon, 1987).

Apart from these general factors, clearly there are individual differences in reactions to combat. Most soldiers do not become psychiatric casualties, and soldiers who serve in the same units in the same operations vary in their reactions. We do not know what causes one soldier to have a combat stress reaction while another who has been through similar combat does not. Logically, even if any person might become a combat stress casualty if in combat of sufficient intensity and duration, we might expect that some preexisting personality trait or disposition makes certain people more likely to become combat stress casualties sooner than others. No single predisposing factor at the individual level, however, has yet been identified. Solomon, Noy, and Bar-On (1986) did find individual differences in likelihood of becoming psychiatric casualties among Israeli soldiers in the 1982 conflict in Lebanon. Those over age 26 who were reservists with a low level of education, low military rank, and a low score on a combat suitability composite measure (computed at time of induction) were found to be most vulnerable. In addition, Noy (1991) also found that personality factors may influence recovery after suffering a combat stress reaction. Bartone (1996) has presented evidence that personality hardiness, a cognitive style that influences the way in which stressful circumstances are processed mentally and integrated into a person's life experience (Kobasa, 1979), may serve as a buffer against stress in noncombat situations, and those results might well extend to combat situations. Such findings provide promising leads for determining individual difference in susceptibility to psychological breakdown in combat, and might in time lead to predictive models. However, at present, the best summary of our knowledge is that while there is evidence for individual differences, we cannot say with any great degree of certainty who is going to break down and when.

Social and Group Factors in Combat Stress

Psychological reactions to combat are, of course, affected by social and interpersonal factors. The importance of social factors has been noted by those interested in military affairs for centuries. Manning and Ingraham (1987) cite Onasander's first century A.D. writings on the importance of comradeship in the army and of commanders' considering relationships in positioning soldiers in combat formations. Centuries later, Ardant DuPicq (1846, p. 110) wrote, "Four brave men who do not know each other will not dare to attack a lion. Four less brave, but knowing each other well, sure of their reliability and consequently of mutual aid, will attack resolutely." Von Clausewitz's (1832/1982, p. 252) comments comparing the value of material factors to moral factors are classic: "We might say that the physical [factors] are almost no more than the wooden handle, whilst the moral are the noble metal, the real bright-polished weapon."

Studies done in the aftermath of World War II (Shils & Janowitz, 1948; Weinstein, 1947) highlighted the importance of morale, cohesion, and *esprit de corps* as buffers against psychological breakdown in combat operations. These terms represent overlapping concepts that have been defined differently by various authors. Manning (1991) defined morale as being demonstrated by the enthusiasm and persistence with which a member of a group engages in the prescribed activities of that group. Morale is differentiated from happiness or mood by the link to group goals (see Britt and Dickinson, this volume). Cohesion and *esprit de corps* both contribute to morale. Cohesion is generally defined as bonding of people to each other in primary groups that have face-to-face interaction (see Seibold, this volume). Johns (1984, p. 9) defines cohesion, for military purposes, as "the bonding together of members of an organization/unit in such a way as to sustain their will and commitment to each other, their unit, and the mission." *Esprit*, a term that is even harder to define precisely, refers to soldiers' sense of identification with larger groups such as their divisions, or their branch of service, or with the nation or cause they serve (Manning, 1991). Morale, cohesion, and *esprit* are related to other factors, such as confidence in the caring and tactical proficiency of leaders, quality of training, and previous mission or training success, all of which serve to build confidence as well as cohesion.

Although there is general agreement on the importance of social factors, the questions of exactly what the social factors are, how they should be measured, how they interact, and the mechanisms by which they operate as buffers against the stresses of combat (and as performance enhancers), have been problematic. Most studies showing the effects of social factors quantitatively have been done in training or garrison settings (e.g., Bliese & Halverson, 1996; Manning & Ingraham, 1987; Seibold & Kelly, 1988; Tziner & Vardi, 1983). Most published studies of soldiers in combat operations over the years have been more qualitative and anecdotal than quantitative (e.g., Gifford, 1995; Gifford, Marlowe, Wright, Barton, & Martin 1992; Martin, Vaitkus, Marlowe, Bartone, Gifford, & Wright, 1992; Shils & Janowitz, 1948).

There are exceptions, however, and there has been a trend in recent years toward more quantitative research in operational theaters. Belenky, Noy, and Solomon (1987) describe the results of studies of Israeli soldiers in that nation's 1973 and 1983 wars, demonstrating the importance of morale, cohesion, and personal and family stability in reducing the incidence of combat stress casualties. Studies conducted by the Walter Reed Army Institute of Research during Operation Uphold Democracy in Haiti in 1994 featured surveys of soldiers in theater, with close to real-time data analysis, and demonstrated that leadership climate and unit cohesion serve as buffers against the deleterious effects of stress (Halverson, Bliese, Moore, & Castro, 1995).

The report of the Army's MHAT in Operation Iraqi Freedom (OIF) extends this trend toward collecting quantitative data in real time during combat operations (Department of the Army, 2004). In July of 2003, an apparent— and highly publicized—increase in the suicide rate among American soldiers serving in OIF caused concern as to whether mental health support in the theater was adequate. In addition, there had been an increase in behavioral health patient evacuation flow through Landstuhl Regional Medical Center in Germany, as well as press reports of stress among soldiers in theater. In response, the surgeon general of the Army and the Army deputy chief of staff for personnel chartered a multidisciplinary Mental Health Advisory Team (MHAT). Over the next few months, MHAT members traveled to Iraq, Kuwait, Landstuhl, and sites within the United States to study behavioral health issues associated with OIF. The MHAT consulted with medical commanders, line leaders, behavioral health units and headquarters, and evacuation chain support personnel. They also collected data from soldiers serving in OIF, using both interviews and surveys. As noted above in discussing the stressors on soldiers in combat operations, the MHAT collected soldiers' reports of exposure to various stressors, and was able to link these stressors to mental health outcomes. The methodologies employed by the MHAT, which included morale and cohesion measures, offer great potential for increasing our understanding of the complex relationships among social/group factors, individual dispositions, and psychological responses to combat and combat operations.

Other Negative Psychological Effects of Combat

There are other potential adverse psychological effects of combat that may not be labeled as combat stress reactions. The United States involvement in Vietnam is often characterized as having had a low rate of combat stress reactions, but there were substance abuse problems, disciplinary problems including attacks on leaders ("fragging"), and evacuations for psychoses that do not appear in the statistics as combat stress reactions (Jones & Johnson, 1975). It is possible that such events were expressions of the stresses of war, even though this cannot be proven at this point. Some psychological effects of combat do not appear until well after return from combat.

Noy (1991) argues that combat stress reactions must be viewed as having an immediate stage lasting hours to days, an acute stage lasting weeks to months, and a chronic stage that may not begin until several months after the combat exposure. The chronic stage may include a variety of psychiatric disorders or problems of family and occupational readjustment.

Friedman (2004) cited a prevalence of current posttraumatic stress disorder (PTSD) of 15 percent among male Vietnam veterans and 8 percent among female veterans when measured in the National Vietnam Veterans Readjustment Study 10 to 20 years after their service. The lifetime prevalence of PTSD in that sample was considerably higher: 30 percent among male veterans and 25 percent among female veterans. Hoge et al. (2004) surveyed Army and Marine units who had served in Iraq or Afghanistan, and found PTSD rates of 12.9 percent and 12.2 percent in the units that had served in Iraq, and 6.2 percent for both units among those who had served in Afghanistan, with the difference in rates between the two combat zones likely attributable to the greater likelihood of the Iraq veterans in the sample having been in intense combat.

Friedman noted that PTSD rates might climb in the months after soldiers return home from war. In a study of Gulf War veterans, the prevalence of PTSD was 3 percent among male veterans and 16 percent among female veterans when they were surveyed at the time of their return to Fort Devens, Massachusetts (Wolfe, Erickson, Sharkansky, King, & King 1999). In a follow-up assessment of the same units two years later, the prevalence had increased to 8 percent among males and 16 percent among females. Thus, Friedman speculates that the PTSD rates among the veterans in Hoge et al.'s study might increase as time goes on.

Gaps in Current Knowledge

Long-term Consequences

The possibility that PTSD rates increase, at least for a while, after return from combat operations, highlights a major gap in our knowledge of the psychological impact of war on those who have participated. There are very few long-term studies of veterans.

One notable exception to this generalization is found in the work of Elder, Shanahan and Clipp (1997), who followed a group of U.S. World War II veterans who had been enrolled in a prospective study before the war started. They found that those who had served in combat were more likely to suffer physical decline or death in the fifteen years after the war. Combat veterans were also more than twice as likely to describe themselves as heavy or problem drinkers. These health and mortality findings were restricted to the first fifteen years after the war. After that period no differences were found in health status, and combat veterans were similar to others in their marital and occupational lives. The group Elder et al. studied was, however, not representative of the general population, being relatively more intelligent and highly educated. Thus, we cannot say that their life course is typical of all U.S. World

War II veterans, let alone veterans of other wars and from other nations. Nevertheless, this study stands out for having premilitary data and following the population for many years after combat service.

Positive Consequences of Combat Service

Another gap in our knowledge is that we know a lot more about the adverse psychological effects of combat service, and especially of clinical syndromes, than we do about the positive effects and personal growth as a result of combat service. As Antonovsky and Bernstein (1986) point out, the research emphasis on clinical populations, or on those who have suffered negative consequences resulting from combat zone service, may give a distorted picture. Antonovsky and Bernstein note that even when research includes successful copers, the emphasis generally is on absence of pathology rather than on what strengths might have enabled these individuals to cope. Given that the studies cited above all found that the majority of soldiers in their samples did *not* exhibit extensive psychopathology, a complete understanding of the psychological effects of combat will require that we learn more about individuals who return from combat operations and somehow process the experience in a manner that allows them to lead healthy, productive lives.

Despite the overall emphasis on clinical populations and negative outcomes, there are studies in the literature that show positive outcomes of military deployments. Britt, Adler, and Bartone (2001) studied psychological outcomes of the deployment of U.S. forces to the former Yugoslavia on a peace enforcement mission. They found that soldiers who scored higher on a measure of personality hardiness were more likely to find meaning in their work while on deployment, and that this sense of meaningful engagement in turn was associated with more reported positive benefits from the experience, such as feeling more aware of problems in the world, having a greater appreciation for the importance of their families, or feeling more able to cope with stress in their lives. Not surprisingly, they also found that where in theater soldiers were assigned and the specific jobs they had were related to their opportunity to have enriching experiences that led to positive outcomes. Some soldiers, by the nature of their jobs, spent most of their time in base camps and were less likely to see the positive results of the operation than soldiers who got out into the countryside and saw both the devastation from the war and the improved quality of life that resulted from the peace enforcement operation.

Newby, McCarroll, Ursano, Fan, Shigemura, and Tucker-Harris (2004) surveyed soldiers who had deployed to Bosnia on a more recent peacekeeping mission. They found that 77 percent reported at least one positive consequence of their service, with 63 percent reporting a negative consequence and 47 percent reporting both. Among the reported positive consequences, ones that might be expected to help them process their deployment experiences in a positive fashion included the reports that the deployment gave them opportunity for self-improvement or time to think, that it improved their relationships with spouses or significant others, that they helped the people of Bosnia, experienced travel to another culture, and saw how good they have it in the United States. Although the studies by Britt et al. (2001) and Newby et al. looked at peacekeeping deployments, there is evidence in the Operation Iraqi Freedom MHAT report to suggest parallel positive effects in combat deployments: 85 percent of the MHAT sample reported satisfaction in encountering grateful civilians and 80 percent in having demonstrated success of their training (Department of the Army, 2004). These findings suggest that future deployment research should include measures to detect positive outcomes as well as negative.

Psychological Consequences of Killing

Perhaps the greatest lack in our understanding of the psychological effects of combat, however, is the effect of killing on the soldiers who do it. Some recent authors have suggested that killing may be the most severe stress of combat in terms of the aftereffects it produces (Grossman, 1996, 2001; MacNair, 2002). The concept that killing is stressful is one that most would accept, and is supported in both literature and anecdotal reports (e.g., Marshall, 1947).

By asserting that killing may be the most severe stressor, however, more even than fear for one's own life, authors such as Grossman and MacNair raise questions that require further examination and research, and perhaps, new conceptual frameworks. Current thinking regarding PTSD and other deleterious effects of stress tends to be oriented toward things that have happened *to* a person as the major cause of debilitating stress, as opposed to viewing actions the person has taken as sources of traumatic stress. The definition of PTSD lists as an essential criterion that

> The person has been exposed to a traumatic event in which both of the following were present: (1) the person experienced, witnessed, or was confronted with an event or events that involved actual or threatened death or serious injury, or a threat to the physical integrity of self or others, and (2) the person's response involved intense fear, helplessness, or horror. (American Psychiatric Association, 1994, pp. 427–428)

This definition implies that the person suffering from the disorder has been a victim in the sense of suffering because of something that happened to him or her, or something that has been witnessed, and does not emphasize psychological suffering as a result of one's own actions.

MacNair (2002) sees this as too limited conceptually, and argues that we need to expand this view of PTSD and pay special attention to what people have done, rather than to what has been done to them, with particular emphasis on killing as an act that can lead to distress for the perpetrator. To contrast this with the traditional view of PTSD, MacNair advanced the concept of perpetration-induced traumatic stress (PITS). Analyzing data from the National Vietnam Veterans' Readjustment Study (NVVRS; see Kulka et al., 1990a, 1990b), MacNair found that veterans who reported that they had killed someone in Vietnam, or thought they might have, reported higher rates of symptoms characteristic of PTSD than those who did not believe they had killed anyone. This finding was not an artifact of intensity of combat experience, since the analysis was based on samples controlled for scores on self-report combat exposure scales also included in the NVVRS.

Of course, since the NVVRS survey was retrospective and the data are correlational, MacNair's analysis does not absolutely prove causality, even though the notion of causality is logical. Wessely et al. (2003) have shown that recall of combat zone hazards changes over time, and that both the nature of the changes and their correlation with various health symptoms appear to vary from conflict to conflict. Thus, one must be cautious in asserting that belief in the probability that having killed caused later symptoms, as, in theory, the reverse could be the case. Nevertheless, in the absence of contrary evidence, MacNair's findings make a strong case that having killed in combat leads to increased vulnerability to PTSD symptoms. The MHAT report supports MacNair's thesis about the stress of killing, in that soldiers who reported on the MHAT survey that they believed they had killed also reported more symptoms. While the MHAT survey was also retrospective, the time difference was a matter of weeks, as opposed to years, for the NVVRS. The MHAT data do not support MacNair's contention that killing is the leading stressor, since although killing, or belief in having killed, predicted symptoms in the weeks following combat, they also found that shortly after combat, the best predictor of symptoms was how often soldiers had believed themselves to be in danger of being seriously wounded or killed. However, the time frames of the MHAT and NVVRS studies are very different, so one cannot use these data sets to resolve the issue of whether belief that one has killed is more important in producing PTSD than belief that one might be killed or maimed. Similarly, whether PITS is really a separate diagnostic category from PTSD or is better considered as a form of PTSD remains to be seen, but clearly the psychological consequences of killing need to be investigated further.

There has been relatively little official interest on the part of the U.S. military in studying the psychology of killing (Baum, 2004). The question of whether killing is the single most potent stressor in combat is open to debate and is probably not resolvable on the basis of current evidence, as noted above. However, as a practical matter, the answer to the question of where killing is in the rank ordering of stressors may not be important. Since both evidence and common sense lead to the conclusion that killing can lead to profound and long-lasting psychological aftereffects, there are important questions that should be answered.

Modern sensibility, at least in Western culture, makes us feel that killing must be highly stressful. After all, most people in our society find killing abhorrent, so we want to believe that normal people would find the act of killing traumatic. While there certainly is truth to that, as the evidence discussed above shows, the issue is much more complex, and poses a number of questions for which current research provides no good scientific answers. Indeed, current science does not even tell us what it is about killing that is stressful for people. It is all too easy to overlook that question and take it for granted that normal people ought to find killing stressful. In fact, while this position is appealing from a moral point of view, we do not have any clear scientific evidence about why it might be so. Since, not that long ago, executions were public entertainment, and more recently, murders of hostages in Iraq have drawn many viewers to Web sites, we can conclude that many people do not find the observation of death to be a source of distress in the absence of other factors. So, logically, we should expect that the effects of killing in combat stem from feeling responsible for death, over and above whatever effects may come from seeing death or dead bodies *in situ*. However, we do not have good evidence as to why, or if, being a perpetrator is essential to developing stress symptoms after killing.

We do know that there are great individual differences among people in how stressful they find killing, but we do not know what underlies those differences. At one extreme, there are a number of people, including serial murderers and suicidal terrorists, for whom killing is actually attractive. Labeling them as aberrant or sociopathic, while satisfying our moral sense that killing is wrong, does absolutely nothing to inform us as to why they want to kill. Indeed, as these two examples suggest, there probably are very different reasons for finding killing satisfying. At the other extreme, there are people who, as best as we can judge, would never kill under any circumstances, even in self-defense. Between these extremes, we have a range of psychological reactions to having killed. While belief in having killed was correlated with later symptoms in both the NVVRS and MHAT samples, not everyone who had killed showed symptoms later on. The data do not tell us whether those who suffer few or moderate symptoms are less affected by the act of killing or whether they are more resilient and capable of dealing with the stress in a fashion that does not lead to later symptoms.

In addition to individual differences, the circumstances of the killing almost certainly make a difference in how perpetrators react. Two obvious issues are how directly responsible the perpetrator feels and whether or not the victim is visible to the one doing the killing. A person who witnesses death on the battlefield, but does not believe he or she caused the death, would be expected to be less likely to suffer PTSD symptoms afterward than a soldier who can be certain of having killed. One would expect that infantry who kill people with small arms at close range might suffer more aftereffects of killing than artillerymen or aircrew members who might never see their victims, even if all felt equally responsible for causing deaths. However, we do not have systematic investigations to verify this, or other aspects of the context in which killing occurs that might affect the long-term adjustment of those who have killed, such as the extent to which the perpetrator identifies with the victim.

Unfortunately, while it is easy to call for more research into the psychology of killing, actually performing such research will prove difficult. Research into killing is necessarily retrospective, but even retrospective research poses ethical issues that will be hard to overcome. Given the evidence that killing is likely to lead to psychiatric symptoms, any questioning of the perpetrators would have to be done in a manner that does not strip away their psychological defenses and exacerbate symptoms. It would be hard to accomplish meaningful research without highlighting issues such as feelings of responsibility, feelings stemming from direct observation of the victim, and feelings of identification with the victim, all of which might increase the psychological distress of the perpetrator. Thus, designing ethical research into the effect of the context in which killing occurs on the psychological aftermath will be a challenge, and one might expect that studies in that area would be met with considerable skepticism by institutional review boards. It may well be that anecdotal reports will be the state of the art for evidence regarding killing for some time to come.

Future Directions for the Study of the Psychology of Combat

Despite all that has been learned about the psychological effects of warfare over the centuries, the phenomenon remains complex and difficult to understand. Combat exacts a psychological toll as well as a physical one. Although we have learned much about the positive and negative psychological consequences of serving in war, there is even more that we do not understand. Resource constraints, combined with the inherent difficulty of studying war, mean that research priorities will have to be set. The paragraphs above highlight three critical areas for future research: Long-term consequences for those who have been in combat, positive and growth-enhancing reactions to having been in combat, and psychological reactions to having killed other people. Each of these areas is challenging, and especially in the case of longitudinal studies, potentially expensive to investigate. Nevertheless, expanded knowledge in these areas is essential to complete our understanding of what it means to have been in combat. However much we might wish for an end to wars, and thus hope that we will be denied the opportunity to increase our knowledge base, it seems certain that for the foreseeable future, there will be all too many wars. The obligation of the researcher is to use the unfortunate opportunity to learn from these wars and thus increase understanding of how the extreme conditions encountered in war affect the human beings who are participants in this most terrible, but most persistent of human endeavors.

References

American Psychiatric Association (1994). *Diagnostic and statistical manual of mental disorders, 4th ed. (DSM-IV)*. Washington, DC: American Psychiatric Association.

Antonovsky, A. & Bernstein, J. (1986). Pathogenesis and salutogenesis in war and other crises: Who studies the successful coper? In N. A. Milgram (Ed.), *Stress and coping in time of war: Generalizations from the Israeli experience* (pp. 52–65). New York: Brunner/Mazel.

Bartone, P. T. (1996). Family notification and survivor assistance: Thinking the unthinkable. In R. J. Ursano & A. E. Norwood (Eds.), *Emotional aftermath of the Persian Gulf War: Veterans, families, communities, and Nations* (pp. 315–350). Washington, DC: American Psychiatric Press.

Baum, D. (2004, July 12 & 29). The price of valor. *New Yorker*, 44–52.

Belenky, G., Noy, S., & Solomon, Z. (1987). Battle stress, morale, cohesion, combat effectiveness, heroism, and psychiatric casualties: The Israeli experience. In G. Belenky (Ed.), *Contemporary studies in combat psychiatry* (pp. 11–20). Westport, CT: Greenwood Press.

Bliese, P. D., & Halverson, R. R. (1996). Individual and nomothetic models of job stress: An examination of work hours, cohesion, and well-being. *Journal of Applied Social Psychology, 26*(13), 1171–1189.

Brill, N. Q., Beebe, G. W., & Lowenstein, R. L. (1953). Age and resistance to military stress. *U. S. Armed Forces Medical Journal, 4*(9), 1247–1266.

Britt, T. W., Adler, A. B., & Bartone, P. T. (2001). Deriving benefits from stressful events: The role of engagement in meaningful work and hardiness. *Journal of Occupational Health Psychology, 6*(1), 53–63.

Clausewitz, K. von. (1982). *On war.* (A. Rapoport, Ed.). London: Penguin. (Original German edition published 1832)

Department of the Army, Mental Health Advisory Team (MHAT) report [38 pages] (2003, December 16). Retrieved March 16, 2004, from http://www.armymedicine.army.mil/news/mhat/mhat_report.pdf

DuPicq, A. (1846). *Battle Studies* (reprint, Harrisburg, PA: Stackpole Books, 1958).

Elder, G. H., Shanahan, M. J., & Clipp, E. C. (1997). Linking combat and physical health: The legacy of World War II in men's lives. *American Journal of Psychiatry, 154*(3), 330–336.

Friedman, M. J. (2004). Acknowledging the psychiatric cost of war. *The New England Journal of Medicine, 351*(1), 75–77.

Fussell, P. (1989). *Wartime: Understanding and behavior in the Second World War.* New York: Oxford University Press.

Gifford, R. K. (1995, Summer). Military field research in Somalia: Findings and implications for military psychology. *The Military Psychologist.*

Gifford, R. K., Marlowe, D. H., Wright, K. M., Bartone, P. T., & Martin, J. A. (1992, November/December). Unit cohesion in Operations Desert Shield/Storm. *Journal of the U .S. Army Medical Department*, PB 8–92–11/12, 11–13.

Glass, A. J. (1973). *Neuropsychiatry in World War II: Vol. II. Overseas theaters.* Office of the Surgeon General, Department of the Army, U.S. Army, Washington, DC.

Graves, R. (1968). *Goodbye to all that: An autobiography.* New York: Anchor Books. (Originally published 1929)

Grossman, D. (1996). *On killing: The psychological cost of learning to kill in war and society.* New York: Little, Brown.

Grossman, D. (2001). On killing II: The psychological cost of learning to kill. *International Journal of Emergency Mental Health, 3*(3), 137–144.

Halverson, R. R., Bliese, P. D., Moore, R. E., & Castro, C. A. (1995). *Psychological well-being and physical health of soldiers deployed for Operation Uphold Democracy: A summary of human dimensions research in Haiti.* Alexandria, VA: Defense Technical Information Center (DTIC: # ADA298125).

Hanson, V. (2003). *Ripples of battle: How wars of the past still determine how we fight, how we live, and how we think.* New York: Doubleday.

Hoge, C. W., Castro, C. A., Messer, S. C., McGurk, D., Cotting, D. I., and Koffman, R. L.(2004). Combat duty in Iraq and Afghanistan, mental health problems, and barriers to care. *The New England Journal of Medicine, 351*(1), 13–22.

Hyams, K. C., Wignall, F. S., & Roswell, R. (1996). War syndromes and their evaluation: From the U.S. Civil War to the Persian Gulf War. *Annals of Internal Medicine, 125*(5), 398–403.

Ingraham, L. H., & Manning, F. J. (1981). Cohesion: Who needs it, what is it, and how do we get it to them? *Military Review, LXI*(6), 2–12.

Johns, J. H. (1984). *Cohesion in the U.S. military.* Washington, DC: National Defense University Press.

Jones, F. D., & Johnson, A. W. (1975). Medical and psychiatric treatment, policy, and practice in Vietnam. *Journal of Social Issues, 31*(4), 49–65.

Kobasa, S. C. (1979). Stressful life events, personality, and health: An inquiry into hardiness. *Journal of Personality and Social Psychology, 37*, 1–11.

Kulka, R. A., Schlenger, W. E., Fairbank, J. A., Hough, R. L., Jordan, B. K., Marmar, C. R., & Weiss, D. S. (1990a). *The National Vietnam Veterans Readjustment Study: Tables of findings and technical appendices.* New York: Brunner/Mazel.

Kulka, R. A., Schlenger, W. E., Fairbank, J. A., Hough, R. L., Jordan, B. K., Marmar, C. R., & Weiss, D. S.(1990b). *Trauma and the Vietnam War generation: Report of findings from the National Vietnam Veterans Readjustment Study.* New York: Brunner/Mazel.

MacNair, R. M. (2002). *Perpetration-induced traumatic stress.* Westport, CT: Greenwood Press.

Mandel, R. (2004). The wartime utility of precision versus brute force in weaponry. *Armed Forces and Society, 30*(2), 171–201.

Manning, F. J. (1991). Morale, cohesion, and esprit de corps. In R. Gal & A. D. Mangelsdorff (Eds.), *Handbook of military psychology* (pp. 453–470). West Sussex, UK: John Wiley.

Manning, F. J., & Ingraham, L. H. (1987). An investigation into the value of unit cohesion in peacetime. In G. Belenky (Ed.), *Contemporary studies in combat psychiatry* (pp. 47–68). Westport, CT: Greenwood Press.

Marshall, S. L. A. (1947). *Men against fire: The problem of battle command.* New York: William Morrow.

Martin, J. A., Vaitkus, M. A., Marlowe, D. H., Bartone, P. T., Gifford, R. K., & Wright, K. M. (1992, September/October). Psychological well-being among U.S. soldiers deployed from Germany to the Gulf War. *Journal of the U. S Army Medical Department*, PB 8–92–9/10, 29–34.

Newby, J. H., McCarroll, J. E., Ursano, R. J., Fan, Z., Shigemura, J., & Tucker-Harris, Y. (2004). Positive and negative consequences of a military deployment. Manuscript submitted for publication.

Noy, S. (1991). Combat stress reactions. In R. Gal & A. D. Mangelsdorff (Eds.), *Handbook of military psychology* (pp. 507–530). West Sussex, UK: John Wiley.

Shalev, A. (2004). Presentation at the workshop War Psychiatry Today: From the Battlefront to the Home Front. Bethesda, MD, July 12–13.

Shay, J. (1994). *Achilles In Vietnam: Combat trauma and the undoing of character.* New York: Scribner.

Shay, J. (2002). *Odysseus in America: Combat trauma and the trials of homecoming.* New York: Scribner.

Shils, E. A., & Janowitz, M. (1948). Cohesion and disintegration in the *Wehrmacht* in World War II. *Public Opinion Quarterly , 12*, 280–315.

Siebold, G. S. & Kelly, D. R. (1988). *The impact of cohesion on platoon performance at the Joint Readiness Training Center* (Tech. Report No. 812). Alexandria, VA: U.S. Army Research Institute for the Behavioral and Social Sciences. (DTIC No. AD-A202 926)

Solomon, Z., Noy, S., & Bar-On, R. (1986). Who is at risk for combat stress reaction syndrome? In N. A. Milgram (Ed.), *Stress and coping in time of war: Generalizations from the Israeli experience* (pp. 78–83). New York: Brunner/Mazel.

Teague, L. M., McNally, R. J., and Litz, B. (2004). Pre-war, war-zone, and postwar predictors of posttraumatic stress in female Vietnam veteran health care providers. *Military Psychology, 16*(1), 99–114.

Tziner, A. & Vardi, Y. (1983). Ability as a moderator between cohesiveness and tank crews performance. *Journal of Occupational Behavior, 4*, 137–143.

Vessey, J. W. (1997). Forward to Army War College edition of *Once an Eagle* by Anton Myrer (pp.xvii–xx). Carlisle, PA: Army War College Foundation Press.

Webb, J. (1978). *Fields of Fire*. New York: Bantam Books.

Weinstein, E. A. (1947). The function of interpersonal relations in the neurosis of combat. *Psychiatry, 10*, 307–314.

Wessely, S., Unwin, C., Hotopf, M., Hull, L., Ismail, K., Nicolaou, V. & David, A. (2003). Stability of recall of military hazards over time: Evidence from the Persian Gulf War of 1991. *British Journal of Psychiatry, 183*, 314–322.

Wolfe, J., Erickson, D. J., Sharkansky, E. J., King, D. W., & King, L. A. (1999). Course and predictors of posttraumatic stress disorder among Gulf War veterans: A prospective analysis. *Journal of Consulting and Clinical Psychology, 67*, 520–528.

CHAPTER 3

PSYCHOLOGICAL RESPONSES TO TERRORISM

William V. Bobo, Richard T. Keller, Neil Greenberg,
Christopher A. Alfonzo, Larry H. Pastor,
and Thomas A. Grieger

This will be a long, hard campaign, measured in years and fought on many fronts.
–Secretary of State Colin L. Powell, 2001

A Growing Asymmetrical Threat

For centuries, so-called terrorist tactics, defined as "illegal use or threatened use of force or violence (with an) intent to coerce societies or governments by inducing fear in their populations" (National Research Council, 2002, p. 13), have been employed in the spirit of anticolonialism, separatism, achievement of political power, control of citizenry, religion, and other motives. During recent decades, the world has witnessed the execution of terrorist tradecraft in the form of aircraft hijackings, embassy seizures, kidnappings, hostage taking, suicide attacks, use of chemical and biological agents, and destruction of government or privately owned property.

Despite wide media coverage of terrorist exploits during much of the Cold War era and in recent decades, terrorism, for many, has been regarded as chiefly a foreign policy issue or, at best, a foreign nuisance. A Department of State report concerning patterns of global terrorism in 2000 documented that the vast majority of terrorist attacks which occurred that year took place in locations outside of the United States, including Asia, Africa, Latin America, and the Middle East (U.S. Department of State, 2001). A separate study released in 2001 by the Congressional Research

The opinions expressed herein are those of the authors and may not reflect the policies of the Federal Government, Department of Defense, Department of the Navy, Department of the Army, the U.K. Ministry of Defence, or any of its branches.

Service indicated that 47 percent of all terrorist incidents worldwide were committed against U.S. citizens orU.S. holdings. The vast majority of these attacks occurred on foreign soil. Together, these reports seemed to suggest that although the United States had remained a popular target for terrorist organizations, the actual attacks were levied against clearly defined U.S. interests in distant locations.

There were, however, reasons for concern about the security of targets within U.S. borders. Specific examples included the bombings of the Murrah Federal Building in Oklahoma City (1995), the World Trade Center in New York (1993), and Centennial Park in Atlanta (1996). Although the incident took place in a foreign port, the suicide bombing of the USS *Cole* (2000) demonstrated the vulnerability of a U.S. military target, and was associated with widespread psychological devastation experienced by sailors from the *Cole*, members of other military units, military family members, and entire communities (Kootte, 2002). These attacks, along with their emotional aftermath, were a prelude to the events that occurred on September 11, 2001. The successful targeting of the Pentagon in Arlington, Virginia and the World Trade Center in New York City—military and commercial facilities symbolic of an entire nation's physical and economic security —resulted in an unprecedented level of widespread property damage, economic burden, and psychological devastation (Galea et al., 2002a; Melnik et al., 2002; Schlenger et al., 2002). The element of surprise achieved in these attacks, which resulted in the complete destruction of the World Trade Center and an entire section of the Pentagon, illustrated very clearly to the population *en masse* that no target—civilian or military—is invulnerable to the practice of terrorism (Wulf, Haimes, & Longstaff, 2003).

New Tactics, New Challenges: Terrorism as War

In the wake of the September 11, 2001, terrorist attacks, Cold War era assumptions about terrorism, and therefore antiterrorism strategies, have required substantial revision (Chyba, 2001; Lesser, 1999a). The traditional archetype of the career terrorist with a clearly defined nationalist or separatist agenda, backed by an identified state sponsor, has become somewhat outdated. Therefore, much previous intelligence and analysis of terrorist organizations and activities may be obsolete (Hopmeier, Ganor, Goodwin & Greinke, 2003). Aging classification schemes, such as those distinguishing between domestic and international terrorist groups, may be less useful. For one, combatants in the Global War on Terror (GWOT) must now confront enemies who are less centralized, less hierarchical in their structure, and more willing to embrace advanced networking and communications technologies—thereby increasing their global reach while simultaneously becoming more difficult to expose. Terrorist organizations now appear to be more diverse in their motivations, ideologies, and sources of funding, posing new challenges for intelligence gathering, profiling, and security planning (Sawyer, 2003).

Lesser (1999b) has proposed an alternative classification scheme centered on the directly communicated or perceived general aims that terror organizations wish to achieve. Terrorist motives under this scheme may be classified as either practical, which represent event-specific goals such as alteration of government policy or public opinion, or systemic and symbolic, which suggests terrorists who may seek more fundamental political or societal change. These groups appear willing to utilize coercive techniques with greater potential for lethality as means to a desired end. From this viewpoint, modern terrorist tactics may be expected to achieve more than conveying a message of specific demand. Instead, many terrorist groups appear to have adopted a warlike mentality, with well-defined "enemies" that may include entire countries, as well as their citizens. Coercion may not be so much the aim as is infliction of damage or harm as an actual end. These scenarios invite the possibility of more ambitious and destructive acts, including the consideration of the use of nuclear devices, conventional explosives designed to disperse radioactive materials upon detonation, chemical agents, and biological weaponry (Chyba, 2001; Johnson, 2003; Krenzelok, Allswede & Mrvos, 2000). Other unconventional but perhaps more devastating tactics may involve attacks upon a population's infrastructure through contamination of its food and water supply or the electronic networks that power its industry and other vital functions (Arquilla, Ronfeldt & Zanini, 1999; Kun, 2002).

Terrorism as Trauma

The erosion of feelings of personal safety and security and disruption of social continuity also characterize traumatic events other than terrorism, including natural disasters, industrial mishaps, and war. Terrorism has been described as a hazard characterized by extremes in terms of dread and uncertainty (Slovic, 1987), as well as its capacity for inducing strong and perhaps disabling psychological effects among an entire populace (Klar, Zakay, Sharvit, 2002). These descriptions beg the following questions: Is terrorism like other traumatic events that have been the subject of more extensive empirical study? If so, do the similarities allow for meaningful extrapolation of results from earlier studies of natural and man-made disasters not involving terrorism?

We believe that terrorism may be regarded as perhaps the most potent form of traumatic stressor. The reason we find "terror" events so terrifying may be based in no small part on their associated degree of intentional, man-made violence, potential for widespread physical and psychological damage, and randomness or unpredictability. One additional distinguishing characteristic may be the enduring nature of the terrorist threat. Modern terrorism, characterized by widespread global reach through strategically placed operative cells, adoption of a warlike doctrine, and willingness to use unconventional and highly destructive modern weaponry (including weapons of mass destruction), may not be amenable to total destruction of a precisely defined enemy. It is therefore less likely that the traditional tools of diplomacy or military force will offer the degree of closure that even the lengthiest of geopolitical campaigns, such as the Cold War, have been characterized by (Lesser, 1999a). Individuals charged with waging the Global War on Terror (GWOT), with its constituent military, law-enforcement, and diplomatic components, will be involved in a lengthy and perhaps indefinite campaign requiring perhaps unprecedented levels of threat vigilance, preparedness, and defensive and preemptive use of force. Diverse motivations, ideologies, funding sources, and highly secretive and clandestine methods of operation that characterize terrorist groups may give rise to sort of an "unseen enemy" mystique. Each of these characteristics may be enough to instill terror among a populace and cause it to question the ability of its government and society to keep them free from harm.

Because terrorists seek to create uncertainty, fear, and terror, terror events may precipitate psychiatric casualties among individuals, groups of individuals, and entire populations. Accordingly, mental health practitioners who serve military forces must be prepared to shift from traditional practices. Instead of focusing on diagnosing and treating psychopathology in a self- or command-directed referral system, practitioners must be equally skilled in public mental health principles, consultation, and liaison to key leadership personnel, outreach mental health practice, and application of lessons learned during previous acts of terrorism and other types of disasters. This latter task requires some familiarity with the psychological effects of disasters and terrorist events.

In this chapter, we attempt to selectively review the available literature concerning the psychological impact of disasters and traumatic stress. We do this in an attempt to also cast terrorism as a particular type of traumatic stressor—one that is potentially more devastating based not only on factors identified in research of other types of disasters, but also on more unique characteristics that serve as "fear multipliers." Because specific interventions and other techniques for prevention against trauma-related psychopathology are reviewed elsewhere in this set, these subjects will not be reviewed in this chapter.

In order to reconcile the relative paucity of studies concerning the direct impact of terrorist events on the mental health and functioning of military forces with what we perceive as a need for some specialized foreknowledge of the topic among mental health care practitioners, we made three basic assumptions when planning the chapter's content:

1. First, the military, along with lead government agencies worldwide, will play an ever-increasing role in the aforementioned mission of combating the modern terrorist threat. One example of this larger role was a significant change in legal doctrine shortly after the terrorist attacks of September 11, 2001. The Enhanced Border Security and Visa Entry Reform Act of 2002 and Military Order for the Detention, Treatment, and Trial of Certain Non-Citizens in the War Against Terrorism (November 13, 2001) expanded the traditional roles of the military by establishing joint military and law enforcement intelligence tracking systems in order to improve border security and by reserving judicial, law enforcement and correctional authority to the secretary of defense (Sawyer, 2003).

2. Military service members are not immune to the emotional impact of terrorism or other disasters (Solomon, 2001) . In fact, military personnel represent a population that reports high rates of psychological trauma even prior to entry into service (Hourani & Yuan, 1999; Merrill et al., 1998, Rosen & Martin, 1996; Stretch, Durand & Knudson, 1998), and experience high levels of acute psychological stress and trauma during active duty

service (Dlugosz et al., 1999; Wolfe, Erickson, Sharkansky, King & King, 1999) that may confer at least equivalent risk of developing significant posttraumatic symptoms as non-military samples.

3. Although terrorism as a stressor likely possesses distinctive characteristics, lessons learned from other types of disasters may still apply, despite limitations in study design and other factors. These limitations will be discussed in the appropriate sections of the text.

The Psychological Impact of Traumatic Events Among Individuals and Communities

In this section, we describe the impact of traumatic events in general, defined as occurrences that are perceived by individuals as life-threatening, unexpected, infrequent, and intense (Ursano, McCaughey, & Fullerton, 1994). Additional characteristics are included in Table 3.1.

Examples of such events, including terrorist attacks, are numerous. With such a wide spectrum of disaster types, associated psychological reactions or effects, individual variations in level of susceptibility to these effects, and other variables that may not be subject to direct measurement, a broad and systematic evaluation of risk for severe psychological sequelae among victims of terrorist activity and other disasters will depend, in part, on the assessor's broad knowledge of known psychological responses—both pathologic and nonpathologic—and mitigating factors as identified in the disaster mental health literature.

The enormous and often cumulative burden of environmental stressors associated with disasters may increase vulnerability to a number of adverse mental and physical health outcomes (Vanitallie, 2002). The most frequently documented negative general outcomes in disaster scenarios, regardless of cause, include specific psychopathologies such as posttraumatic stress disorder (PTSD), depression, nonspecific distress symptoms (e.g., demoralization, other subsyndromal affective states), health problems or related concerns (e.g., somatic complaints, sleep problems), perceived decreases in psychosocial support and heightened financial, occupational, or family related stress (Norris, Friedman & Watson, 2002a).

Table 3.1
Qualitative Aspects of Trauma and Associated Psychological Response

Quality of Traumatizing Stressor	Predominant Psychological Reaction
Threat to bodily integrity ("near-miss")	Anxiety, hyperarousal
Loss (death of a colleague or family member)	Grief, traumatic grief
Horror (exposure to horrific injury)	Intrusive thoughts and imagery
Bad outcome (botched execution of mission)	Shame and blame or self-blame

Individuals

Emotional and behavioral sequelae of traumatic stressors are believed to occur in a somewhat predictable manner, and many common psychological reactions to disaster are considered to be ordinary responses to extraordinary stressors (McMillen, North & Smith, 2000; Ursano, Fullerton & Norwood, 1995). Some of the common emotional and behavioral reactions to traumatic stress are listed in Table 3.2.

According to Ursano et al. (1995), most of these psychological symptoms are mild and transient, although negative emotional states can be cued in the future upon encountering reminders of the traumatic event. Subsequent reactions such as these are also believed to be relatively short-lived. The symptoms listed in Table 3.2 appear with considerable variability in frequency, intensity, and duration among individuals. Although exposure to traumatic events may be quite prevalent in the general population, the development of overt psychopathology in association with these exposures is still believed to be rare (Breslau et al., 1998). Posttraumatic symptoms and ongoing distress will persist in significant numbers of victims, particularly those with high exposure and those with physical injury. Despite these changes from baseline, most will continue to engage in personal and professional duties and most will not seek treatment (Waldrep, Grieger & Lovasz, 2004). In fact, "benefited responses" (Ursano, Fullerton & Norwood, 1995) have been observed among survivors of combat trauma and among civilian subjects. Assessors of those who have been subject to potentially traumatic events, including acts of terrorism, are likely to find that resilience rather than the adoption of victim status is the norm (Bisson, 2003; Green & Solomon, 1995).

Unfortunately, severe psychopathologic reactions resulting in disabling symptoms can also occur. The more common of these are summarized in Tables 3.2, 3.3, and 3.4. While these varied responses have been consistently described in empirical studies, what has been less clear is the division point between pathologic and nonpathologic responses to extreme events. Even among individuals who fulfill operationalized criteria for PTSD, their natural course of illness likely favors significant reduction in symptomatology by three months, with further improvement expected thereafter (Kessler, Sonnega, Bromet, Hughes & Nelson, 1995). Several related issues remain to be determined, including at what point universal responses to trauma such as fear, horror, and grief become pathologic, and what significance should be assigned to intense psychological reactions early in the posttrauma period.

Sleep problems and medically unexplained symptoms are also frequently reported (Escobar, Canino, Rubio-Stipic & Bravo, 1992; Hassett & Sigal, 2002), the latter of which may overwhelm health care delivery systems in the immediate postrecovery phase (Jones et al., 2002; Miller, 1988; Pillar, Malhotra & Lavie, 2000; van der Kolk et al., 1996). Several specific symptoms are listed in Table 3.2. Similar to the transient psychological and behavioral symptoms related to traumatic event exposure, most medically unexplained symptoms may be expected to remit over time without specific medical intervention. In the clinical setting, however, it may be difficult to distinguish between transient psychophysiological responses to an inordinate stress

Table 3.2
Emotional, Behavioral and Physiological Responses to Traumatic Events

"Normal" Emotional	Behavioral/Cognitive	Physiological	Course/Impairment
Frustration	Blame	Tachycardia	Temporary symptoms
Nervousness	Self-reproach	Headache	Especially prevalent in immediate aftermath of disaster
Anxiety	Decreased self-efficacy	GI discomfort	Still considered normal responses to extreme events
Irritability	Inability to enjoy activities	Muscle tension	Subsyndromal
Discouragement	Interpersonal withdrawal	Sleep deprivation	Rare impairment or dysfunction
Anger	Interpersonal conflict	Fatigue	
"Numbness"	Interpersonal mistrust	Easy startle	
Shock/denial	Loss of libido	Appetite loss	
Sadness	Cognitive dulling	Lightheadedness	
Helplessness	Poor work performance	Dizziness	
Hopelessness	Poor school performance	Dry mouth	
Perceived lack of support		Hyperventilation	

Table 3.2 Continued

"Abnormal" Emotional	Behavioral/Cognitive	Physiological	Course/Impairment
Severe dissociation	Severe insomnia	Persistence of symptoms listed above, with associated impairment	Considered pathological
Severe intrusive reexperiencing	Substance abuse		Associated with clear impairment and dysfunction
Severe phobic avoidance	Episodic violence		Symptoms follow unremitting (sometimes progressive) course
Severe depression	Inability to concentrate		Symptoms often cluster into definable psychiatric syndromes such as major depression, PTSD, acute stress disorder, and others
Suicidal ideation	Severe interpersonal conflict, mistrust, withdrawal		
Psychotic symptoms	Preoccupation with medically unexplained symptoms		
Episodic panic reactions			
Severe anxiety/worry			
Severe hypervigilance			

Sources: Lacy & Benedek, 2003; Norris et al., 2002a; Ursano et al., 2003; Ursano, Fullerton & McCaughey, 1994; Weisaeth & Eitinger, 1993.

Table 3.3
Ten Overlapping Trauma Themes Following a Suicide Bombing

Anxiety and hyperarousal. Nervousness, fearfulness, startle response. Sensory or cognitive stimuli precipitate physiological arousal and intense, affectively charged memories.

Preoccupation with the trauma. The victim relived the underlying event and could not otherwise get the event out of his or her mind. A victim who was in the embassy that was destroyed, when walking into another building, had concerns about the building's structural integrity, scanned for possible escape routes, etc.

Altered sense of self, foreshortened future. Whereas the pretraumatic self-concept did not conceptualize the self as victim, afterward the survivor experienced a sense of inefficacy about controlling his or her fate. Guilt over survival when others did not is additional alteration of self-concept.

Depression and psychic pain. Feelings of loss of innocence about life and doubts about previously held religious and metaphysical belief system.

Avoidance and phobias. Victims attempted to avoid reminders of the attack. For some, to remember was tantamount to painfully reliving the experience. This symptom cluster included flashbacks, especially when visual, auditory, or olfactory stimuli precipitated sudden reexperiencing of the initial trauma.

Emotional isolation and failed relationships. Victims restricted their lives to avoid coming into contact with reminders of the trauma, to the point of avoiding any kind of unpredictable affective arousal.

Insomnia, fatigue, and nightmares. Victims experienced nightmares and secondary sleep avoidance, with consequent fatigue.

Pain and physical discomfort. Muscle tension, physical pain, and disrupted sleep were frequent occurrences.

Deterioration of performance in major life areas. Emotional resources were deployed in the service of control over anxiety, leaving fewer mental resources for use elsewhere and impacting performance at work and in relationships.

Personality change. Affected persons came across as withdrawn from life. Others saw them as inflexible and volatile, or passive and helpless.

load and acute medical illness. Alternatively, several chronic medical problems may become exacerbated by disaster-related allostatic load (Miller, 1988; Resnick, Acierno & Kilpatrick, 1997; Vanitallie, 2002; Weisberg et al., 2002). Stress-related precipitation of myocardial infarction and aggravation of diabetes mellitus and hypertension are among the best described of these (Cwikel, Abdelgani, Goldsmith, Quastel & Yevelson, 1997; Leor & Kloner, 1996; Pickering, 2002; Rubinstein, Koffler, Villa & Graff, 1993; Suzuki et al., 1997).

Table 3.4
Potential Psychiatric Consequences of Large-Scale Terrorist Attacks

Acute stress disorder (ASD)

Posttraumatic stress disorder (PTSD)

Other anxiety disorders

Major depression

Adjustment disorder

Substance abuse

Delirium (secondary to head injury, dehydration, biochemical exposure, etc.)

Chronic, subsyndromal problems in living (financial problems, occupational difficulties, interpersonal conflicts, feelings of demoralization, grief reactions, family violence)

Other forms of social disruption

Medically unexplained symptoms

Sources: Dooley & Gunn, 1995; Goenjian et al., 2000; McFarlane, 2000; Norris et al., 2002a; Norris et al., 2002b; Rundell, 2003; Rundell, Ursano, Holloway & Silberman, 1989; Solomon et al., 1992; Stimpson, Thomas, Weightman, Dunstan & Lewis, 2003; Zahava, 2001.

Communities

Patterns of response to disaster, when viewed from a macroscopic level of community or population, may also be somewhat predictable (Ursano et al., 1995). Such response patterns have been reported to occur in phases (Norwood, Ursano & Fullerton, 2000; Oster, 1997; Ursano et al., 1995). These are illustrated in Figure 3.1.

In this model, a set of adaptational challenges are posed and, in most cases, overcome. As with the prediction of recovery among individuals exposed to disaster, it is assumed that communities will also recover and function independently once more. This restoration of self-efficacy and establishment of a new emotional or physiologic equilibrium may take years to accomplish. Although these patterns are subject to variability, they seem to occur with consistency, suggesting that each disaster carries with it a certain predictable life cycle. The successful management of the emotionally destructive effects of disaster may depend, in part, on the coordinated phase-specific responses that meet basic needs, rapidly restore a sense of safety, preserve community cohesion, and bolster its sense of self-efficacy during trying times.

Community responses such as mass panic, ranging from extreme, reflexive or desperate action (e.g., mass exodus from a disaster area, improper overuse of prophylactic measures) to extreme inaction (e.g., unwillingness to venture from one's home, refusal to accept medical care), are believed to be rare (Glass & Schoch-Spana, 2002; Pastel, 2001); however, they are often a prime concern among disaster relief planners, due to their potentially far-reaching disruptive effects on social functioning (Lacy & Benedek, 2003). By assuming that mass panic is inevitable,

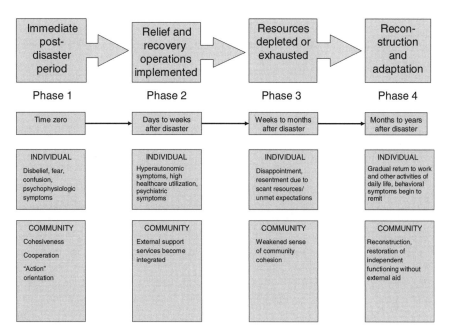

Figure 3.1
A Stage Model of Community Responses to Disasters

authorities may unwittingly bring about public mistrust and a sense of being pla-
cated rather than informed. Since it appears as though most communities are quite
resilient and therefore capable of participating in their own recovery, a valuable
opportunity to capitalize on existing resources or strengths may also be lost if panic
reactions are overanticipated.

Physical symptoms of autonomic arousal and medically unexplained symptoms discussed briefly above and reviewed elsewhere in this set, may be misattributed
to an "as yet undiagnosed" medical illness (Benedek, Holloway & Becker, 2002;
Lacy & Benedek, 2003). In other cases, somatic complaints may be manifestations
of an affective or anxiety disorder that was precipitated or exacerbated by disaster
(Kroenke, 2003), or may be plausible consequences of chemical or other harmful
exposure (DiGiovanni, 1999; Engel, Adkins, & Cowan, 2002). Many of these
symptoms may affect entire groups of individuals at once, with a pattern of spread
suggestive of mass outbreak of disease (Boss, 1997), but without a medially verifiable explanation. This phenomenon, referred to by Boss (1997) as epidemic hysteria, has been clearly documented in the setting of environmental and combat-
related incidents (DiGiovanni, 1999; Jones et al., 2002; Kipen & Fiedler, 2002),
and may be anticipated in the event of a chemical, biological or radiological disaster.
Recalling that most symptoms that appear in the setting of traumatic stress are transient, differential diagnostic formulation may be quite challenging, due to the

unspecific nature of the symptoms themselves, as well as the sheer number of individuals that may present to primary and emergency room settings for care of what
many believe may be symptoms related directly to toxic exposure. Further complicat-
ing the matter is the inevitable overlap of these symptoms, many of which may be
reported with a high degree of consistency from individual to individual, with a host
of traditionally verifiable medical illnesses (Pastel, 2001; Rundell, 2003). Additional
challenges are imposed if medically unexplained symptoms experienced collectively
within a population do not remit over time in the anticipated manner. Considerable
disability and antagonism between patients and caregivers may result (Page &
Wessely, 2003).

Empirical Studies of Terror Events

Having discussed some of the responses to traumatic events, we wish to focus now
on those dimensions that may pertain directly to terrorist acts as stressors. According
to Fullerton, Ursano, Norwood and Holloway (2003), large-scale terrorist attacks
may be a uniquely destructive type of stressor. Like natural catastrophes (e.g., floods,
hurricanes) or technological disasters (e.g., nuclear leaks, massive toxic spills), terrorist attacks may increase local fear among a populace, alter its sense of safety, and cause
widespread community disruption (Kroll-Smith & Couch, 1993). Factors that may
be more particular to terrorist attacks include their man-made nature, as well as the
intentional infliction of pain, suffering, and intense fear upon other human beings
(Benedek, Holloway & Becker, 2002). As we have seen, certain features of disaster
scenarios such as high perceived threat, human-made cause, achievement of extensive
death or destruction, significant interpersonal or property loss, perceived lack of con-
trol/unpredictability, or being otherwise severely violent have been associated with
the development of posttraumatic psychological sequelae, or are believed to confer
more severe psychological risk (Antony & Barlow, 2002; Breslau et al., 1998; Brewin, Dalgleish & Joseph, 1996; Figley, 1985; Garb, Bleich & Lerer, 1987; McFarlane,
1986; Milgram, 1993; Rothbaum, Marshall, Foa, Lindy & Mellman, 2001; Simon,
1999; Ursano & McCarroll, 1990; Yehuda, 2002; Zatzick, Kang & Hinton, 2001).
Because so many of these variables identified in empirical research have come to all
but define modern terrorist threats of scenarios, such stressors may be thought of as
prototypic if one aims to inflict a high degree of psychological damage upon a target
population. Indeed, research concerning the psychological effects of terrorist acts
consistently documents both widespread and intense psychological effects and
behavioral disruption, although this is not always the case.

Studies of Terrorist Events in the United States

Although terrorism may carry with it a potentially greater and more far-reaching
psychological impact than other disasters, a general review of the disaster mental
health literature seems to illustrate more shared similarities to other types of disaster,
with a few noteworthy exceptions. Studies conducted after the World Trade Center

and Pentagon airliner attacks in New York City and Arlington, Virginia documented consistently that posttraumatic symptoms such as syndromal anxiety (e.g., PTSD), depression, and others were far more prevalent during the first several weeks after the disaster and seemed to decay during the months following in both nationally representative samples (Silver, Holman, McIntosh, Poulin & Gil-Rivas, 2002) and the general populace in the New York/New Jersey area (Chen, Chung, Chen, Fang & Chen, 2003; Galea et al., 2003). Studies of nationally representative samples also clearly documented a significant degree of symptomatology across the nation among all age groups. Proximity to the epicenter of the disaster, younger age, female gender, low social support, preexisting depressive or anxiety symptoms, physical illness, and markers of challenged coping such as self-blame, denial, or disengagement were associated with increased emotional symptoms of posttraumatic stress (Cardenas, Williams, Wilson, Fanouraki & Singh, 2003; Schuster et al., 2001; Schlenger et al., 2002; Silver et al., 2002). In regional studies of the same attacks, Hispanic ethnicity, higher exposure severity, presence of multiple psychological stressors prior to the events, interpersonal loss, job loss, and low social support were associated with higher rates of both PTSD and depression (Galea et al., 2002a; Galea et al., 2002b). The most profound finding from the pooled literature was the presence and persistence, in many cases, of significant stress symptomatology in people who were only indirectly exposed to the terrorist attacks (Neria, Gross & Marshall, 2003). Two other interesting findings were relatively lower-reported prevalence rates of posttraumatic symptoms in the Washington, DC area samples and a relationship between extensive television viewing and PTSD symptoms in nationally representative samples. Some studies of New York area residents documented lower prevalence of PTSD among lower Manhattan residents who were presumably more proximal to the attack site versus the remainder of the New York City metropolitan area (Neria, Gross & Marshall, 2003). These results seemed to suggest that an anticipated proximity effect reported in other trauma studies appeared less consistently during this event. Besides psychological symptomatology, other outcomes such as increased physical symptoms among workers surveyed near the World Trade Center site, persistence of physical symptoms several months after the attack, and increased alcohol, tobacco, and drug use were also observed (Bernard et al., 2002; Melnik et al., 2002). In Pentagon employees evaluated two years after the September 11 attack, direct exposure to the attack, physical injury, and exposure to the dead were all risk factors for ongoing PTSD. In those without direct exposure, there was no association between hours of television watching after the attack and PTSD symptoms at two years (Waldrep et al., 2004).

Studies of the emotional and behavioral effects of the Murrah Federal Building bombing in Oklahoma City in 1995 documented similar findings, including higher rates of psychiatric illness among survivors of the direct blast, particularly PTSD (North et al., 1999). Increased symptom severity or high association with the development of posttraumatic stress symptoms were observed among children and adolescents (especially those who knew someone who was injured or killed), those who experienced intense psychological arousal and fear during the event, and individuals who received high degrees of television and emotional exposure to the disaster (Peak, 2000; Pfefferbaum et al., 2001b; Tucker, Pfefferbaum, Nixon & Dickson, 2000).

Studies of Terrorist Events Outside of the United States

Research on psychological consequences of terrorist events outside the United States also revealed similarities between terrorist attacks and other types of disasters. Obhu et al. (1997) reported the occurrence of significant and persistent stress-related symptoms among exposed individuals at one-, three-, and six-month follow-up following the Aum Shinrikyo sarin gas attacks in Tokyo (1995). Although 11 people were killed and over 1,000 were hospitalized, more than 4,000 people who had no signs of exposure sought emergency care. Persistent somatic symptoms and psychological distress were also reported by Kawana, Ishimatsu and Kanda (2001) at two-, three-, and five-year follow-up. In a small sample of attack victims, 8 of 34 individuals developed PTSD (Tochigi et al., 2002). Similar results were documented in a review by Karsenty et al. (1991): Of over 1,000 patients who presented to emergency departments in Israel following Iraqi Scud missile attacks between January and February 1991, only 22 percent of individuals were injured due to missile blast (direct exposure), while 78 percent were believed to be psychiatric and behavioral casualties. Together, these studies documented significant stress-related symptomatology, much of which probably resulted in extensive seeking of relief in medical care delivery systems. The possibility that medical care delivery systems may become overwhelmed by individuals who were not directly exposed to attack was also illustrated.

In a study of civilian terrorist attack victims in France (1982–1987) involving mostly bombings, the occurrence of PTSD was related to extent of injury suffered (8.3 percent of moderately injured victims versus 30.7 percent of the more severely injured), with no significant correlation discovered with respect to sex or age of the victims (Abenhaim, Dab & Salmi, 1992). Interestingly, 10.5 percent of individuals diagnosed with PTSD were uninjured. Major depression was also prevalent (13.3 percent), with no correlation observed between its occurrence and level of injury.

Smaller studies of terrorist attack survivors have documented the presence of a substantial amount of posttraumatic symptoms (PTSD) and depression between 6 and 12 months after the incident event. Shalev (1992) reported a high incidence of PTSD (33 percent) among survivors of a terrorist attack on a civilian bus with a persistence of symptoms measured ten months later. The relatively small sample size (n = 14) limited broader interpretation, although the level of exposure to the trauma may be presumed to have been similar throughout the sample. In another small sample of 21 subjects who had been directly exposed to the terrorist bombing of the U.S. Embassy in Dar es Salaam, Tanzania, report of injury predicted posttraumatic stress eight months later (Pfefferbaum et al., 2001a). A high prevalence of PTSD was also observed among survivors of the Enniskillen bombing (1987), which claimed the lives of 11 people and injured 60 (Curran et al., 1990). At six months' follow-up, 50 percent of those surveyed had developed PTSD. Although female sex was associated with the development of PTSD, no correlation was found between psychological or physical injury and the development of the disorder. This latter finding stood in contrast with other studies that documented an association between the development of PTSD and degree of exposure or injury, sometimes several years after the event (see e.g., Abenhaim et al., 1992; Desivilya, Gal & Ayalon, 1996).

The longevity of the aftereffects of trauma and traumatic grief are illustrated by the findings of Pastor (2004), who conducted an in-depth examination of survivors and family members of the suicide truck-bombing of the American Embassy in Beirut, Lebanon in April, 1983. A constellation of ten interrelated trauma and traumatic loss themes were identified up to 20 years after the precipitating event (Table 3.3). One individual's experience was especially poignant (Figure 3.2).

In contrast to these reviewed studies, other investigations documented evidence of remarkable resiliency, especially among populations who had received some chronic degree of exposure to violent acts over time (Ayalon, 1993). Northern Irish and Israeli populations are good examples of possible longitudinal stress habituation effects that may be expected to occur in societies that have been subject to civil disorder, high community tension, and social disruption due to terrorist-motivated violence for a period of several years. Indeed, according to data from community surveys, hospital admission records, and surveys of psychotropic drug usage and suicide rates in Northern Ireland, the impact of terrorist violence was believed to be relatively negligible (Curran, 1988). In a large epidemiologic survey of a nationally representative sample in Israel, relatively high degrees of direct (16.4 percent) and indirect (37.3 percent) exposure to terrorist violence were reported (Bleich, Gelkopf & Solomon, 2003). Despite such prevalent exposure, only 9.4 percent of the sample satisfied symptom criteria for PTSD, while a significant proportion (76.7 percent) of individuals had at least one stress-related symptom. Another key finding in the study was the high degree of optimism among survey respondents about their personal futures (82.2 percent), as well as the future of their country (66.8 percent), and a high degree of self-efficacy (74.6 percent) despite a low sense of safety with regard to themselves (60.4 percent) and their relatives (67.9 percent). The most frequently reported coping mechanism was actively searching for information about the safety of loved ones and the use of available social support.

Studies of Military Members

Despite somewhat routine exposure to dangerous and highly stressful duties, surprisingly little research has been conducted on military populations from combat and combat support units. There are a number of anecdotal reports of the nature of the psychological impact and efforts at early intervention following the terrorist attacks on the USS *Cole* (Grieger et al., 2003a) and the Pentagon on September 11, 2001 (see, e.g., Keller & Bobo, 2002; Hoge et al., 2002; Waldrep & Waits, 2002). There has been scant empirical study of the impact of terrorist events on active duty military members. Two recent studies have examined the psychological manifestations of terrorist attacks against military personnel and federal employees within the United States. These studies specifically examined the role of early psychological

Figure 3.2
For one survivor of the suicide attack upon the American embassy in Beirut in 1983
(top), viewing photographs of the truck bombing of the federal office building in Oklahoma City in 1995 (bottom) precipitated the sudden reemergence of posttraumatic
symptoms.

symptoms in the development of subsequent psychiatric illness. The first study examined members of one of the commands at the Pentagon following the terrorist attack of September 11, 2001 (Grieger, Fullerton & Ursano, 2003b). The study population was surveyed using the full-version (ten-item) Peritraumatic Dissociative Experiences Scale (Marmar, Weiss & Metzer, 1997) at the time of the attack and at seven months postevent, using an assessment scale for PTSD. A high level of peritraumatic dissociation was strongly associated with the development of PTSD seven months later.

In a related study of military hospital staff members following a three-week series of random sniper shootings that killed ten individuals in the Washington, DC metropolitan area, study subjects were sampled during a two-week period that began five days after the apprehension of the suspected snipers using an abbreviated version of the Peritraumatic Dissociative Experiences Scale (Greiger, Fullerton, Ursano & Reeves, 2003c). A high level of dissociation on this scale was also found in those who reported symptoms consistent with acute stress disorder or major depression. The association between dissociation, acute stress disorder, and PTSD—as well as the high comorbidity between these illnesses—suggests a link between difficulty in cognitive processing of the situation at the time of the event and subsequent psychiatric illness. In addition, the hospital staff was also assessed with an instrument that measured the degree of perceived safety in routine activities and changes in the number of routine activities altered due to the sniper attacks. Those with acute stress disorder reported a nearly twofold reduction in the number of activities compared to those who did not meet diagnostic criteria. This suggested that, following a large-scale terrorist attack, a significant proportion of health care providers could be expected to substantially modify their behavior patterns, including the decision to come to work, as a result of perception of high risk to themselves or family members. Interestingly, the exposure of the medical staff to the psychological trauma associated with the sniper shootings was based solely on media exposure, since none of the shooting victims were taken to the hospital from where that study sample was drawn, and none of the victims were related to the staff members surveyed. This result achieved further conceptual significance, since individuals were responding to a series of shootings that did not significantly increase the level of baseline violence, including murder, in the nation's capital during that period. During that actual period of the shootings and for several weeks thereafter, media coverage was extensive, and included repeated reports of the limited advances of law enforcement and personal background information relating to the victims. Similar coverage had followed other terrorist activities, including the anthrax attacks delivered through the mail in the Washington, DC and Maryland mail distribution centers. Although the matter of classification of the DC sniper shootings as a terrorist event is subject to debate, this incident, which lasted several weeks, shares a number of aforementioned characteristics with terror events: This was an intentional, man-made series of incidents involving death or serious injury to randomly chosen victims that resulted in widespread fear among a large populace.

There have been no published empirical studies, to our knowledge, of the psychological impact of terrorist actions among deployed troops. Clues are provided, however, by studies of the psychological consequences of modern peacekeeping missions, discussed elsewhere in this set.

Why We Find Terror Events So Terrifying: A Theoretical Framework

We have illustrated in our review that while traumatic stressors of all types have the potential of wreaking much devastation upon an individual's and community's psyche, recovery and resilience remain the norm. Terrorism, a particular type of disaster, seems to involve a bit more devastation than other forms of trauma. A traditional view of terrorism as a traumatic stressor would suggest that its man-made nature and sheer violence would explain a high degree of psychological destructiveness; however, it would not necessarily explain, as one example, the American population's willingness to give up some freedoms, assurances of privacy, and certain conveniences such as rapid transit through airport security. It is reasonable to assume that this willingness would have been relatively unheard of prior to terrorist attacks on U.S. soil.

We believe that terrorism differentiates itself from both natural disasters and from criminal enterprises by its distinguishing characteristic: the deliberate instillation of fear and insecurity in a target audience far larger than the subset of specific victims attacked. This intentional demoralization of a populace may then be thought of as a unique hazard of terrorism as psychological warfare. A common theme of all terrorist activity is the achievement of a political or ideological goal through fear-based acquiescence to their demands by that larger, target audience. As Boaz Ganor (2002) observes: "The way to the terrorist's ultimate political goal runs through a vital interim objective—the creation of an unremitting, paralyzing sensation of fear in the target community." Ganor observes that if the fear of becoming the next victim of an act of terror were entirely rational and proportional to the statistical probability, terrorism would have little chance of instilling fear on a widespread basis. It is the irrational anxiety—the amplification of fear via the unpredictability and shocking methods of the attack (such as conveyed by suicide attacks)—which acts as a "fear multiplier" in the psychological warfare waged by terrorists. The social cohesion of a civilian population, or the fighting effectiveness of a military unit, can be eroded by such irrational anxiety. As force multipliers, military mental health professionals should be prepared to foster resiliency against the psychological dimension of terrorist activity. Because fear of horrifying consequences may be quite large among a populace, despite an often negligible probability of such an outcome actually occurring (Rottenstreich & Hsee, 2001), the manner in which risk is communicated to a target population also requires careful consideration. The balance between informing people about serious risks and creating exaggerated and therefore harmful fear can be difficult to achieve.

At the outset of this chapter, terrorism was defined as the "illegal use or threatened use of force or violence (with an) intent to coerce societies or governments by inducing fear in their populations." Terrorists employ tactics such as suicide bombings not solely for instrumental purposes of evading security countermeasures, but additionally to effect maximum psychological impact: impressions of the suicide bomber as supernaturally courageous or unstoppable serve to irrationally multiply fear and insecurity in the target audience (Pastor, 2004). Terrorists seek to maintain a campaign of fear and insecurity in between actual attacks by purely psychological tactics such as threats, rumors, and misinformation. The media acts as an inevitable multiplier of the frightening intentions of terror groups.

Perhaps the most far-reaching potential effect of terrorism is a society's loss of a sense of safety, cohesion, and belief in a safe and predictable world. It seems reasonable to assume that it is these "fear multipliers" that pave a pathway from rational concern to irrational anxiety about perceived individual risk. In so doing, factors that promote individual, community, and societal resilience may be inevitably challenged, necessitating that drastic measures be employed and tolerated in order to reassure a worried public. These challenges will continue to test, and likely retest, a target population's capacity for resilience and adaptation as long as terror organizations continue to employ their tactics of surprise, misinformation, threats, and graphic brutality.

Summary and Future Directions

By all indications, modern terrorism appears to have become a more widespread global threat, and antiterrorism tactics must now be utilized against an unconventional enemy. It has also become clear that the military, as well as other government institutions, will be primary combatants in the global war on terror. As such, military forces may become engaged in even more dangerous and highly stressful activities over a lengthier period of time than what is typical of their routine work during other conflicts. Empirical studies of military service members have revealed high rates of exposure to traumatic stressors both prior to entry into the service and during periods of active duty. Moreover, it has been shown that members of military forces may not enjoy any significant degree of protection against potentially devastating psychological effects of these exposures as was once perhaps believed (Whealin, Morgan & Hazlett, 2001). Our forces then, as individuals and as a group, remain vulnerable to terrorism as both physical and psychological warfare. As terrorism threatens society's social fabric, so too does it pose a "sociolytic" threat against military unit cohesion and morale.

From the disaster literature, we have achieved a cursory understanding of the nature of traumatic stressors. Those that are man-made, involve significant degrees of dread or terror, are associated with low levels of perceived predictability or controllability, result in widespread death or devastation, and display a high degree of violence are especially potent with respect to their ability to disrupt the social fabric and sense of safety among community members and to result in severe psychiatric illness among the exposed. Beyond these characteristics that are well expressed among terror activities, we believe that terrorism's unique destructiveness and potential to elicit fundamental changes in societal norms stem from fear multipliers that include graphic brutality, use of the media for widespread exposure, threats, and misinformation. The target population remains sensitized, uneasy about their own safety, and in some cases, mistrustful. This sociolytic effect—the loss of a sense of safety and belief in a safe and predictable world—is itself perhaps the most devastating aspect of terrorism as a unique stressor.

While symptoms at an individual, unit, or community level are to be expected, in the majority of victims these will be self-limited (Ehlers & Clark, 2003; Boscarino, 2004). The long-term impact of terrorism occurs when individuals and communities change their cognitive processing of events and behavioral interactions in the months and year following a terrorist attack. These changes, more than simple rates of psychiatric illness over time, are the ultimate outcome measure. Some resilience and recovery-promoting factors have been identified through empiric research (Figure 3.3); however, because terrorist events are so rare, much remains to be done in terms of identifying factors that impact individual and community responses to terror attacks and evaluating interventions em-

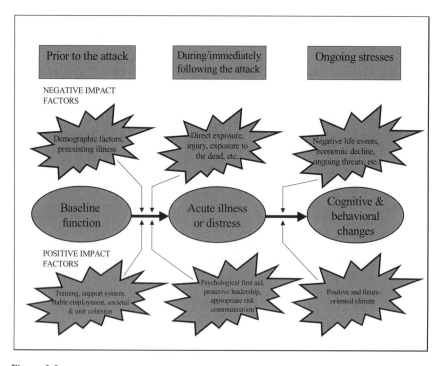

Figure 3.3
Determinants of Responses to Terrorist Attacks

ployed to restore individual and community health (Ozer, Best, Lipsey & Weiss, 2003).

As such, victims of terrorist attacks—both individuals and communities— should be studied on a longitudinal basis, from factors present before the attack, exposures during the attack, and subsequent life events. In this manner we may be able to identify factors which foster resiliency and those which erode it.

This approach is in keeping with the notion that terrorism appears to target direct victims, but may also wreak psychological devastation upon first-responders, family members, community members, and societies at large, with predictable behavioral responses that may be observed among individuals, as well as large groups or communities. These reactions have been documented in studies of both civilian and military samples after traumatic events, including terrorist attacks of varying intensity. Because such patterns among military members may be predictably similar to those seen in civilian cohorts, the model could be applied to military disaster planning operations. Factors such as strong unit cohesion, sound leadership, and communication of risk in a manner that strikes the tenuous balance between informing and oversensitizing—principles that have been applied successfully in civilian disasters—may have important preventive effects (Slovic, Fischhoff & Lichtenstein, 1982) that could be subject to direct measurement. Other important areas for future research are presented in Figure 3.4. Resilience factors, both positive and potentially harmful, may include biological factors (Charney, 2004), individual psychological factors, public health-based preventive measures (Ahern et al., 2002), specific health care interventions (Watson, Friedman, Ruzek & Norris, 2002), and policy/leadership factors.

We close with some comments about the delivery of mental health services in the face of such uncertainty. Mental health force multipliers should remember that resiliency is innate, need only be augmented (not created *de novo*), and its appearance often surprises clinicians who are prepared for psychopathological responses in the face of potentially traumatizing events. The absence of mass panic or hysteria among Londoners surviving repeated Nazi bombardment in World War II, the resilience of New Yorkers following the attacks of September 11, 2001, and even the unexpected resistance of hijacked passengers aboard United Flight 93 on that same day (Longman, 2002) provide ample evidence of the ability of populations under attack to refuse to be terrorized by terrorism.

Whether through direct service provision or consultation to unit or higher command, the mental health force multiplier may have the opportunity to bolster resilience against psychological manipulation by terrorist campaigns through providing education, insight, and empowerment (Ganor, 2002). Service members should be educated as to the nature and goals of what they are fighting for and against. Troops can be reminded that terrorism is a weapon of the weak against the strong, that a vibrant democracy has never been toppled by terrorism, and that democracies are the favorite target of terrorist groups worldwide precisely because of the high value that democracies place upon the worth of the individual. The insight that the terrorist attack is an attempt to manipulate the thinking and behavior of the target

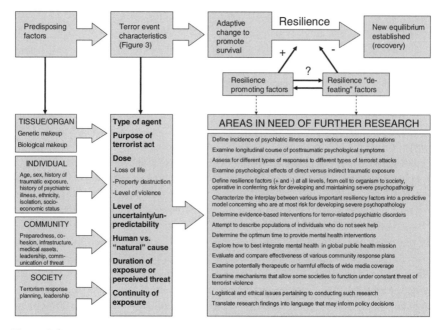

Figure 3.4
A Model for Future Research on the Psychology of Terrorism

audience is often sufficiently empowering to enable a subject to refuse to be a co-operating party to his or her own psychological manipulation. Presence of a credible, trusted authority also plays a central role in strengthening the resolve of a threatened population, and timely messages from leadership during times of crisis serve as *de facto* public mental health interventions.

While risk assessment and provision of treatment are familiar roles for most health care providers, important decisions regarding risk communication, public education, troop morale, and preparedness may depend, to a large extent, on recommendations provided by mental health practitioners to unit commanders. It is therefore essential that military mental health practitioners be familiar with these principles, as well as their application in settings other than the clinic or office. We may safely argue that consultation regarding each of the principles mentioned in this paragraph to the chain of command and other key leadership figures will fall under the purview of mental health (Cozza & Hales, 1991). As the specialty that deals most closely with behavior, this follows quite logically, and we are most fortunate to be in a position of such importance.

References

Abenhaim, L., Dab, W., & Salmi, L. R. (1992). Study of civilian victims of terrorist attacks (France 1982–1987). *Journal of Clinical Epidemiology, 45,* 103–09.

Ahern, J., Galea, S., Resnick, H., Kilpatrick, D., Bucuvalas, M., Gold, J., & Vlahov, D. (2002). Television images and psychological symptoms after the September 11 terrorist attacks. *Psychiatry, 65*, 289–300.

Antony, M. M., & Barlow, D. H. (2002). Specific phobia. In D. H. Barlow. *Anxiety and its Disorders: The Nature and Treatment of Anxiety and Panic* (2nd ed, pp. 380–417). New York: Guilford Press.

Arquilla, J., Ronfeldt, D., & Zanini, M. (1999). Networks, netwar, and information-age terrorism. In I. O. Lesser, B. Hoffman, J. Arquilla J, et. al. (Eds.) *Countering the New Terrorism* (pp. 39–84). MR-989-AF: RAND Corporation.

Ayalon, O. (1993). Posttraumatic stress recovery of terrorist survivors. In J. P. Wilson & B. Raphael (Eds.). *International Handbook of Traumatic Stress Syndromes* (pp. 855–866). New York: Plenum Press.

Benedek, D. M., Holloway, H. C., Becker, S. M. (2002). Emergency mental health management in bioterrorism events. *Emergency Medicine Clinics of North America, 20*, 393–407.

Bernard, B. P., Baron, C. L., Mueller, C. A., Driscoll, R. J., Tapp, L. C., Wallingford, K. M., & Tepper, A. L. (2002). Impact of September 11 attacks on workers in the vicinity of the World Trade Center—New York City. Centers for Disease Control: *Morbidity and Mortality Weekly Report, 51* (Special Issue), 8–10.

Bisson, J. I. (2003). Early intervention following traumatic events. *Psychiatric Annals, 33*, 37–44.

Bleich, A., Gelkopf, M., & Solomon, Z. (2003). Exposure to terrorism, stress-related mental health symptoms, and coping behaviors among a nationally representative sample in Israel. *Journal of the American Medical Association, 290*, 612–620.

Boscarino, J. A. (2004). Posttraumatic stress disorder and physical illness: Results from clinical and epidemiologic studies. *Annals of the New York Academy of Sciences, 1032*, 141–153.

Boss, L.P. (1997). Epidemic hysteria: A review of the published literature. *Epidemiologic Reviews, 19*, 233–43.

Breslau, N., Kessler, R. C., Chilcoat, H. D., Schultz, L. R., Davis, G. C., & Andreski, P. (1998). Trauma and posttraumatic stress disorder in the community: The 1996 Detroit Area Survey of Trauma. *Archives of General Psychiatry, 55*, 626–632.

Brewin, C. R., Dagliesh, T., & Joseph, S. (1996). A dual representation theory of posttraumatic stress disorder. *Psychological Review, 103*, 670–86.

Cardenas, J., Williams, K., Wilson, J. P., Fanouraki, G., & Singh, A. (2003). PTSD, major depressive symptoms, and substance abuse following September 11, 2001, in a Midwestern university population. *International Journal of Emergency Mental Health, 5*, 15–28.

Charney, D.S. (2004). Psychobiological mechanisms of resilience and vulnerability: Implications for successful adaptation to extreme stress. *American Journal of Psychiatry, 161*, 195–216.

Chen, H., Chung, H., Chen, T., Fang, L., & Chen, J. P. (2003). The emotional distress in a community after the terrorist attack on the World Trade Center. *Community Mental Health Journal, 39*, 157–165.

Chyba, C. F. (2001). Biological security in a changed world. *Science 293*, 2349.

Congressional Research Service. (2001). CRS Issue Brief for Congress: *Terrorism, the Future, and U.S. Foreign Policy.* September 12, 2001.

Cozza, K., & Hales, R. E. (1991). Psychiatry in the Army: a brief historical perspective and current developments. *Hospital and Community Psychiatry, 42*, 413–418.

Curran, P. S. (1988). Psychiatric aspects of terrorist violence: Northern Ireland 1969–1987. *British Journal of Psychiatry, 153*, 470–475.

Curran, P. S., Bell, P., Murray, A., Loughrey, G., Roddy, R., & Rocke, L.G. (1990). Psychological consequences of the Enniskillen bombing. *British Journal of Psychiatry, 156*, 479–82.

Cwikel, J., Abdelgani, A., Goldsmith, J. R., Quastel, M., & Yevelson, I. I. (1997). Two-year follow-up study of stress-related disorders among immigrants to Israel from the Chernobyl area. *Environmental Health Perspectives, 105* (Suppl. 6), 1545–1550.

Desivilya, H. S., Gal, R., & Ayalon, O. (1996). Extent of victimization, traumatic stress symptoms, and adjustment of terrorist assault survivors: A long-term follow-up. *Journal of Traumatic Stress, 9*, 881–889.

Di Giovanni, C. (1999). Domestic terrorism with chemical or biological agents: Psychiatric aspects. *American Journal of Psychiatry, 156*, 1500–05.

Dlugosz, L. J., Hocter, W. J., Kaiser, K. S., Knoke, J. D., Heller, J. M., Hamid, N. A., Reed, R. J., Kendler, K. S., & Gray, G. C. (1999). Risk factors for mental disorder hospitalization after the Persian Gulf War: U.S. Armed Forces, June 1, 1991–September 30, 1993. *Journal of Clinical Epidemiology, 52*, 1267–1278.

Dooley, E., & Gunn, J. (1995). The psychological effects of disaster at sea. *British Journal of Psychiatry, 16*, 233–237.

Ehlers, A., & Clark, D. (2003). Early psychological interventions for adult survivors of trauma: a review. *Biological Psychiatry, 53*, 817–826.

Engel, C. C., Adkins, J. A., & Cowan, D. N. (2002). Caring for medically unexplained physical symptoms after toxic environmental exposures: Effects of contested causation. *Environmental Health Perspectives, 110* (Suppl. 4), 641–647.

Escobar, J., Canino, G., Rubio-Stipic, M., & Bravo, M. (1992). Somatic symptoms after a natural disaster: A prospective study. *American Journal of Psychiatry, 149*, 965–967.

Figley, C.R. (Ed.). (1985). *The Study and Treatment of Posttraumatic Stress Disorder* New York: Brunner Mazel.

Fullerton, C. S., Ursano, R. J., Norwood, A. E., & Holloway, H. H. (2003). Trauma, terrorism, and disaster. In R. J. Ursano, C.S. Fullerton & A. E. Norwood (Eds.). *Terrorism and Disaster: Individual and Community Mental Health Interventions* (pp. 1–22). Cambridge, UK: Cambridge University Press.

Galea, S., Ahern, J., Resnick, H., Kilpatrick, D., Bucuvalas, M., Gold, J., & Vlahov, D. (2002a). Psychological sequelae of the September 11 terrorist attacks in New York City. *New England Journal of Medicine, 346*, 982–987.

Galea, S., Resnick, H., Ahern, J., Gold, J., Bucuvalas, M., Kilpatrick, D., Stuben, J., & Vlahov, D. (2002b). Posttraumatic stress disorder in Manhattan, New York City, after the September 11th terrorist attacks. *Journal of Urban Health, 79*, 340–353.

Galea, S., Vlahov, D., Resnick, H., Ahern, J., Susser, E., Gold, J., Bucuvalas, M., Kilpatrick, D. (2003). Trends of probable posttraumatic stress disorder in New York City after the September 11 terrorist attacks. *American Journal of Epidemiology, 158*, 514–524.

Ganor, B. (2002, July 15). Terror as a Strategy of Psychological Warfare. *International Policy Institute for Counter-Terrorism*. Retrieved June 8, 2005, from http://www.ict.org.il/articles/articledet.cfm?articleid=443

Garb R., Bleich A., & Lerer, B. (1987). Bereavement in combat. *Psychiatric Clinics of North America, 10*, 421–36.

Glass, T. A, & Schoch-Spana, M. (2002). Bioterrorism and the people: How to vaccinate a city against panic. *Clinical Infectious Disease, 34*, 217–223.

Goenjian, A.K., Steinberg, A. M., Najarian, L. M., Fairbanks, L. A., Tashjian, M., Pynoos, R. S. (2000). Prospective study of posttraumatic stress, anxiety, and depressive reactions after earthquake and political violence. *American Journal of Psychiatry, 157,* 911–916.

Green, B., & Solomon, S. (1995). The mental health impact of natural and technological disasters. In J. Freedy & S. Hobfoll (Eds.), *Traumatic Stress: From Theory to Practice* (pp. 163–180). New York: Plenum Press.

Grieger, T. A., Bally, R. E., Lyszczarz, J. L., Kennedy, J. S., Griffeth, B. T., & Reeves, J. J. (2003a). Individual and organizational interventions after terrorism: September 11 and the USS *Cole.* In R. J. Ursano, C. S. Fullerton & A. E. Norwood (Eds). *Terrorism and Disaster: Individual and Community Mental Health Interventions* (pp. 71–89). Cambridge, UK: Cambridge University Press.

Grieger, T. A., Fullerton, C. S., & Ursano, R. J. (2003b). Posttraumatic stress disorder, alcohol use, and safety after the terrorist attack on the Pentagon. *Psychiatric Services, 54,* 1380–1383.

Grieger, T. A., Fullerton, C. S., Ursano, R. J., Reeves, J. J. (2003c). Acute stress disorder, alcohol use, and perception of safety among hospital staff after the sniper attacks. *Psychiatric Services, 54,* 1383–1387.

Hassett, A. L., & Sigal, L. H. (2002). Unforeseen consequences of terrorism: Medically unexplained symptoms in a time of fear. *Archives of Internal Medicine, 162,* 1809–1813.

Hoge, C. W., Orman, D. R., Robichaux, R. J., Crandell, E. O., Patterson, V. J., Engel, C. C., Ritchie, E. C., & Milliken, C. S. (2002). Operation Solace: Overview of the mental health intervention following the September 11, 2001 Pentagon attack. *Military Medicine, 167* (Suppl. 4), 44–47.

Hopmeier, M., Ganor, B., Goodwin, T., & Greinke, D. S. (2003, July). "There are no dangerous weapons...": Suicide attacks and potential responses. *Journal of Homeland Security.* Retrieved June 8, 2005, from http://www.homelandsecurity.org/journal/Articles/displayarticle.asp?article=94

Hourani, L. L., & Yuan, H. (1999). The mental health status of women in the Navy and Marine Corps: Preliminary findings from the perceptions of wellness and readiness assessment. *Military Medicine, 164,* 174–181.

Johnson, R. J., Jr. (2003). Facing the terror of nuclear terrorism. *Occupational Health and Safety, 72,* 44–48, 50.

Jones, E., Hodgins-Vermaas, R., McCartney, H., Everitt, B., Beech, C., Poynte, D., Palmer, I., Hyams, K., & Wessely, S. (2002). Post-combat syndromes from the Boer war to the Gulf war: A cluster analysis of their nature and attribution. *British Medical Journal, 324,* 321–324.

Karsenty, E., Shemer, J., Alshech, I., Cojocaru, B., Moscovitz, M., Shapiro, Y., & Danon, Y. L. (1991). Medical aspects of the Iraqi missile attacks on Israel. *Israel Journal of Medical Sciences, 27,* 603–607.

Kawana, N., Ishimatsu, S., & Kanda, K. (2001). Psycho-physiological effects of the terrorist sarin attack on the Tokyo subway system. *Military Medicine, 166* (Suppl. 12), 23–26.

Keller, R. T., & Bobo, W. V. (2002). Handling human remains following the terrorist attack on the Pentagon: Experiences of 10 uniformed health care workers. *Military Medicine, 167* (Suppl. 4), 8–11.

Kessler, R. C., Sonnega, A., Bromet, E., Hughes, M., & Nelson, C. B. (1995). Posttraumatic stress disorder in the National Comorbidity Survey. *Archives of General Psychiatry, 52,* 1048–1060.

Kipen, H. M., & Fiedler, N. (2002). Environmental factors in medically unexplained symptoms and related syndromes: The evidence and the challenge. *Environmental Health Perspectives, 110* (Suppl. 4), 597–599.

Klar, Y., Zakay, D., & Sharvit, K. (2002). "If I don't get blown up...": realism in the face of terrorism and an Israeli nationwide sample. *Risk Decision and Policy, 7*, 203–219.

Kootte, A. F. (2002). Psychosocial response to disaster: the attacks on the *Stark* and *Cole*. *Medicine, Conflict and Survival, 18*, 44–58.

Krenzelok, E. P., Allswede, M. P., & Mrvos, R. (2000). The poison center role in biological and chemical terrorism. *Veterinary and Human Toxicology, 42*, 297–300.

Kroenke, K. (2003). Patients presenting with somatic complaints: Epidemiology, psychiatric comorbidity and management. *International Journal of Methods in Psychiatric Research, 12*, 34–43.

Kroll-Smith, J. S., & Couch, S. R. (1993). Technological hazards: Social responses as traumatic stressors. In J. P. Wilson & B. Raphael. *International Handbook of Traumatic Stress Syndromes* (pp. 79–91). New York: Plenum Press.

Kun, L.G. (2002). Homeland security: the possible, probable, and perils of information technology. Information technology is a key component in both defending against and aiding terrorism threats. *IEEE Engineering in Medicine and Biology Magazine, 21*(5), 28–33.

Lacy, T. J., & Benedek, D. M. (2003). Terrorism and weapons of mass destruction: Managing the behavioral reaction in primary care. *Southern Medical Journal, 96*, 394–399.

Leor, J., & Kloner, R. A. (1996). The Northridge earthquake as a trigger for acute myocardial infarction. *American Journal of Cardiology, 77*, 1230–32.

Lesser, I. O. (1999a). Changing terrorism in a changing world. In Lesser, I. O., Hoffman, B., Arquilla, J, Ronfeldt, D. F., Zanini, M., Jenkins, B. M. (Eds.) *Countering the New Terrorism* (pp. 1–5), MR-989-AF: RAND Corporation.

Lesser, I. O. (1999b). Countering the new terrorism: implications for strategy. In Lesser, I. O., Hoffman, B., Arquilla J., Ronfeldt, D. F., Zanini, M., Jenkins, B. M. (Eds.), *Countering the New Terrorism* (pp. 85–144). MR-989-AF: RAND Corporation.

Longman, J. (2002). *Among the Heroes: United Flight 93 and the Passengers and Crew Who Fought Back*. New York: Harper-Collins.

Marmar, C. R., Weiss, D. S., & Metzer, T. J. (1997). The peritraumatic dissociative experiences questionnaire. In J. P. Wilson & T. M. Keane (Eds.), *Assessing Psychological Trauma and PTSD*. New York: Guilford Press.

McFarlane, A. C. (1986). Posttraumatic morbidity of a disaster. A study of cases presenting for psychiatric treatment. *Journal of Nervous and Mental Disease, 174*, 4–14.

McFarlane, A. C. (2000). Traumatic stress in the 21st century. *Australian and New Zealand Journal of Psychiatry, 34*, 896–902.

McMillen, J., North, C., & Smith, E. (2000). What parts of PTSD are normal: Intrusion, avoidance, or arousal? Data from the Northridge, California, earthquake. *Journal of Traumatic Stress, 13*, 57–75.

Melnik, T. A., Adams, M. L., O'Dowd, K., Mokdad, A. H., Murphy, W., Giles, W. H., & Bales, V. S. (2002). Psychological and emotional effects of the September 11 Attacks on the World Trade Center—Connecticut, New Jersey, and New York, 2002. Centers for Disease Control: *Morbidity and Mortality Weekly Report, 51*(35), 784–786.

Merrill, L. L., Newell, C. E., Milner, J. S., Koss, M. P., Hervig, L. K., Gold, S. R., Rosswork, S. G., & Thornton, S. R. (1998). Prevalence of premilitary adult sexual victimization and aggression in a Navy recruit sample. *Military Medicine, 163*, 209–212.

Milgram, N. (1993). War related trauma and victimization: Principles of stress prevention in Israel. In J. P. Wilson & B. Raphael. *International Handbook of Traumatic Stress Syndromes* (pp. 811–820). New York: Plenum Press.

Miller, T. W. (1988). Advances in understanding the impact of stressful life events on health. *Hospital and Community Psychiatry, 39,* 615–22.

Neria, Y., Gross, R., & Marshall, R. (2003, April). Mental health consequences of the Sept. 11 terrorist attacks. *Psychiatric Times,* pp. 41–43.

Norris, F. H., Friedman, M. J., & Watson, P. J. (2002a). 60,000 disaster victims speak: Part II. Summary and implications of the disaster mental health research. *Psychiatry, 65,* 240–260.

Norris, F. H., Friedman, M. U., Watson, P. J., Byrne, C. M., Diaz, E., & Kaniasty, K. (2002b). 60,000 disaster victims speak: Part I. An empirical review of the empirical literature, 1981–2001. *Psychiatry, 65,* 207–239.

North, C. S., Nixon, S. J., Shariat, S., Mallonee, S., McMillen, J. C., Spitznagel, E. L., & Smith, E. M. (1999). Psychiatric disorders among survivors of the Oklahoma City bombing. *Journal of the American Medical Association, 282,* 755–62.

Norwood, A. E., Ursano, R. J., & Fullerton, C. S. (2000). Disaster psychiatry: Principles and practice. *Psychiatric Quarterly, 71,* 207–226.

Ohbu, S., Yamashina, A., Takasu, N., Yamaguchi, T., Murai, T., Nakano, K., Matsui, Y., Mikami, R., Sakurai K., & Hinohara S. (1997). Sarin poisoning on Tokyo subway. *Southern Medical Journal, 90,* 587–593.

Oster, N. S. (1997). Disaster medicine. *Mount Sinai Journal of Medicine, 64,* 323–328.

Ozer, E. J, Best, S. R., Lipsey, T. L., & Weiss, D. S. (2003). Predictors of posttraumatic stress disorder and symptoms in adults: A meta-analysis. *Psychological Bulletin, 129,* 52–73.

Page, L. A., & Wessely, S. (2003). Medically unexplained symptoms: Exacerbating factors in the doctor-patient encounter. *Journal of the Royal Society of Medicine, 96,* 223–227.

Pastel, R. H. (2001). Collective behaviors: Mass panic and outbreaks of multiple unexplained symptoms. *Military Medicine, 166* (Suppl. 12), 44–46.

Pastor, L. H. (2004). Culture as casualty. *Psychiatric Annals, 34,* 616–22.

Peak, K. S. (2000). Oklahoma City: Posttraumatic stress disorder and gender differences. *Dissertation Abstracts International: Section B: the Sciences & Engineering,* 60(9–B), 4901.

Pfefferbaum, B., North, C. S., Flynn, B. W., Ursano, R. J., McCoy, G., DeMartino, R., Julian, W. E., Dumont, C. E., Holloway, H. C., & Norwood, A. E. (2001a). The emotional impact of injury following an international terrorist incident. *Public Health Reviews, 29,* 271–280.

Pfefferbaum, B., Nixon, S. J., Tivis, R. D., Doughty, D. E., Pynos, R. S., Gurwitch, R. H., & Foy, D. W. (2001b). Television exposure in children after a terrorist incident. *Psychiatry, 64,* 202–211.

Pickering, T. G. (2002). Terror strikes the heart—September 11, 2001. *Journal of Clinical Hypertension, 4,* 58–60.

Pillar, G., Malhotra, A., & Lavie, P. (2000). Posttraumatic stress disorder and sleep—what a nightmare! *Sleep Medicine Reviews, 4,* 183–200.

Resnick, H. S., Acierno, R., & Kilpatrick, D. G. (1997). Health impact of interpersonal violence. 2: Medical and mental health outcomes. *Behavioral Medicine, 23,* 65–78.

Rosen, L. N., & Martin, L. (1996). Impact of childhood abuse history on psychological symptoms among male and female soldiers in the U.S. Army. *Child Abuse and Neglect, 20,* 1149–1160.

Rothbaum, B. O., Marshall, R. D., Foa, E. B., Lindy, J., & Mellman, L. (2001) Posttraumatic stress disorder. In G. O. Gabbard (Ed.), *Treatments of Psychiatric Disorders* (3rd ed., Vol. 2, pp. 1539–1566). Washington, DC: American Psychiatric Press.

Rottenstreich, Y., & Hsee, C. K. (2001). Money, kisses, and electric shocks: On the affective psychology of probability weighting. *Psychological Science, 12*, 185–190.

Rubinstein, A., Koffler, M., Villa, Y., & Graff, E. (1993). The Gulf War and diabetes mellitus. *Diabetic Medicine, 10*, 774–776.

Rundell, J. R. (2003). A consultation-liaison psychiatry approach to disaster/terrorism victim assessment and management. In R. J. Ursano, C. S. Fullerton, & A. E. Norwood (Eds.), *Terrorism and Disaster: Individual and Community Mental Health Interventions* (pp. 107–120). Cambridge, UK: Cambridge University Press.

Rundell, J. R., Ursano, R. J., Holloway, H. C., & Silberman, E. K. (1989). Psychiatric responses to trauma. *Hospital and Community Psychiatry, 40*, 68–74.

Sawyer, M. (2003, July). Connecting the dots: The challenge of improving the creation and sharing of knowledge about terrorists. *Journal of Homeland Security.* Retrieved June 8, 2005, from http://www.homelandsecurity.org/journal/Articles/displayarticle.asp?article=93

Schlenger, W. E., Caddell, J. M., Ebert, L., Jordan, B. K., Rourke, K. M., Wilson, D., Thalji, L., Dennis, J. M., Fairbank, J. A., & Kulka, R. A. (2002). Psychological reactions to terrorist attacks: Findings from the National Study of Americans' Reactions to September 11. *Journal of the American Medical Association, 288*, 581–88.

Schuster, M. A., Stein, B. D., Jaycox, L. H., Collins, R. L., Marshall, G. N., Elliott, M. N., Zhou, A. J., Kanouse, D. E., Morrison, J. L., Berry, S. H. (2001). A national survey of stress reactions after the September 11, 2001, terrorist attacks. *New England Journal of Medicine, 345*, 1507–1512.

Shalev, A. Y. (1992) Posttraumatic stress disorder among injured survivors of a terrorist attack. Predictive value of early intrusion and avoidance symptoms. *Journal of Nervous and Mental Disease, 180*, 505–509.

Silver, R. C., Holman, E. A., McIntosh, D. M., Poulin, M., & Gil-Rivas, V. (2002). Nationwide longitudinal study of psychological responses to September 11. *Journal of the American Medical Association, 288*, 1235–1244.

Simon, R. I. (1999). Chronic posttraumatic stress disorder: a review and checklist of factors influencing prognosis. *Harvard Review of Psychiatry, 6*, 304–12.

Slovic, P. (1987). Perception of risk. *Science, 236*, 280–285.

Slovic, P., Fischhoff, B., & Lichtenstein, S. (1982). Why study risk perception? *Risk Analysis, 2*, 83–94.

Solomon, Z. (2001). The impact of posttraumatic stress disorder in military situations. *Journal of Clinical Psychiatry, 62* (Suppl. 17), 11–15.

Solomon, Z., Waysman, M., Levy, G., Fried, B., Mikulincer, M., Benbenishty, R., Florian, V., & Bleich, A. (1992). From front line to home front: A study of secondary traumatization. *Family Process, 31*, 289–302.

Stimpson, N. J., Thomas, H. V., Weightman, A. L., Dunstan, F., & Lewis, G. (2003). Psychiatric disorders in veterans of the Persian Gulf War of 1991. Systematic review. *British Journal of Psychiatry, 182*, 391–403.

Stretch, R. H., Durand, D. B., & Knudson, K. H. (1998). Effects of premilitary and military trauma on the development of posttraumatic stress disorder symptoms in female and male active duty soldiers. *Military Medicine, 163*, 466–470.

Suzuki, S., Sakamoto, S., Koide, M., Fujita, H., Sakuramoto, H., Kuroda, T., Kintaka, T., & Matsuo, T. (1997). Hanshin-Awaji earthquake as a trigger for acute myocardial infarction. *American Heart Journal, 134* (5 Pt. 1), 974–977.

Tochigi, M., Umekage, T., Otani, T., Kato, T., Iwami, A., Asukai, N., Sasaki, T., & Kato, N. (2002). Serum cholesterol, uric acid and cholinesterase in victims of the Tokyo subway sarin poisoning: A relation with posttraumatic stress disorder. *Neuroscience Research, 44,* 267–272.

Tucker, P., Pfefferbaum, B., Nixon, S. J., & Dickson, W. (2000). Predictors of post-traumatic stress symptoms in Oklahoma City: Exposure, social support, peri-traumatic responses. *Journal of Behavioral Health Services and Research, 25,* 406–416.

Ursano, R. J., Fullerton, C. S., & McCaughey, B. G. (1994). Trauma and disaster. In R. J. Ursano, B. G. McCaughey & C. S. Fullerton (Eds.), *Individual and Community Responses to Trauma and Disaster: The Structure of Human Chaos* (pp. 3–27). Cambridge, UK: Cambridge University Press.

Ursano, R. J., Fullerton, C. S., Norwood, A. E. (Eds.). (2003). *Terrorism and Disaster: Individual and Community Mental Health Interventions.* Cambridge, UK: Cambridge University Press.

Ursano, R. J., Fullerton, C. S., & Norwood, A. E. (1995). Psychiatric dimensions of disaster: Patient care, community consultation, and preventive medicine. *Harvard Review of Psychiatry, 3,* 196–209.

Ursano, R. J., & McCarroll, J. E. (1990). The nature of a traumatic stressor: Handling dead bodies. *Journal of Nervous and Mental Disease, 178,* 396–398.

Ursano, R. J., McCaughey, B. G., & Fullerton, C. S. (Eds.). (1994). *Individual and Community Responses to Trauma and Disaster: The Structure of Human Chaos.* Cambridge, UK: Cambridge University Press.

U.S. Department of State. (2001, April). Patterns of Global Terrorism, 2000.

van der Kolk, B. A., Pelcovitz, D., Roth, S., Mandel, F. S., McFarlane, A., Herman, J. L. (1996). Dissociation, somatization, and affect dysregulation: The complexity of adaptation of trauma. *American Journal of Psychiatry, 153* (Suppl. 7), 83–93.

Vanitallie, T. B. (2002). Stress: A risk factor for serious illness. *Metabolism, 51,* 40–45.

Waldrep, D., Grieger, T., & Lovasz, M. (2004). The enduring impact of terrorism: follow up of Pentagon employees two years after the attack. Poster presented at the American Psychiatric Association Annual Meeting (New York).

Waldrep, D., & Waits, W. (2002). Returning to the Pentagon: The use of mass desensitization following the September 11, 2001 attack. *Military Medicine, 167* (Suppl. 4), 58–59.

Watson, P. J., Friedman, M. J., Ruzek, J. I., & Norris, F. (2002). Managing acute stress response to major trauma. *Current Psychiatry Reports, 4,* 247–253.

Weisberg, R. B., Bruce, S. E., Machan, J. T., Kessler, R. C., Culpepper, L., & Keller, M. B. (2002). Nonpsychiatric illness among primary care patients with trauma histories and posttraumatic stress disorder. *Psychiatric Services, 53,* 848–854.

Whealin, J. M., Morgan, C. A., and Hazlett, G. (2001, Winter). The role of military studies in enhancing our understanding of PTSD. *PTSD Research Quarterly, 12,* 1–4.

Wolf, J., Erickson, D. J., Sharkansky, E. J., King, D. W., & King, L. A. (1999). Course and predictors of posttraumatic stress disorder among Gulf War veterans: a prospective analysis. *Journal of Clinical Psychiatry, 67,* 520–528.

Wulf, W. A., Haimes, Y. Y., & Longstaff, T. A. (2003). Strategic alternative responses to risks of terrorism. *Risk Analysis, 23,* 429–444.

Yehuda, R. (2002). Posttraumatic stress disorder. *New England Journal of Medicine, 346*, 108–114.

Zahava, S. (2001). The impact of posttraumatic stress disorder in military situations. *Journal of Clinical Psychiatry, 62* (Suppl. 17), 11–15.

Zatzick, D. F., Kang, S. M., Hinton, L. et al. (2001). Posttraumatic concerns: A patient-centered approach to outcome assessment after traumatic physical injury. *Medical Care, 39*, 327–39.

CHAPTER 4

Psychological Operations in Combat, Peacekeeping, and Fighting Terrorism

Steven Collins

The United States throughout its history has attempted to develop policies, doctrines, and structures, whether in war or peace, to guide the activities of its policy makers and military commanders in the conduct of persuasion activities focused upon the opposition. Today, these activities have many names, all with similar meanings: psychological operations (PSYOP), persuasion operations, information operations, perception management, and so on. The term "propaganda" has been discarded by many due to association with Nazism and Communism (Taylor, 1995). PSYOP are "operations planned to convey selected information and indicators to foreign audiences to influence their emotions, motives, objective reasoning, and ultimately the behavior of foreign governments, organizations, groups, and individuals" (U.S. Department of Defense, 1996; see also Hoffman, 2002; Leonard, 2002; and Peterson, 2002). The intent of these operations is to create a behavior that supports U.S. national policy objectives and theater combatant commanders' intentions at the strategic, operational, and tactical level. Experience clearly shows that the successful integration of PSYOP with more conventional activities during peace and war saves lives, combatant and noncombatant alike.

Despite the success of its strategic information efforts during the Cold War, the United States quickly dismantled this apparatus during the 1990s (Johnson, 2004). Ironically, the United States, with arguably the greatest capacity to wield the media tool, found itself in the 1990s reacting to the information activities of its opponents rather than setting the agenda (Centner, 1997; Nye & Owens, 1996). The truth is that Americans are uncomfortable with "spin" of any type. Innately, they understand the importance of freedom of the press, having grown up on a steady diet of an explication and defense of the significance of this liberty from an early age. Therefore, Americans view information management of any type, even if directed toward an enemy or potential enemy, and even during a time of crisis or conflict, with trepidation. This is true even if this effort is effectively benign and primarily a counter to hostile propaganda from abroad. However, U.S. rivals were often more flexible, less restricted by egalitarian views of freedom, and willing to use the information tool in any manner possible to gain an advantage (Becker, 1999).

The watershed events of 9/11 and the U.S.-led invasion of Iraq during the spring of 2003 changed U.S. priorities and put the related topics of public diplomacy, persuasion, information operations, and PSYOP squarely in the center of the discussion with respect to national security funding and policy priorities. This change has been welcomed by those who recognize the importance of persuasion and information, but the process to reach this stage has been painfully slow, and much work still remains to be done to provide the United States with effective organizations who can wield the information instrument.

In the present chapter, I first present current models of psychological operations, including the content of these operations and how they are hypothesized to exert their effects. I then emphasize the importance of placing the use of psychological operations in an historical context. The use of psychological operations in different military operations is then discussed. Finally, I turn to the lessons learned from prior operations with an emphasis on how psychological operations should be conducted in the future.

Models of Psychological Operations

Used properly, PSYOP can help, in the words of the Chinese philosopher Sun Tzu, "subdue the enemy's army without battle." In an era when any loss of life is politically sensitive, the ability of PSYOP to be a "combat reducer" and save the lives of U.S. troops and citizens, as well as the lives of the opposition, is exceedingly important. PSYOP forces offer U.S. policy makers and war fighters a more discreet and often more politically palatable tool than conventional military activities, which are primarily designed to bring the adversary to heel through death and destruction. Figure 4.1 describes the types of psychological operations activities that an organization can employ as part of the strategic, operational, and technical levels of conflict.

Strategic PSYOP is commonly defined as having global implications and is planned, initiated, and executed at the national level. The audience of strategic PSYOP, like all PSYOP activities, is limited to foreign populations. Normally the objectives of strategic PSYOP are long-term and political in nature. They aim to undermine the real or potential adversary's readiness for conflict, will to fight, and reduce his war-making capability, while gaining the support and cooperation of neutral and friendly audiences. Strategic PSYOP is often intertwined with diplomacy and is therefore intrinsically an instrument developed and executed at the political level. The military can support strategic PSYOP through planning, and if tasked, through the dissemination of PSYOP materials (television or radio broadcasts, etc.).

Operational PSYOP consists of persuasion activities in support of a deployed military task force. Operational PSYOP actions impact throughout the entire military theater of operations and typically include widespread television and radio broadcasts, and newspaper, magazine, and leaflet dissemination.

Tactical PSYOP consists of actions taken in a local area with focused impact and are directed at opposition military forces and civilians in the specified area of operations, with the aim of reducing the adversary's combat power by eliminating its will to continue aggression, as well as supporting the maneuver freedom of the commander. Loudspeaker operations, handbills, local radio broadcasts, and television programming are typical tactical PSYOP actions. Today's PSYOP capability at the tactical level is quite well developed. These types of activities are described in Figure 4.1 below.

The key to PSYOP, and the area most related to psychology, is the so-called 14-step process that makes up the Target Audience Analysis (TAA) outlined in Figure 4.2. This involves the systematic study of people to enhance the understanding of the military psychological environment in order to achieve PSYOP objectives. The aim of TAA is to identify the target audience's attitudes and vulnerabilities. Then it is vital to determine lines of persuasion for the target audience, symbols to express the lines of persuasion, and the appropriate media to disseminate the PSYOP

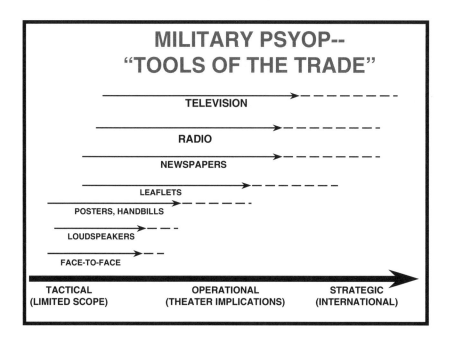

Figure 4.1
Psychological Operations Techniques as a Function of Level of Employment

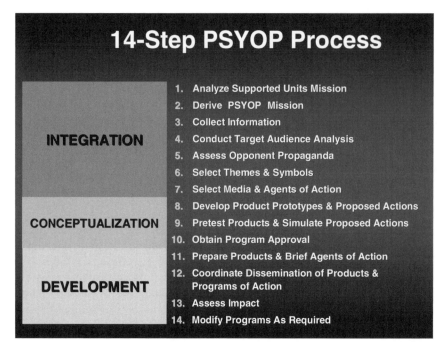

Figure 4.2
The 14-Step PSYOP Process

messages. TAA vulnerabilities are derived from the analysis of the target audience's conditions and attitudes indicating potential issues, positive and negative, which can be exploited to promote the behavior desired to reach the PSYOP objectives.

Historical Perspective

Even before becoming a nation, America used PSYOP to help further its foreign policy objectives. George Washington's *To the Inhabitants of Canada* in 1775 was an attempt to encourage Canadian surrender and defection during the ill-fated invasion of Quebec led by Benedict Arnold. The timing and wording of the Emancipation Proclamation during the Civil War is best understood as a PSYOP message aimed at stabilizing shaky northern support and to encourage the defection of African-American slaves, who served as the primary labor force in the southern states (Taylor, 1995).

Nonetheless, U.S. PSYOP activities came of age during the twentieth century. During the First World War, two organizations had the responsibility for U.S. PSYOP. The Committee on Public Information or "Creel Committee," headed by George Creel, was a civilian agency; the propaganda section under Hebert Blankenhorn, a part of the American Expeditionary Forces in France, was a military outfit

(Bruntz, 1938). The close coordination and synchronization between the Creel and Blankenhorn efforts was a large reason for the success of the United States and the associated Allied strategic PSYOP efforts in prompting the capitulation of Germany and the other Central Powers. Creel and Blankenhorn thus provided a model upon which similar efforts were made during the Second World War.

The major difference between the PSYOP efforts of the two world wars was in scope. U.S. PSYOP efforts in the Second World War involved tens of thousands of personnel and employed the talents of such luminaries as Frank Capra (prominent movie director), David Sarnoff (former CEO of NBC), and William Paley (former CEO of CBS). Two organizations participated in PSYOP planning and execution during this conflict. The Office of War Information had dominion over national public information and overt PSYOP disseminated abroad, while the Office of Strategic Services controlled covert strategic PSYOP overseas. United States strategic PSYOP efforts during the Second World War were, by all accounts, very successful and contributed significantly to the ultimate Allied victory. Significant achievements included the Doolittle Raid against Japan and the deceptions regarding the location of the Allied invasion of the French coast in 1944 (Lerner, 1971).

The United States disbanded its PSYOP capability after 1945 but quickly reactivated it in 1950 as part of the conflict on the Korean peninsula. It was in the early 1950s that the Office of the Chief of PSYOP was established under the Secretary of the Army. At the same time, Major General Robert McClure, General Eisenhower's former Chief of PSYOP in Europe, established the Psychological Warfare School at Fort Bragg, North Carolina, which also spawned U.S. Special Forces (Paddock, 2002). It was also during the 1950s that a variety of U.S. agencies were established that were essentially arms of U.S. strategic information (e.g., the United States Information Agency, the Voice of America, and Radio Free Europe).

U.S. PSYOP played a role during the Vietnam conflict as part of the Joint Special Operations Group (Katagiri, 1976), but PSYOP capabilities atrophied in the 1970s. However, in January 1983, as part of National Security Decision Directive (NSDD) 77 ("Management of Public Diplomacy Relative to National Security"), President Ronald Reagan created a "Special Planning Group" to address information synchronization and reinvigorate strategic PSYOP capabilities (Snyder, 1995). NSDD 77 created four subcommittees: public affairs, international information, international political activities, and international broadcasting. This group was chaired by the National Security Advisor and designed to improve the coordination of public diplomacy and strategic PSYOP (Lord, 1997). The dramatic success of information activities in defeating Communism is difficult to question. The impact of Ronald Reagan's "Mr. Gorbachev, tear down this wall!" speech in Berlin (Reagan, 1987) was indelible, and the desire of the people of the Warsaw Pact countries to cast off the yoke of Soviet domination was significantly energized.

The end of the Cold War put U.S. PSYOP at all levels in a crisis. The great ideological struggle against the Soviet Union was won and "history was over" (Fukuyama, 1992). Funding for strategic PSYOP structures was dramatically cut or disbanded. America's soft-power capabilities were allowed to wither (Nye & Owens, 1996).

On the military side, the approximately 3,000 U.S. Army PSYOP soldiers focused on delivering messages by loudspeaker and leaflets, and became virtually obsolete due to a lack of funding and support from the policy levels.

Despite significant PSYOP activities in support of military operations in Panama (1989), Desert Storm (1990), Somalia (1992), and Haiti (1994) (Walko, 1996), PSYOP funding and emphasis at the tactical and operational level continued to decline. At the strategic level, this process of neglect was even more dramatic as the United States Information Service was absorbed into the Department of State and funding was drastically cut (Kiehl, 2003).

It took the U.S. interventions in Bosnia (1995) and Kosovo (1999) to compel policy makers to question the logic of abandoning activities that could proactively change attitudes and persuade target audiences to act differently. Albeit reluctantly, the long-term nature of the commitments to both Bosnia and Kosovo forced an extensive examination of how the United States was able influence the thoughts and beliefs of foreign audiences.

Bosnia

The Bosnian War (1992–1995) and the subsequent NATO intervention (1995–present), led by the United States, is best explained as a struggle for perception, with the forces on the ground playing merely a supporting role. Many pointed to the centrality of perception during the Bosnian conflict and subsequent peacekeeping operation as a harbinger of future conflicts (Jacobson, 1997; Siegel, 1997; Thompson, 1994). The manipulation of the media by the political leaders in the region was vitally important in igniting and exploiting latent ethnic hatred. While the actual conflict on the ground occurred in fits and starts, the battle of words and perception was continuous and endures today.

In the war, Serb forces very early on made the capture of various radio and television transmitters a priority military objective, seizing control of as much local electronic media as possible (Thompson, 1994). Radovan Karadzic, the political leader of the Bosnian-Serb forces and a psychiatrist, understood the importance of perception management and manipulation and made it a priority effort. While the Bosnian-Muslim side initially had fewer tools with which to wage media war, they were even more focused on the importance of PSYOP. While the Serbs channeled their efforts toward the people of the region, the Bosnian-Muslims took great care to influence the international audience, as their very survival depended upon massive intervention on their behalf by the international community. The Bosnian government of Alija Izetbegovic hired two public relations firms in the United States to assist in their perception manipulation efforts—Hill & Knowlton and Ruder Finn (Owen, 1995). These firms ensured that the point of view presented to the people of America regarding the Bosnian conflict was predominantly a Bosnian-Muslim perspective.

The Bosnian-Muslim effort to portray themselves as hapless victims was assisted by the fact that nearly all the international correspondents assigned to Bosnia stayed in Sarajevo. Because of this concentration of journalists in a city ringed by besieging

Serbs, many succumbed to the "Stockholm Syndrome"—sympathizing too much with the Sarajevans and losing a measure of journalistic objectivity, as both journalist and Sarajevan suffered through privations caused by the traumatic siege of the city (Brock, 1993–1994).

It was into this environment of extremely sophisticated perception management, where the target audience was well educated, media savvy, and already the product of more than three years of elaborate propaganda bombardment, that the NATO PSYOP effort, led by the United States, began in December 1995. At first, NATO's information activity, much like the entire Implementation Force (IFOR) mission, was agonizingly hesitant. Frustratingly, months were spent getting the PSYOP media effort underway. Particularly distressing was the lack of facilities and personnel in Sarajevo to conduct early operations, and most importantly, a muddled policy and wrongheaded command direction that often gave PSYOP little priority. These factors played havoc with the ability of the PSYOP Task Force to contribute effectively to the early part of the mission in Bosnia (Collins, 1999).

The appointment of U.S. General Wesley Clark as NATO's military commander in July 1997 signaled a willingness by the international community to widen the scope of action of NATO. Intimately involved with the Dayton discussions as an aide to diplomat Richard Holbrooke, Clark was extremely familiar with the situation in Bosnia. During the same period of time, Carlos Westendorp replaced Carl Bildt as the head of the Office of the High Representative in Bosnia, an organization agreed to by the signatories to the Dayton Agreement to implement the civilian aspects of the General Framework Agreement for Peace in Bosnia. The placement of Clark and Westendorp ensured a new aggressive attitude by the renamed NATO Stabilization Force (SFOR) in Bosnia.

Clark and Westendorp soon found their excuse to exert the information tool. During the summer of 1997, Bosnian-Serb radio and television juxtaposed images of SFOR soldiers with the Nazi SS and, cleverly playing upon the similarity in the two abbreviations, referred to the force in Bosnia as "SS-FOR" ("Anti-NATO Images," 1997). A crisis, popularly termed the "transmitter war," began to take shape (Collins, 1998). After more broadcasts by the Bosnian-Serbs to discredit the work of Louise Arbour, Chief Prosecutor for the International War Criminal Tribunal at The Hague, SFOR was asked on October 1 to seize four Republika Srpska radio and television transmitters and shut down its network. This was accomplished, and the anti-SFOR stance of the Republika Srpska television was quickly moderated.

NATO PSYOP activities in Bosnia continued to grow and diversify. Soon, an annual operating budget of nearly $3 million was in place, producing hundreds of thousands of print items, radio programs, television commercials, and so on. During 1998, the bulk of the PSYOP activities in SFOR transferred from a U.S.-led task force to a multinational effort predominately led by Germany and continued the effort to put out information in Bosnia. Today, the PSYOP effort continues with joint input from NATO and the new European Union Force (EUFOR), which has largely taken over military security in Bosnia.

Despite the importance of PSYOP and perception management to the mission in Bosnia, little was done in a concrete manner to strengthen the ability of U.S. government organizations to change minds and influence behavior. For some at the policy level, the hope was that Bosnia was an anomaly. Events in Kosovo would prove otherwise.

Kosovo

Serbian leader Slobodan Milosevic was aware, as were NATO leaders, that the most vulnerable aspect of the NATO effort to exert pressure on the Serbian regime in 1999 during the Kosovo conflict was United States and Western European public opinion. Milosevic believed that American public opinion was particularly susceptible to Serbian perception management. The Kosovo crisis was occurring in an area most Americans could not identify on a map, much less understand why the Serbs and ethnic Albanians were killing each other, or why America should get involved. Once again, as in Bosnia, perception management played a central role in each side's strategy (Collins, 2000).

For those in the United States and Europe who favored intervention in Kosovo to support the ethnic Albanians, the powerful images caused by the deaths of innocents at the hands of Serbian security forces was an opportunity that needed to be exploited. The use of photographs and video from horrific massacres to justify intervention is nothing new. Just as the second Sarajevo Marketplace massacre in August 1995 was the trigger for decisive NATO bombing in Bosnia, the Racak massacre on January 15, 1999, was the incident that began the final spiral toward NATO bombing in Kosovo. The deaths of 45 ethnic Albanians in Racak, the quick arrival of the press at the scene before the Serbs could sanitize the area, and the emotional statements of the Organization for Security and Cooperation in Europe representative in Kosovo, American William Walker, proved to be a powerful push for intervention. Tellingly, at the subsequent Rambouillet Conference, an anonymous, and evidently frustrated U.S. official in the Clinton administration confided to a reporter from *The New York Times*, "It may turn out that we may need another Srebrenica [Bosnian massacre] before we have a Dayton. But wasn't Racak sufficient?" (Perlez, 1999). Ultimately, the Racak massacre was sufficient to cause the United States and NATO to intervene. The mass executions in Kosovo attributed to the Serbs helped advance a policy that many in the West wanted to enact.

While Western officials publicized Serbian atrocities committed against the ethnic Albanians to pull policy toward intervention, once NATO's military involvement began, the Serbs did their best to use NATO's bombing errors and the deaths of innocent civilians to break Western public support for intervention. One observer of the situation opined:

> It's enough to portray the people as hapless and demonize the leaders....Clinton and Secretary of State Madeline Albright sold Kosovo in that fashion: as a quarrel with Milosevic

rather than the Serbian people. But surgical propaganda is risky business. What happens when bombs miss the villains—Milosevic and his generals—and land on their people instead? You are, by your own terms, killing innocents. (Powell, 1999, p. C1)

NATO bombing errors were, in terms of percentages, extremely small. But while small in number, they were still exploited exceedingly well by the Serbs, as Milosevic hoped to derail NATO's prosecution of the war (Judah, 2000). As a result of the cumulative effect of the 55 killed on a train crossing a bridge at Leskovac on April 12, the 75 ethnic Albanians killed by NATO near Djakovica, the 15 killed in Nis, the three dead as a result of the Chinese Embassy bombing in downtown Belgrade on May 7, and the death of 16 at a retirement home in Surdulica on May 31, the Serbs hoped Western public pressure would bring an end to NATO's attacks.

But, just as President Clinton admitted to *underestimating* the steadfastness of Milosevic and his capacity to endure the physical destruction of large sections of Serbian civilian infrastructure, it is also clear Milosevic *overestimated* the sympathetic impulses of the West—especially the American people. Milosevic correctly identified the center of gravity for the NATO effort—American public opinion—but the American public showed tremendous indifference to Serbian civilian casualties. While American support for the intervention was paper thin, as long as the U.S. military suffered few casualties, it seemed as though few Americans really cared what occurred in Yugoslavia. When Milosevic grasped the depth of this American apathy, and realized he could not cause the casualties to the American military that were necessary to shake U.S. public opinion, he must have realized he had no chance to outlast NATO.

During NATO's Kosovo bombing campaign, the Serbs found their outlets to the world gradually choked off by NATO's air strikes. NATO's commanders placed a high priority on destroying Serbian cellular phone relays and satellite up-links. Because of communications interruptions, Serbian Internet Web sites were forced offline. Also noteworthy was the decision by the European consortium controlling the communications satellite EUTELSAT, many of them NATO members, to suspend dissemination of the Serbian government Radio Television Service (RTS) at the end of May. When NATO suspended the air strikes, Serbia was largely cut off from outside contact.

In the early portion of the NATO bombing campaign, Milosevic's government benefited from a patriotic outpouring by a wide cross section of Serbs. "Turbo-folk" concerts, combining traditional Serbian folk and modern rock music, as well as nightly vigils on bridges in the major cities in Serbia, with participants holding paper "bulls-eye" targets daring NATO bombers to strike, seemed to indicate deep support for Milosevic. RTS cleverly reinforced these early perceptions of a plucky, guiltless, nation standing up to the most powerful military coalition the world had yet known by comparing NATO actions to Nazi bombings on Belgrade and frequently playing the eerily prophetic American movie, "Wag the Dog," a film about a U.S. President, dogged by sexual embarrassments, attempting to divert public attention to a contrived conflict in Albania.

As days added up into weeks, and then into months, however, early Serbian enthusiasm wilted under the NATO bombardment. Early Serbian jingoist attitudes became extinguished by the daily struggles with water and electricity shortages, as well as the collapse of nearly all organized commercial enterprise. NATO's bombing campaign started to chip away Milosevic's support. Wary of Milosevic because of his previous lies and broken promises, the Serbs were skeptical of any information coming from the government. Moreover, the predilection of RTS to exaggerate, such as claiming Serbian forces downed several NATO aircraft each night, and to tell the really big lie rather than work in the gray areas where truth and lies coexist, caused the Serbs to become increasingly distrustful of *any* news. This universal distrust worked against NATO information efforts in Serbia, too, as the Serbs became unlikely to "listen to anyone's truth anymore" and to turn toward light entertainment on the radio and television rather than news (Pancic, 1996).

Additionally, in contrast to the previous conflicts in Croatia and Bosnia, when Milosevic had near full control of the information flow to the Serbian people, Serbs during the Kosovo conflict had access to news sources other than state-controlled RTS. In conjunction with its normal bombing, NATO attacked Serbia with nonlethal weapons—leaflet drops and radio/television broadcasts—to get information from a different slant to the Serbs. NATO dropped over 100 million leaflets over the course of the 78-day bombing campaign—nearly nine leaflets for every man, woman, and child in the country. Reports were that in some areas of Serbia, the three-by-six-inch paper leaflets covered the ground like snow for many kilometers. *New York Times* reporter Steven Erlanger (1999), who spent much of the bombing campaign in Belgrade, noted:

> What began as a campaign against the Yugoslav military to get Slobodan Milosevic to capitulate quickly over Kosovo, veered, perhaps out of frustration, into a psy-ops war aimed also at civilians, at their electricity and their water and their heating plants. (p. 86)

Without his traditional information monopoly, Milosevic's ability to control perceptions in his own country was undermined. Ironically, the actions by Milosevic to shut down many independent indigenous stations, coupled with NATO bombings, temporarily cleared the crowded airwaves and made transmission into the region much less difficult (Lansner, 1999). NATO military commander, General Clark, noted in his book on the Kosovo campaign: "In this war, a camera inside Kosovo [to show Serb activities against ethnic Albanians] would have been worth a dozen strikes on Serb vehicles" (Clark, 2001, p. 443).

After the capitulation by Milosevic to NATO in June 1999 and his agreement to withdraw Serbian forces from Kosovo, the United States attempted to maintain the psychological momentum it had achieved within Serbia and unseat Milosevic from power. The United States built a series of six transmitters to encircle Serbia in order to beam anti-Milosevic radio and television programming (Waller, 1999). Eventually, the impact of effective perception management helped magnify the activities of the Serbian dissidents. Milosevic was overthrown in October 2000 and was eventually surrendered by Serbian authorities in June 2001 to stand war crimes charges in The Hague.

One would have thought that the experiences in Bosnia and Kosovo would convince the civilian and military leadership in the United States that PSYOP was at the heart of 21st century foreign policy and warfare. Nevertheless, despite hundreds of journal articles and tens of books attesting to this trend, there was no real movement at the policy level to invigorate this discipline until the horrific events of 9/11.

After 9/11

In the aftermath of the terrorist attacks on September 11, 2001, the United States realized that the headlong rush to dismantle its public diplomacy apparatus in the 1990s was, to say the least, shortsighted. U.S. leadership believed that in the post-Soviet era the need to explain its policies globally, trying to build good will through cultural exchanges, and so on was no longer needed in a world where the United States and Russia called one another allies. Perhaps some in the United States believed that its dominating culture, the so-called "Coca Cola Colonialism," coupled with support for free markets and open government, was ultimately enough to carry the day, and that any organized activity to promote its agenda abroad was redundant and might even appear overbearing. Unfortunately, the world was not a less threatening place after the fall of Soviet Communism, and the need for a vigorous information effort at all levels, targeted toward all audiences, was still very much required.

The task facing the United States after 9/11—to tell its side of the story and to defend its policies—was enormous. After some false starts, notably the strange rise and rapid demise of the Pentagon's Office of Strategic Influence in February 2002 (Garfield, 2002), the United States attempted to put its public diplomacy house in order. Within a year of the terrorist bombings of 9/11, the United States had built its most coordinated strategic perception management structure since the 1980s, focused on the Islamic World, and heavily funded—with over $750 million for the Middle East area alone (Leonard, 2002). One of the most notable new additions is Radio Sawa (Radio Together), which features Western and Arab pop music, interspersed with news featuring a U.S. perspective. Within months of its debut, Radio Sawa's advocates announced that it was one of the most popular radio stations among young Arabs (Youssef, 2003; but see Hassan, 2002).

Tested in its nascent stages during military operations in Afghanistan during October and November of 2001, the United States, along with its ally the United Kingdom, was ready to use its revitalized PSYOP apparatus to full effect during Operation Iraqi Freedom. In addition to attempting to control the spin of stories, the Pentagon's spokesperson Victoria "Torie" Clarke (former general manager of the Washington, DC office of Hill and Knowlton, a global public relations and marketing firm) made the decision to embed reporters with military units scheduled to deploy. Although, in retrospect, this was a brilliant move, initially many in the U.S. defense establishment were not so sanguine about the decision. It proved to be the right choice on many levels. First, reporters that wanted to embed were forced to undergo a mandatory miniboot camp, which gave many their first appreciation of the challenges faced by the average military member. Second, embedding created an inevitable bond between reporters and the units they covered. Even if only subconsciously, an unavoidable jingoism crept into the reporting of many of those embedded with Coalition troops. Finally, embedding made sense because it insured the safety of the reporters and gave the world its first real-time coverage of a battlefield. Because of the fluid nature of Operation Iraqi Freedom, had reporters been allowed to be free agents and roam the battlefield, many more would have been killed and captured.

Still, despite all the effort, in reality there was very little demonstrated success in the Coalition's public diplomacy effort prior to Operation Iraqi Freedom. In one notable *faux pas*, the Coalition Information Centre set up by the United Kingdom's Alistair Campbell in Whitehall handed out a dossier purported to be gleaned from secret intelligence, but it subsequently proved to be largely plagiarized from a graduate student's dissertation work posted on the Internet (Brown & Coman, 2003).

U.S. Secretary of State Colin Powell's 78-minute speech to the U.N. Security Council broadcast live around the world on February 5, 2003, failed to convince representatives from the key nations on the council—France, Germany, and Russia—that military action needed to be taken immediately against Iraq. By contrast, French Foreign Minister Dominique de Villepin's subsequent speech before the United Nations, casting doubt on every aspect of Powell's presentation, was greeted with cheers and wild applause within the usual staid council. As a result, the United States and United Kingdom made little headway in gaining support among their traditional allies, and a second U.N. Security Council resolution authorizing military action against Iraq was never put to a vote, as it was obvious it would inevitably fail to garner the required support.

Within the Islamic world, U.S. information activities to gain support for the Iraqi invasion also failed. In retrospect, immediate positive results may have been impossible to achieve. Effective PSYOP takes a sustained effort and a long-term view. For the foreseeable future, as Osama Sibliani, the publisher of *Arab American News* noted: "The United States could have the Prophet Muhammad doing public relations and it wouldn't help" (Miller & Rampton, 2001, p. 12).

During the actual conduct of the military operation, the U.S.-led Coalition attempted to favorably shape the worldwide perception of the conflict through perception operations. One factor that makes it difficult to have an effect on world opinion today is the vast proliferation of news sources. In particular, the large increases in satellite television news services and Internet connections make it ever more difficult to influence opinions and attitudes globally, or even regionally. The explosion in the number of news providers allows the viewer to read or see the news that reinforces his or her own prejudices and fixed opinions. An Arab viewer who finds the reporting on CNN to be contrary to his or her own news bias can switch to al-Jazeera and see a perspective of the world perhaps more consistent with his or her own.

Reportedly, during the conflict the Iraqi Information Agency recognized the power of al-Jazeera and went so far as to infiltrate that organization with its agents in order to help slant the coverage to be more pro-Iraqi (Colvin, 2003). Likewise, the Coalition attempted to take Iraqi television news service off the air through both bombing and electronic jamming—as much, if not more, for the impact it was having outside Iraq than for the impact it was having within the country.

While the results of PSYOP at the strategic level by the United States and United Kingdom were mixed at best, the employment of PSYOP within Iraq at the military operational and tactical level was more successful. As noted in *Jane's Defense Weekly*, "When the full story of the PSYOP campaign in 'Iraqi Freedom' comes to be written, there is little doubt that it will be deemed to have been hugely successful" (Burger, Cook, Koch, & Sirak, 2003, p. 21). The use of mass media like radio and leaflets, and targeted media like emails against key decision makers and loudspeakers during ground operations, seems to have accrued better results.

Over 40 million leaflets were dropped on Iraq before the first attack on March 20, 2003, and another 40+ million were dropped during the conflict. Some leaflets threatened to destroy any military formation that stood and fought, while others encouraged the Iraqi populace and military to ignore the directives of the Ba'athist leadership. In retrospect, they did seem to have the effect intended. The problem, as with all PSYOP actions, is the difficulty in determining the proximate cause of an action during a war.

Certainly, Coalition forces did not see the level of Iraqi surrenders of the 1991 Gulf War, which reached 70,000. About 250 Iraqis surrendered the first day during the seizure of Umm Qasr, and it was hoped that this initial trickle would soon turn into a flood of surrenders, but this did not happen. During the first days of the conflict, the manner in which the Coalition approached the entire military campaign was arguably psychological, with the hope that the use of overwhelming force and precision munitions would induce "shock and awe" and the Iraqi regime would collapse like a house of cards. The failure of the plan forced a change by the conventional U.S. military forces, and no doubt also caused the PSYOP forces to rethink their themes and messages. They came to rely more upon steady activity and pressure rather than hoping one knockout blow would do the job.

In addition to leaflets, the Coalition also heavily used radio. Broadcasting from fixed transmission towers as well as from the United States flying airborne broadcast platform (the EC-130E aircraft—COMMANDO SOLO), the Coalition used a similar format to Radio Sawa, a great deal of popular music interlaced with news and a few announcements. The name for this Iraqi-wide PSYOP radio broadcast was the rather uninspiring "Information Radio" (Radio Nederland Wereldomroep, n.d.). Local PSYOP radio stations were also set up outside of major population centers— one being the U.K. PSYOP radio station, Radio Nahrain ("Two Rivers"), an FM radio station established on the periphery of Basra. In addition to setting up its own radio transmitters, the Coalition attempted to electronically jam Iraqi radio stations to gain a monopoly on the information available to the Iraqi people through this medium.

The PSYOP radio stations and leaflets discussed thus far are examples of so-called "white PSYOP" that openly and accurately declares who is sponsoring the PSYOP product. During the Iraqi conflict there was also "black PSYOP"—PSYOP that purportedly is produced by one source, but is actually created by someone else. It has been reported that the U.S. Central Intelligence Agency, with the assistance of the U.S. public relations firm the Rendon Group, set up black PSYOP radio stations as early as February 2003 (Grace, 2003). One such station, so-called "Radio Tikrit," tried to build up its credibility with a classic black PSYOP tactic by stating that it was managed by loyal Iraqis in the Tikrit area and by maintaining an editorial line slavishly supportive of Saddam Hussein. But within a few weeks, the tone changed and the station began to become more and more critical of Saddam. The hope of black PSYOP is that the target audience does not see through the ruse and truly believes the PSYOP is coming from the wrongly attributed source, which it sees as more credible. The risk, of course, is that if the ruse is discovered, the trustworthiness of the entire PSYOP effort, both white and black, is damaged—perhaps irreparably.

One of the more innovative means used by Coalition PSYOP in the build-up to the Iraqi invasion was mobile phone messaging and emails sent directly to key decision makers in the Iraqi regime (Sennitt, 2003). At the start of 2003, there were only 60 Internet cafes in Iraq, and the connection fee of U.S. $25 per home was beyond the means of many ordinary Iraqis (Sennitt, 2003). Also, the Iraqi regime was very wary indeed of allowing access to the Internet throughout Iraq. So, while many ordinary Iraqis did not have access to the Internet, most of the Iraqi Ba'athist leadership did, and the Coalition used this means to specifically outline to each personally why continued support of Saddam would dearly cost both Iraq collectively, and the members of the Iraqi elite individually.

On the Iraqi side, the quirky "Baghdad Bob," Information Minister Mohammed Saeed al-Sahhaf, provided material for many comics in the West. The climax of his tragic hilarity was his pronouncements that Coalition forces were nowhere near Baghdad, while simultaneously live television pictures from embedded reporters were broadcast showing U.S. armored vehicles passing under highway signs for "Baghdad Center." While Baghdad Bob may not have had much credibility abroad, his news releases and press conferences were attributed by an Iraqi authority as *significantly bolstering Iraqi military morale—perhaps by as much as 50 percent* (Walt, 2003).

Also very active were tactical PSYOP elements, involving attaching PSYOP troops with a loudspeaker vehicle and a translator directly to army and marine units. As in past conflicts, these units proved their worth by convincing isolated Iraqi elements to surrender, helping to maintain control of Iraqi prisoners, and even conducting deception operations against Iraqi military elements by playing sound effects of tanks and helicopters through the loudspeakers.

Mysteriously, it appears that not much thought was given by the Iraqi Freedom military planners to the postconflict challenges. Developing a postconflict PSYOP capability in advance appears to have similarly been forgotten. This lack of forethought is even more puzzling when one reads study after study emphasizing that effective PSYOP is a key to establishing a lasting peace.

In some cases, Iranian agents, especially in southern Iraq, filled the information vacuum in postconflict Iraq (DeYoung & Pincus, 2003). The United States tried to fill the void by contracting for assistance, offering millions of dollars to companies who could put anything on the air. This led to some unintentionally amusing moments, especially as the attention of the U.S. media turned away from Iraq, and these contracted companies beamed U.S. news stories to what to be sure were quizzical Iraqis scratching their heads about the applicability of the Lacy and Scott Peterson murder case to the average Iraqi (DeYoung & Pincus, 2003). The effort to win hearts and minds by all sides continues unabated in Iraq today, and will continue for years to come. It is the outcome of this struggle that will ultimately determine whether the conflict was worth the effort in the first instance.

Lessons Learned and Relearned

Despite the unctuous nature of the term, one must unavoidably speak of the lessons learned from the recent attention that persuasion operations (including PSYOP) have earned. First, it is clear that persuasion activities cannot gain results overnight, and even if you invest a lot of money and allocate a lot of personnel, as the United States has, positive achievements may be scanty—especially initially. But this does not mean that PSYOP should be ignored. Changing ingrained attitudes can take generations; persuasion activities take time and sustained effort.

Second, as the United States learned in Iraq, do not forget PSYOP in the postconflict phase. Since there is often an informational gap to be filled, this is really where PSYOP can be of considerable help. It is during the aftermath of a conflict that people psychologically need reassurance and comforting. Whether in the Balkans or Iraq, PSYOP can bridge the perception gap between whether the military forces in the area are viewed as heartless occupier or helpful partner.

Third, it is becoming acceptable to use the word PSYOP. It was surprising, even to PSYOP practitioners, how often the term PSYOP was used in military briefings and by the press during Operation Iraqi Freedom. In other recent military operations, there has been a tendency to blur connotations and meanings by using fuzzier terminology, avoiding terms like psychological operations and opting for more politically correct terms, or avoiding the subject altogether. As in the Cold War, it is now acceptable to acknowledge that the U.S. is involved in an ideological struggle where ideas mean as much, if not more, than bullets. Changing views and influencing perceptions are the primary weapons in combating terrorism.

Today, in an era where the United States can find that its greatest challenge is not the opposition's military but its attempts to manipulate world opinion in its favor, a continual review and strengthening of the United States' PSYOP capabilities is all the more important. The overriding purpose of the U.S. defense establishment is to deter war, not to fight. Deterrence is a psychological phenomenon, not a simple reflection of the quantity and quality of military forces. PSYOP can help shape foreign perceptions and strengthen the deterrent effect of U.S. forces, and strengthen overall U.S. security policy.

References

Anti-NATO images on Bosnian Serb TV. (1997, August 23). *New York Times*, p. 6.

Becker, E. (1999, October 15). Military leaders tell Congress of NATO errors in Kosovo. *New York Times*, p. A8.

Brock, P. (1993–1994). Dateline Yugoslavia: The Partisan Press. *Foreign Policy, 93*, 152–172.

Brown, C. & Coman, J. (2003, February 9). How not to win a propaganda war. *London Sunday Telegraph*, p. 1.

Bruntz, G. G. (1938). *Allied propaganda and the collapse of the German Empire in 1918*. Stanford, CA: Stanford University Press.

Burger, K, Cook, N., Koch, A., & Sirak, M. (2003, April 30). What went right? *Jane's Defense Weekly*, p. 21.

Centner, C.M. (1997). Precision-guided propaganda: Exploiting the U.S. information advantage in peacetime. *Strategic Review, Spring*, 35–41.

Clark, W. K. (2001). *Waging modern war: Bosnia, Kosovo, and the future of combat*. New York: Public Affairs.

Collins, S. (1999). Army PSYOP in Bosnia: Capabilities and constraints. *Parameters: U.S. Army War College Quarterly, Summer*, 57–73.

Collins, S. (1998). The antenna war and the transformation of Bosnian-Serb television. *Peacekeeping and International Relations: Journal of the Pearson Peacekeeping Centre, August-September*, 9–11.

Collins, S. (2000). Perception conflict in the 'modern' Balkan Wars. In A.D. Campen & D.H. Dearth (Eds.), *Cyberwar 3.0: Human Factors in Information Operations and Future Conflict* (pp. 191-201). Fairfax, VA: AFCEA International Press.

Colvin, M. (2003, May 11). How Saddam's agents targeted Al-Jazeera. *London Sunday Times*. Retrieved August 29, 2005, from http://www.freerepublic.com/focus/fr/909285/posts

DeYoung, K. & Pincus, W. (2003, May 11). U.S. to take its message to Iraqi airwaves. *Washington Post*, p. 17.

Erlanger, S. (1999, June 13). Lives; Beneath the falling bombs. *New York Times Magazine*, p. 86.

Fukuyama, F. (1992). *The end of history and the last man*. New York: Free Press.

Garfield, A. (2002). The Offence of Strategic Influence: Making the case for perception management operations. *Journal of Information Warfare, May*, 30–39.

Grace, N. (2003, March 17). Bush address underscores importance of radio psyop. Retrieved September 22, 2005, from http://www.rnw.nl/realradio/features/html/iraq-analysis030318.html

Hassan, A. (2002, September 26). Spin unspun. *World Press Review Online*.

Hoffman, D. (2002). Beyond public diplomacy. *Foreign Affairs, March/April*, 83–95.

Jacobson, M. R. (1997). Tactical PSYOP support to Task Force Eagle. In L.Wentz (Ed.), *Lessons from Bosnia: The IFOR experience* (pp. 189–224). Washington, DC: Department of Defense Command and Control Research Program.

Johnson, S. C. (2004). Improving U.S. public diplomacy toward the Middle East: Heritage Lecture #838. Delivered May 24, 2004, at The Heritage Foundation. Retrieved June 9, 2005, from http://www.heritage.org/Research/NationalSecurity/hl838.cfm

Judah, T. (2000). *Kosovo: War and revenge.* New Haven: Yale University Press.

Katagiri, T. (1976, April). A former PSYOP group commander in Vietnam looks back. In D.C. Pollock (Ed.), *The art and science of psychological operations: Case studies of military application* (DA PAM 525–7–1), Vol. 1. Washington, DC: Department of the Army.

Kiehl, W. P. (2003). Can Humpty Dumpty be saved? Retrieved August 29, 2005, from http://www.unc.edu/depts/diplomat/archives_roll/2003_10-12/kiehl_humpty/kiehl_humpty.html

Lansner, T. R. (1999, September). Same spin, different war. *The New Presence: The Prague Journal of Central European Affairs,* 6–7.

Leonard, M. (2002, September/October). Diplomacy by other means. *Foreign Policy,* 48–56. Retrieved September 22, 2005, from http://www.bintjbeil.com/articles/en/020929leonard.html

Lerner, D. (1971). *Psychological warfare against Nazi Germany: The Sykewar Campaign, D-day to VE-Day.* Cambridge, MA: MIT Press.

Lord, C. (1997). The psychological dimension in national strategy. In F. R. Barnett & C. Lord (Eds.), *Political warfare and psychological operations: Rethinking the U.S. approach* (pp. 13–37). Washington, DC: NDU Press.

Miller, L. & Rampton, S. (2001). The Pentagon's information warrior: Rendon to the rescue. *PR Watch, October–December,* 12.

Nye, J. & Owens, W. A. (1996). America's information edge. *Foreign Affairs, 75,* 20–36.

Owen, D. (1995). *Balkan odyssey.* New York: Harcourt Brace & Company.

Paddock, A. H., Jr. (2002). *U.S. Army Special Warfare—Its Origins* (Rev. ed.). Lawrence, KS: University of Kansas Press.

Pancic, T. (1996). *On the air in Serbia: Freedom of media unsealed.* Retrieved June 9, 2005, from http://www.aimpress.ch/dyn/trae/archive/data/199906/90626-002-trae-pod.htm

Perlez, J. (1999, March 15). U.S. hope is slim as talks restart on Kosovo crisis. *New York Times,* pp. A1, A6.

Peterson, P. G. (2002). Public diplomacy and the war on terrorism. *Foreign Affairs, September/October,* 74–94.

Powell, M. (1999, May 27). How to bomb in selling a good war. *Washington Post,* p. C1.

Radio Nederland Wereldomrop (n.d.). Iraq: Psychological warfare. Retrieved June 9, 2005, from http://www.rnw.nl/realradio/features/html/iraq-psywar.html

Reagan, R. (1987). Remarks at the Brandenburg Gate (speech delivered June 12). Retrieved June 9, 2005, from http://www.reaganfoundation.org/reagan/speeches/wall.asp

Sennitt, A. (2003, May 14). The Internet under Saddam. Retrieved June 9, 2005, from http://www.rnw.nl/realradio/features/html/iraq-internet.html

Siegel, P. C. (1997). Information activities. In L.Wentz (Ed.), *Lessons from Bosnia: The IFOR experience* (pp. 167–187). Washington, DC: Department of Defense Command and Control Research Program.

Snyder, A. A. (1995). *Warriors of disinformation: American propaganda, Soviet lies, and the winning of the Cold War.* New York: Arcade.

Taylor, P. M. (1995). *Munitions of the mind: A history of propaganda from the ancient world to the present day.* Manchester, UK: Manchester University Press.

Thompson, M. (1994). *Forging war: The media in Serbia, Croatia, and Bosnia-Hercegovina.* Avon, UK: Bath Press.

U.S. Department of Defense. (1996, July). Doctrine for joint psychological operations. Joint Pub. 3–53 (125 pp.). Retrieved June 9, 2005, from http://www.iwar.org.uk/psyops/resources/doctrine/psyop-jp-3-53.pdf

Walko, D. P. (1996). Psychological operations in Panama during Operations Just Cause and Promote Liberty. In F. L. Goldstein & B. F. Findley (Eds.), *Psychological operations: Principles and case studies* (pp. 249–277). Maxwell Air Force Base: Air University Press.

Waller, D. (1999, July 12). Tearing down Milosevic. *Time*, pp. 37–38.

Walt, V. (2003, May 13). Bob is believed to be in Baghdad. *USA Today*, p. 9.

Youssef, N. (2003, March 11). U.S. radio station in Jordan sounds like a hit with young. Retrieved September 22, 2005, from http://www.freep.com/news/nw/propa11_20030311.htm

PART III

PHYSIOLOGICAL AND COGNITIVE DIMENSIONS OF MILITARY OPERATIONS

CHAPTER 5

SLEEP LOSS: IMPLICATIONS FOR OPERATIONAL EFFECTIVENESS AND CURRENT SOLUTIONS

Nancy J. Wesensten, Gregory Belenky, and Thomas J. Balkin

In this chapter, we describe the contribution of sleep to operational effectiveness—specifically, cognitive effectiveness. In the first section, we provide an overview of sleep-loss effects on those cognitive capacities relevant to military operations. Next, we present a solution—a sleep management system—for minimizing the effects of sleep loss on cognitive performance.

How does sleep sustain cognitive performance? One would not dispute that falling asleep while on duty in an operational setting can lead to errors, accidents, and even catastrophe. Less well appreciated is that sleep deprivation systematically degrades performance long before people become so sleepy that they fall asleep. Although the underlying physiological mechanisms by which sleep sustains cognitive effectiveness are still under investigation, the subtle yet devastating consequences of sleep loss on operational effectiveness are clear, as one case history from the Gulf War exemplifies.

Case History

Schematic depictions of the series of events in this case history are shown in Figure 5.1. At 1800 hours on February 25, 1991 during the 100-hour ground war, a platoon of Bradley fighting vehicles from the Second Armored Cavalry Regiment (2ACR) were ordered to halt their advance and go into a screen line (Figure 5.1,

The views expressed in this chapter are those of the authors and do not reflect the official policy or position of the U.S. Department of Defense or the U.S. Government. This material has been reviewed by the Walter Reed Army Institute of Research, and there is no objection to its presentation and/or publication.

panel A). They were to resume their advance the next morning. They remained awake monitoring their thermal sights for "hot spots" indicating possible Iraqi approach to their position.

About seven hours later—at approximately 0100 hours on February 26, 1991—the Bradley crews observed hot spots approaching (Figure 5.1, panel B). They were uncertain as to whether these were friend or foe and continued to observe. The Iraqis had no thermal sights of their own; therefore, the Iraqis were unaware of the Bradley screen line and proceeded forward. Only when the lead Iraqi vehicles reached the screen line did the Bradley crews realize that these were the enemy. A brief firefight ensued, during which all the Iraqi vehicles were destroyed (Figure 5.1, panel C). During the firefight the two Bradleys at the right flank of the screen line had turned to their left; they were no longer parallel to the other Bradleys but were instead facing into their own screen line (Figure 5.1, panel D). The crews of these two Bradleys, however, were unaware that they had turned to face their own screen line. They still believed that they were facing in the correct orientation to the other Bradleys; therefore, they also believed that forward of them was the enemy. Because of this disorientation, the crews mistook the two Bradleys on the left flank (which were maneuvering around burning Iraqi vehicles) for enemy vehicles and proceeded to enfilade their

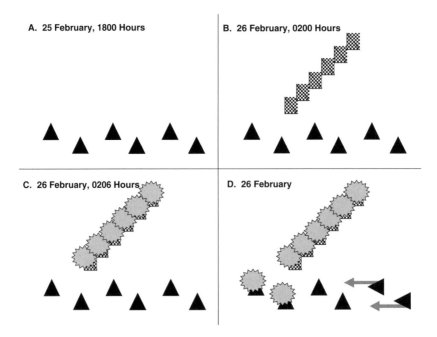

Figure 5.1
Sequence of Events from the 100-Hour Ground War Friendly Fire Incident, Gulf War 1991 (Solid triangles represent U.S. Bradley fighting vehicles. Checkered triangles represent enemy vehicles.)

own line with fire. They destroyed the two Bradleys on the left flank (Figure 5.1, Panel D).

Because the Bradley fighting vehicles were equipped with Kevlar spall curtains and Halon fire suppression and the crew members were wearing Nomex fire-retardant suits, all escaped without injury. One of us (G.B.) was a medical officer with the parent unit of the Bradley platoon and was able to assemble all crew members of the platoon a few days later and conduct a reconstructive debriefing of this incident (Belenky, Martin & Marcy, 1996).

By their own self-report, the Bradley crews had obtained only 3 to 4 hours of sleep per night over the previous five days. Thus, the crews were chronically sleep deprived. Second, the firefight ensued during the early morning hours, at a time of day when the crew members' complex mental operations would be waning as a function of circadian rhythmicity.

The sleep-deprived crew members, however, were still able to fire rounds accurately down-range, as evidenced by their ability to destroy the Bradleys on the left flank. The problem was that the disoriented crew lost the situational awareness critical for distinguishing friend from foe. This misperception was particularly devastating because the crew was operating under the axiom that "if it's in front of us, it dies." The problem was that once disoriented, the crew misperceived where "front" was.

Early in the debriefing, crew members maintained that they had destroyed only Iraqi vehicles. It was only after Bradley 25 mm antitank rounds were recovered from the destroyed Bradleys that the crew understood what had happened on the battlefield.

This friendly fire incident had all the marks of sleep-loss effects on cognitive effectiveness.

Military Effectiveness Defined

The above case history illustrates that even as weaponry becomes more sophisticated, the soldier—particularly his cognitive effectiveness—remains central to the success of military operations. Effective operational outcomes generally depend on speed of responding (which translates into operating inside of the enemy's decision cycle) and attention to context directed toward accomplishing the commander's intent. This in turn feeds cognitive integration at the highest levels (complex mental operations). Such complex mental operations are facilitated by a networked force, described next, and include situational awareness; adaptability, mental agility, and judgment; initiative; anticipation and planning; and course-of-action determination. These are all mental operations known to be impaired by the various stressors to which today's war fighter is routinely exposed, including environmental extremes (heat, cold), dehydration, operational tempo, and sleep loss.

Network-centric operations refers to computer network-based provision of an integrated picture of the battlefield available in detail to all levels of command and control down to the individual soldier level. The latter is achieved through command post, vehicle, and helmet-mounted displays; and individual soldier computers (all linked by radio-frequency networks). The point of greatest vulnerability in network-centric operations is the war fighter's ability to make use of the information provided by the network (i.e., to facilitate predictive planning and preemption; integrated force management; execution of time-critical missions) (Wesensten, Belenky, & Balkin, 2005)—a vulnerability potentially compounded by reduced human redundancy in modern military operations.

Impact of Sleep Loss on Cognitive Effectiveness

Of the stressors affecting war fighter *cognitive* performance, sleep loss is the most thoroughly studied.

Total Sleep Deprivation

Total sleep deprivation exerts substantial deleterious effects on complex mental operations (cognitive performance). Figure 5.2 shows that cognitive performance on a task requiring decision making, short-term memory, and mathematical processing declines by approximately 25 percent for every 24 hours of wakefulness (from Wesensten, Killgore & Balkin, 2005). After three nights without sleep, complex cognitive performance can be degraded by as much as 75 percent.

Partial Sleep Deprivation (Restricted Sleep)

Eight hours of sleep per day will sustain maximal cognitive performance indefinitely. But can we get by with less than eight hours of sleep per day? The answer appears to be that we can, but we will pay a performance penalty for it. To date, only two studies have been published in which the effects of *chronic* (7 days) restricted sleep were characterized (Belenky et al., 2003; Van Dongen, Maislin, Mullington & Dinges, 2003). Figure 5.3 shows results from one of these (Belenky et al., 2003) in which cognitive performance was evaluated across 7 days on a fixed nightly sleep schedule comprised of 9, 7, 5, or 3 hours time in bed (TIB). As shown, 9 hours TIB (which translated into approximately 8 hours of sleep) sustained cognitive performance for the entire 7 days. Seven hours TIB (6.5 hours of sleep) resulted in small but immediate declines in cognitive performance; the difference between 7 hours TIB and 9 hours TIB was clearly obvious after the fourth day. Five hours TIB (4.5 hours of sleep) resulted in immediate and fairly substantial cognitive performance deficits. Deficits in the 5-hour TIB group leveled off after about 4 days, but performance remained well below the 9-hour TIB group. Finally, 3 hours TIB per night (nearly all of which was spent sleeping—a well-documented effect of sleep restriction) resulted in immediate and devastating cognitive performance deficits that did not level off but continued to accumulate across days. After seven nights of sleep restricted to three hours, performance was reduced by 58 percent of levels maintained by the 9-hour TIB group. Van Dongen et al. (2003) evaluated effects of 2, 4, 6, and 8 hours TIB across 7 days and found similar patterns of degradation.

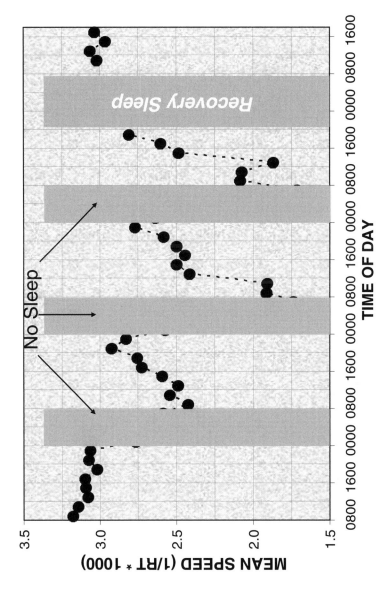

Figure 5.2
Effect of 85 Hours Total Sleep Deprivation on Speed of Cognitive Operations (Shaded areas represent nighttime periods [approximate] during which volunteers would otherwise be sleeping.)

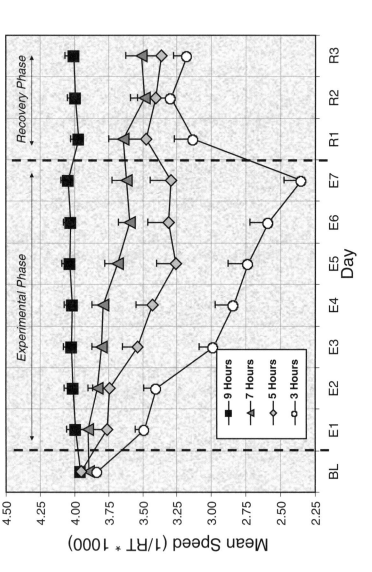

Figure 5.3
Effects of 3, 5, 7, or 9 Hours Time in Bed (TIB) Per Night for Seven Nights (BL = baseline phase [each day preceded by 8 hours TIB]; E = experimental phase [each day preceded by 3, 5, 7, or 9 hours TIB]; R = recovery phase [each day preceded by 8 hours TIB].)

Disrupted (Disturbed) Sleep

Individuals may spend 8–9 hours in bed per night, but during this time, sleep may be disrupted or "fragmented" due to noise, attempting to sleep during daytime hours, and so on. Disrupting sleep exacts a toll on cognitive performance and alertness (Balkin, Badia, Harsh & Klempert, 1985). The more frequent the disruptions, the more difficult it is to maintain next-day alertness and mental performance. When sleep is highly disrupted (e.g., every minute, as is the case in certain sleep disorders and under some operational conditions), next-day alertness is degraded to a level not much different from getting no sleep at all. Disrupting sleep impairs cognitive performance by effectively increasing wake time and thus decreasing total sleep time. Second, and far less obvious, is that sleep can be disrupted without causing a full awakening and still impair mental performance. That is, if disrupting sleep increases the amount of light sleep (even in the absence of frank awakenings), cognitive performance will be impaired. Light sleep (e.g., dozing, or "stage 1") appears to have no value for sustaining mental operations (Wesensten et al., 2001). Thus, disrupting sleep amounts to decreasing recuperative sleep time, just the same as restricting sleep.

Recovery from Sleep Loss

Although the effects of sleep loss on cognitive performance have been described, the effects of recovery sleep (specifically, the amount of sleep needed to recover from sleep loss) have received less attention. In particular, cognitive performance recovery from chronic, restricted sleep (a much more common phenomenon in both military and civilian sectors) has not been well characterized, but it appears to take longer than recovery from acute, total sleep deprivation. In the Belenky et al. (2003) study, cognitive performance recovery from the various TIB schedules was evaluated: volunteers from all 4 TIB conditions were subsequently allowed 8 hours TIB per night across 3 nights (see Figure 5.3). As shown in Figure 5.3, following chronic, severe (3 hours TIB) sleep restriction, substantial cognitive performance recovery was accrued following the first night of recovery sleep (8 hours TIB). This substantial recovery (Figure 5.3) appeared to be similar to the large performance recovery seen following total sleep deprivation (as illustrated in Figure 5.2). However, cognitive performance was not restored to presleep restriction (baseline) levels. Smaller performance gains were accrued following the second and third night of recovery sleep; however, even after the third night, cognitive performance was not restored to baseline levels. These results suggest that unlike acute, total sleep deprivation, in response to chronic sleep restriction the brain undergoes adaptive changes that serve to sustain a stable (albeit reduced) level of performance; the findings further suggest that these changes persist into the recovery period and prevent rapid return to baseline performance. Such adaptive changes may act as a rate-limiter or governor that reduces (caps) the brain's operational capacity, allowing the brain to operate in the face of a restricted sleep budget. They may serve to prevent injury from occurring in the brain if it continued to perform at full capacity in the face of restricted sleep.

Summary of Sleep Deprivation Effects

In sum, sleep deprivation exerts two main effects. First, it makes the individual more susceptible to falling asleep in a boring or nonstimulating environment—as evidenced by difficulty with maintaining alertness while performing a boring, monotonous task or watching television. Second, even in a stimulating environment (where the susceptibility to falling asleep is minimal), sleep deprivation directly impairs higher order mental operations. Tasks that are most susceptible to sleep deprivation are those that are novel (not well learned), multifaceted (complex), and/or requiring a novel solution. In short, whenever recuperative sleep time is reduced, mental operations are impaired—whether via total sleep deprivation, partial sleep deprivation (restricted sleep), or the far less obvious situation in which sleep is disrupted or fragmented.

Further, performance recovery following acute total sleep deprivation and chronic sleep restriction differ. Rapid recovery is typical following acute total sleep deprivation. In contrast, chronic sleep restriction leads to long-time-constant cognitive performance decrements that are not rapidly reversed when sleep durations are once again increased. From an operational standpoint, the failure to rapidly recover from chronic sleep restriction implies that operator recycle rates will be slower.

Sleep-loss/Recovery Effects: Current Unknowns

As noted above, sleep loss impairs cognitive performance. For the most part, however, such deficits have been quantified using simple psychomotor (reaction time) and computerized cognitive (e.g., addition/subtraction) tasks. The degree to which effects on these tasks reflects effects on more operationally relevant functions (such as those exemplified by the Gulf War friendly fire incident) is unknown. These so-called cognitive "executive functions" include mental abstraction, critical reasoning, planning, sequencing, organizing, and coordinating willful and directed action, flexible thought, self-monitoring, selective attention, and conflict resolution—functions which effectively translate into situational awareness, course-of-action determination, and discriminating friend from foe. The lack of data pertaining to sleep deprivation effects on executive functions is probably due to the fact that (1) most tasks of executive function are nonrepeatable (thus, performance under both rested and sleep-deprived conditions cannot be obtained in the same individual); and (2) administration of executive function tasks is labor intensive and requires substantial expertise. Despite these drawbacks, available evidence indicates that sleep deprivation impairs some aspects of executive functioning, including creative thinking, sentence completion, estimation, and impulsivity (Harrison & Horne, 1998; 1999; Killgore, Balkin & Wesensten, 2005).

As reviewed in the next section, impairment of executive functioning (as well as the more widely documented impairment in vigilance) is consistent with the neurophysiological changes associated with sleep loss.

Neurophysiological Changes Underlying Sleep Deprivation and Recovery Sleep

Until recently, little was known about the neurophysiological changes underlying sleep deprivation and reversal of these changes during sleep. The advent of imaging techniques such as positron emission tomography (PET) has made it possible to image the living human brain during sleep deprivation and during recovery sleep.

Recent results show that sleep deprivation decreases brain glucose utilization (Thomas et al., 2002). Glucose utilization is most affected in brain areas mediating (1) the ability to maintain alertness and vigilance, and (2) executive functions. During sleep, those brain regions most affected by sleep deprivation are deactivated (Braun et al., 1997); and upon awakening, activity is restored (Balkin et al., 2002). Thus, the primary function of sleep appears to be restoration/sustainment of metabolic activity in brain regions that mediate (1) the ability to maintain wakefulness under nonstimulating conditions, and (2) higher order mental operations (i.e., executive functions).

Consequences for Cognitive Effectiveness

As indicated earlier, sleep deprivation exerts two main effects: it decreases the ability to resist sleep under boring, repetitive circumstances; and it also directly impairs cognitive performance even in a stimulating environment. Thus, whether a task or job is likely to be affected by sleep deprivation depends on the extent to which it involves these components. A task likely to be very sensitive to sleep deprivation is manning a screen line (as described in the case history above).

On the surface, manning a screen line appears to be a simple task, easily learned, and thus resistant to sleep deprivation. However, it involves all the components affected by sleep deprivation. First, it contains conditions that increase the likelihood of falling asleep: it is a long-duration task very infrequently punctuated with exciting events, and therefore presents very little in the way of mental or physical stimulation. Second, should a critical event occur, manning a screen line involves correctly discriminating friend from foe.

What about the decision makers at higher levels of command and control? Even if they are sleep deprived, they are not likely to fall asleep in a high operational tempo environment; nonetheless, their decision-making skills are impaired. They will be less likely to generate novel solutions to problems, and they are likely to perseverate on "tried and true" solutions, even in the face of evidence that these solutions are not working (Harrison & Horne, 1999). They also will be less likely to keep up with continuously evolving situations or make sense of and integrate newly emerging information.

The implications of the above are clear: even in well-equipped, well-trained, highly motivated soldiers operating within cohesive units with good morale, sleep will remain a critical factor for maintaining the operational capabilities enabled (and required) by a network-centric environment. To date, however, no study has been published in which sleep-loss effects have been described under actual combat conditions. In several studies, sleep-loss effects during field training exercises have been evaluated. The most notable of these was published by Diana R. Haslam and Peter Abraham (see Haslam & Abraham, 1987). In a series of studies, Haslam and Abraham evaluated the effects of sleep loss (total or severely restricted) on militarily relevant aspects of performance. In the first (Early Call I), platoons were assigned to 0, 1.5, or 3.0 hours of sleep per 24 hours (one platoon per sleep group) for 9 days. Shooting, weapon handling, digging, marching, patrolling, and cognitive performance, including map plotting, encoding/decoding, short-term memory, and logical reasoning, were evaluated periodically throughout the exercise. Haslam and Abraham reported that all soldiers in the 0-hour sleep platoon withdrew from the exercise after four nights without sleep (approximately 96 hours of total sleep deprivation); 39 percent of the 1.5-hour sleep platoon withdrew after five nights; 52 percent of the 1.5-hour and 91 percent of the 3-hour sleep platoons completed the entire 9-day exercise. Encoding performance (number correct) decreased across the exercise in all groups. Number of hits during a 20-minute shooting task decreased across days in all 3 platoons; and across the last 5 days performance appeared to drop more precipitously in the 1.5-hour group compared to the 3-hour group. In contrast to number of hits, "grouping capacity" (ability to fire five rounds in as small an area as possible) did not vary across days or among sleep groups. Haslam and Abraham also observed that personal hygiene, self-care, and leadership deteriorated across the exercise. Leadership deterioration was marked by a change from direct order to exhortation (i.e., urging, requesting, or advising). In the second exercise (Early Call II), ten experienced infantry soldiers were sleep deprived for 90 hours. This total sleep-deprivation period was then followed by 4 hours sleep per 24 hours for 6 days. Similar to Early Call I, performance on the 20-minute shooting task in this group degraded across the 90-hour sleep deprivation period and showed some rebound during the 4-hour sleep phase. This ten-soldier unit was marked by a high level of unit cohesion and morale. Nonetheless, as the sleep deprivation period continued, the section leader reported increased isolation from his soldiers (who became more docile and more united) and progressive difficulty keeping his soldiers going.

Based on the results from Early Call I and Early Call II, Haslam and Abraham concluded that soldiers are likely to be militarily ineffective in a defensive role after 48 hours without sleep. Results from the Early Call field exercises are consistent with those reported from laboratory studies and support the previously stated implications that well-equipped, well-trained, highly motivated soldiers operating within cohesive units with good morale are not resistant to the effects of sleep loss.

A Solution for Maintaining Cognitive Effectiveness

As reviewed above, sleep is critical to successful operational (both military and nonmilitary) outcomes. Under operational conditions, obtaining adequate sleep can be viewed as presenting management problems similar to other items of logistic resupply such as water, food, fuel, and ammunition. For example, to effectively manage fuel consumption, a commander must know (1) how much fuel is on hand and, given the anticipated mission profile, (2) how far that fuel will take the unit. These pieces of information are critical to planning for timely and adequate resupply. The same is true for sleep. Historically, commanders could not manage sleep effectively to sustain operational readiness because (1) they did not know how much sleep their soldiers had obtained over the previous days or weeks (i.e., they had no means of measuring the relative amounts of sleep versus wake in the field); and (2) they were unable to predict how long any sleep obtained would sustain readiness (i.e., they had no "miles to the gallon" equivalent for sleep).

For purposes of managing sleep to sustain performance before and during deployments, the Walter Reed Army Institute of Research (WRAIR) has developed a sleep management system. The sleep management system currently is comprised of the following elements: (1) a means to unobtrusively measure sleep/wake amounts (via a wristwatch-like device) in each individual soldier continuously both in garrison and in theatre; (2) a mathematical model to predict each individual soldier's cognitive readiness as a function of his measured sleep/wake amounts; (3) guidelines for the use of stimulants to sustain some level of cognitive effectiveness temporarily when no sleep is possible (e.g., during surge operations) or to improve performance during unavoidable chronically restricted sleep (e.g., during sustained operations); (4) guidelines for behavioral (i.e., nonpharmacological) strategies to promote recuperative sleep; and (5) guidelines for pharmacological strategies (i.e., sleep-inducing agents) to promote recuperative sleep. A final component includes guidelines and tools for monitoring performance in real time in the operational environment (either via embedded metrics or some other means). This component is the least developed and will not be discussed here. For a review of relevant issues, the interested reader is referred to Dinges and Mallis (1998) and Balkin et al. (2004).

The key to any sleep management system is its integration around the various activities that must be coordinated for any mission—that is, training, briefings, meals, vehicle/aircraft maintenance, refueling, and so on. A full discussion of this coordination is beyond the scope of this chapter. The interested reader is referred to the comprehensive guide on crew rest and mission coordination by Comperatore (1996).

Measuring Sleep and Wake Amounts under Operational Conditions

The cornerstone of the sleep management system is the means for measuring amount of sleep and wake time under operational conditions to determine how much is on hand. Wrist-mounted actigraphy (developed in the 1970s and 1980) is a portable, fieldable method for determining sleep and wake amounts based on movement data. Compared to the laboratory-based gold standard for recording sleep and wake time (polysomnography or PSG), actigraphy is a reliable, valid, and fieldable means of measuring sleep and wake amounts under operational conditions (see Balkin et al., 2000 for an historical review). Wrist-worn actigraphy presents a logistically practical and cost-effective way to measure daily sleep amounts in large numbers of individuals for weeks at a time.

In a series of studies, we used actigraphy to quantify sleep/wake amounts during training exercises at the U.S. Army Ranger School and the National Training Center. In the U.S. Army Ranger School exercise, soldiers wore the actigraph continuously throughout the 58 days of training across all four phases. As shown in Figure 5.4 (which includes a photo of an actigraph), soldiers were severely sleep deprived across all four training phases. Average sleep amounts for each phase were less than 4 hours per day (amounts that are inadequate to sustain cognitive readiness, as described above; see Belenky et al., 2003).

We also actigraphically recorded sleep/wake amounts in soldiers during another field exercise conducted at the National Training Center in Ft. Irwin, CA. Figure 5.5 shows average sleep per day across the three training phases, broken down by rank and type of activity. Soldiers of the lowest rank obtained on average a little over 8 hours of sleep per night—adequate to sustain cognitive performance indefinitely. However, the highest ranking individuals obtained the least sleep, on average about 5 hours per night—an amount that is insufficient for sustaining cognitive performance at high levels. This discrepancy was particularly noteworthy during the force-

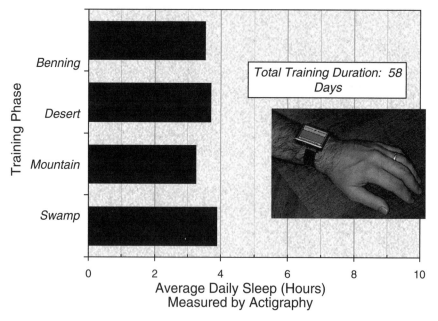

Figure 5.4
Average Daily Sleep Amounts Obtained by Soldiers during 58 Days of U.S. Army Ranger School, Ft. Benning, GA (Broken down by terrain phase. "Benning" phase is conducted at Ft. Benning [hot, humid pine forest on flat terrain]. Current ranger school curriculum does not include a desert phase.)

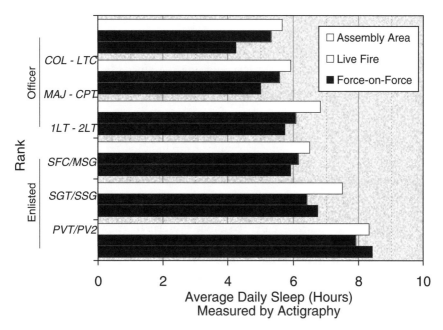

Figure 5.5
Average Daily Sleep Amounts of Military Personnel during Military Exercises Conducted
at the National Training Center in Ft. Irwin, CA (Data are broken down by rank. Assem-
bly Area = drawing, repairing, and organizing equipment. Live Fire = firing actual tank
and artillery shells while advancing through terrain dotted with simulated enemy targets.
Force-on-force = battle using laser systems to simulate killing and being killed by a live
enemy.)

on-force training phase. This phase most realistically simulates combat in that live
people and machines were fighting against each other. During this phase, key leaders
were getting inadequate sleep.

The above-described field studies highlight the utility of and need for an objective
means for determining sleep/wake amounts in the field. To date, wrist-worn actigraphy is the most reliable method for accomplishing this goal.

Knowing an individual's sleep/wake history is useful only if this information can
be used to predict the individual's current or projected state of cognitive readiness.
In order to translate sleep/wake data into such a predictive tool, useful for
commanders in planning, we have developed a mathematical model that predicts
cognitive performance based on sleep/wake history. This model is discussed next.

Predicting Cognitive Readiness as a Function of Sleep/Wake Amounts

As part of the sleep management system, we developed a mathematical Sleep Performance Model (SPM) to predict cognitive performance based on sleep/wake

history. The SPM provides commanders with the "miles to the gallon" equivalent for sleep and performance. Unlike previous modeling efforts, in which sleepiness, sleep onset, or some other variable was predicted, the SPM describes and predicts cognitive performance directly and mathematically. It is comprised of the following functions: (1) a *sleep function* describing restoration of cognitive performance during sleep; (2) a *wake function* describing cognitive performance degradation during wakefulness, and (3) a *circadian modulator* that describes improvements and decrements in performance as a function of time of day. These three functions were selected for modeling based on empirical evidence indicating that they contribute the bulk of variance in cognitive performance across the day.

Figure 5.6 illustrates predicted performance output from the SPM in which an idealized sleep/wake schedule was assumed (i.e., uninterrupted nightly sleep from 2300 to 0700; daily wakefulness without naps from 0700 to 2300). Panel A illustrates sleep and wake function outputs with the circadian function set to zero, thereby isolating the contributions of the sleep and wake functions). Panel B illustrates the circadian function output with the sleep/wake functions set to zero, thereby isolating the contribution of the circadian function. Panel C illustrates the actual predicted performance output by the SPM based on the mathematical combination of all three model functions (sleep, wake, and circadian functions).

Sleep Function

The SPM sleep function mathematically describes the recovery or restoration of performance during sleep (Figure 5.6, Panel A). It is based on empirical data indicating that the recuperative value of sleep on cognitive performance accumulates in a nonlinear fashion (e.g., Lumley, Roehrs, Zorick, Lamphere & Roth, 1986). That is, the rate of recuperation is higher initially during sleep and slows as sleep continues. For example, following a 16-hour day, during the ensuing sleep period cognitive restoration initially accumulates rapidly. As sleep continues, the rate of restoration declines (and therefore cognitive restoration asymptotes). Following sleep deprivation, predicted cognitive performance at the start of the sleep period is even lower than it would be following a normal 16-hour day; therefore, the rate of cognitive restoration is even higher than at the beginning of a normal night of sleep. During chronic partial sleep deprivation (restricted nocturnal sleep), the rate of cognitive restoration also is higher than after a 16-hour day. However, cognitive restoration is not complete at the end of each night because sleep is restricted.

Wakefulness Function

The SPM wakefulness function describes the progressive decrement in performance that occurs during waking (Figure 5.6, Panel A). The current model iteration is based upon three sets of results from our laboratory: (1) near-100 percent performance is maintained from day to day when individuals obtain eight hours sleep each night; (2) during total sleep loss, performance declines by approximately 25 percent for every 24 hours of wakefulness; (3) a single, daily 30-minute nap over 85 hours of sleep deprivation has substantial recuperative value, slowing the rate of performance

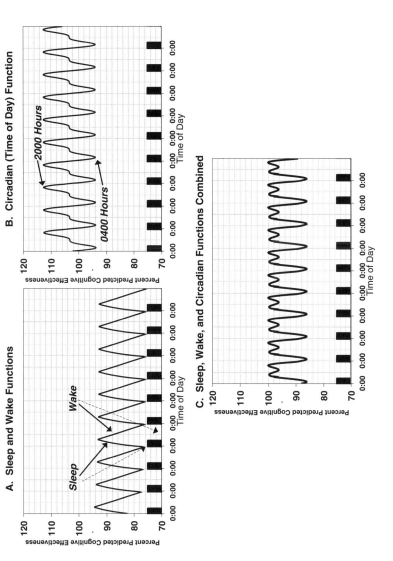

Figure 5.6
Sleep and Wake (Panel A), Circadian (Panel B), and Combined Sleep, Wake, and Circadian (Panel C) Functions of the Sleep Performance Model

decline [described below in section, "Behavioral Strategies for Promoting Sleep"]. The latter results corroborate one aspect of the sleep function, i.e., that recuperation during sleep is front-loaded. As a first approximation, we modeled the wakefulness function as a linear decline. The wakefulness function thus depletes performance linearly across time spent awake at a rate of approximately 1 percent per hour (Panel A, Figure 5.6).

Circadian Modulation Function

The circadian (time of day) modulation function mathematically describes the well-characterized, cyclic daily variation in cognitive performance (Panel B, Figure 5.6). Note that in this illustration, because mean predicted performance is assumed to be 100 percent when individuals obtain 8 hours of sleep per day, the range of the circadian function includes predicted performance greater than 100 percent. This performance variation closely resembles the circadian rhythm in body temperature (except that the cognitive performance rhythm appears to lag body temperature by approximately two hours). Empirical observations indicate that across a 24-hour period cognitive performance varies by +/− 10 to 20 percent of mean performance (the percentage of variation differs across individuals). Under certain conditions, the percentage of daily performance variation approaches zero (i.e., "flattens"); however, this flattening generally occurs only following time zone travel (as the circadian system slowly realigns with new local time). A biphasic, asymmetrical waveform appears to best describe empirical data (i.e., a mathematical embodiment in which performance improves slowly during the day to its peak [acrophase], and then decrements more quickly during the night to its lowest point [nadir]). Therefore, in the current SPM, circadian modulation shows slow rise across the day and peaks at approximately 2200 hours (the acrophase); this peak is followed by rapid decline to a nadir at approximately 0800 hours.

Sleep, Wake, and Circadian Functions Combined

The mathematical combination of the sleep, wake, and circadian function contributions to predicted performance is illustrated in Figure 5.6, Panel C. The mathematical descriptions of these functions are a first approximation fit to laboratory-based data and will likely be revised as new findings become available. In addition, should additional factors be identified that contribute meaningfully to variations in cognitive performance, those factors will be mathematically described and incorporated into the SPM. Two such factors are *time on task* (i.e., fatigue) and *time of day preference* (morning or evening). Currently, sufficient data to mathematically describe these two factors is lacking. SPM-based predictions will continuously undergo laboratory and field validation.

Both military and commercial applications of the SPM exist. For example, commercial motor vehicle (CMV) drivers could be instrumented with actigraphs to record daily sleep amounts. Each individual CMV driver's work hours could then be regulated based on cognitive performance predictions derived from objective measurement of sleep duration (via actigraphy). Such individualized regulation could replace the current "hours of service" (HOS) regulations, which are based solely on amount of on-duty and off-duty time, regardless of how much off-duty time is actually spent sleeping.

Stimulants to Sustain Cognitive Effectiveness during Unavoidable Sleep Loss

Sleep is the best (and only permanent) strategy to combat sleep-deprivation-induced cognitive deficits. However, military exigencies often preclude adequate sleep. Under such circumstances, strategies for augmenting mental performance can be implemented. Currently, the most effective pharmacological strategy for improving mental performance during sleep deprivation is administration of central nervous system stimulants. Agents tested for fieldability in our and other laboratories include: caffeine, dextroamphetamine (d-amphetamine), nicotine, and the relatively new stimulant modafinil. Because results from our laboratory show that nicotine is ineffective for improving cognitive performance during sleep deprivation (Newhouse et al., 1992), and because nonpharmacological strategies (e.g., cold air, loud noise) are ineffective for improving cognitive performance (except perhaps momentarily; Reyner & Horne, 1998), neither will be discussed here. In fact, there may be a danger to using substances such as nicotine, which may increase feelings of alertness without actually improving cognitive performance. If one misinterprets *feeling* more alert as indicating improved performance, then appropriate actions to objectively augment cognitive performance likely will not be taken.

Caffeine

Over-the-counter formulations of caffeine (pills, gum, beverage) are routinely used to minimize/reverse performance and alertness-impairing effects of both total and partial sleep deprivation, and caffeine's effectiveness is well established (Bonnet et al., 2005). Caffeinated gum (which may be more desirable than other caffeine formulations such as coffee because it is more fieldable) also has been shown to sustain operationally relevant aspects of performance during sleep deprivation (marksmanship and urban operations vigilance during military training in a simulated Military Operations in Urban Terrain or "MOUT" exercise) (McLellan et al., 2005). Subjectively, caffeine improves self-ratings of fatigue, confusion, sleepiness, vigor, alertness, confidence, and energy level; and caffeine also increases ratings of talkativeness, anxiety, and jitteriness (Penetar et al., 1993).

Caffeine can also interfere with sleep. Caffeine may decrease recuperative sleep time, even though sleep is not initiated until 12 hours after caffeine ingestion. However, whether caffeine-impaired sleep translates into next-day performance impairments (as a result of partial sleep deprivation) depends on the total amount of actual recuperative sleep time obtained. For example, in one study, caffeine 300 mg reduced recuperative sleep duration by an hour compared to a placebo group (Penetar et al., 1993). However reduced sleep did not translate into next-day performance impairments, probably because the overall amount of recuperative sleep obtained was more than seven hours. Had the sleep period been shorter, the impact of this 1-hour loss may have been more apparent. Similarly, had the sleep period commenced nearer to caffeine administration (e.g., 4 hours after administration versus 12), and/or had the sleep deprivation period been shorter (the long sleep deprivation period drastically increased sleep propensity, which may have offset caffeine-induced decrements in sleep propensity), caffeine's effect on sleep may have been more devastating.

In sum, caffeine reverses the two effects of sleep deprivation: it restores the ability to remain awake under boring, nonstimulating conditions, and it restores complex mental operations. Caffeine also exerts mild subjective effects, both negative and positive, and can interfere with sleep.

Dextroamphetamine and Modafinil

Two prescription stimulants, dextroamphetamine (Dexedrine®) and modafinil (Provigil®) are currently available to certain military groups such as aviators (under guidance of a flight surgeon). However, for the most part, prescription stimulants are not widely available in operational settings. Therefore, they will be discussed only briefly here.

The cognitive performance-enhancing effects of dextroamphetamine and modafinil during sleep deprivation are similar to those of caffeine: both dextroamphetamine and modafinil restore cognitive performance, and both agents can impair recovery sleep. Subjectively, dextroamphetamine and modafinil improve self-ratings of fatigue, vigor, and alertness. After equally potent doses (i.e., doses that restored cognitive performance to the same degree), performance-restoring effects of dextroamphetamine and modafinil last longer than those of caffeine (see Figure 5.7, from Wesensten, Killgore & Balkin, 2005). This differential duration of efficacy is most likely a function of each drug's duration of action, with caffeine possessing the shortest duration of action. Operationally, a short duration of action may be beneficial should a mission be aborted and an opportunity for sleep present itself. Alternatively, another dose of caffeine could be ingested to further sustain cognitive performance.

Caveat: Stimulant Use

Although stimulants such as caffeine, dextroamphetamine, and modafinil improve sleep-loss-induced performance deficits on simple psychomotor tasks and computerized cognitive tasks, their effects on executive functions during sleep deprivation have received virtually no attention. All three stimulants have some costs associated with their use. However, the currently available data suggest that caffeine is safe and effective. Based on this, its low cost and wide availability, judicious, well-informed use of caffeine may constitute a reasonable first line of defense.

Behavioral Strategies for Promoting Sleep

Because sleep is the best (and only permanent) strategy to combat sleep-deprivation-induced cognitive deficits, and because pharmacological means of promoting sleep (discussed below) are generally precluded in operational settings,

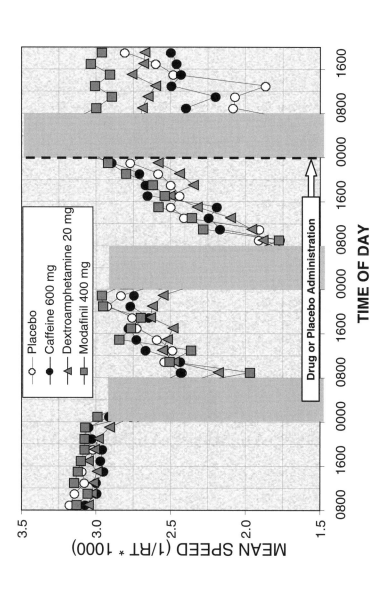

Figure 5.7
Effect of Stimulant Intervention after 65 Hours of Sleep Deprivation on Speed of Cognitive Operations (Shaded areas represent nighttime periods [approximate] during which volunteers would otherwise be sleeping.)

behavioral strategies for promoting sleep are critical. The benefit of obtaining even small amounts of sleep (a nap—i.e., any sleep period outside the main sleep period) cannot be overemphasized. In separate studies, volunteers were deprived of sleep for three nights. In one study, in addition to nighttime sleep deprivation, volunteers were allowed no daytime sleep; in the other study, volunteers had a 30-minute daily nap opportunity (an unavoidable consequence of their being in a PET scanner, during which time they could not be disturbed). Figure 5.8 illustrates the performance degradation curves from these two studies. After three nights without sleep, individuals who were allowed only 30 minutes per day to sleep (a total of 1.5 hrs sleep across 72 hours) were performing about 20 percent better than the volunteers who obtained neither daytime nor nighttime sleep. We also found that sleep during the daily 30-minute nap was extremely efficient. Volunteers spent nearly the entire nap time in the deeper stages of sleep, and almost no time awake or in light, nonrecuperative sleep. Thus, even short bouts of sleep will offset sleep-loss-induced cognitive performance degradation.

The key to naps is that they actually consist of *sleep*. Dozing and resting do not restore and sustain cognitive effectiveness (Wesensten, Balkin & Belenky, 1999), although a few minutes benefit may be derived from taking time off task (Pigeau et al., 1995). A rule-of-thumb recommendation is to provide individuals with

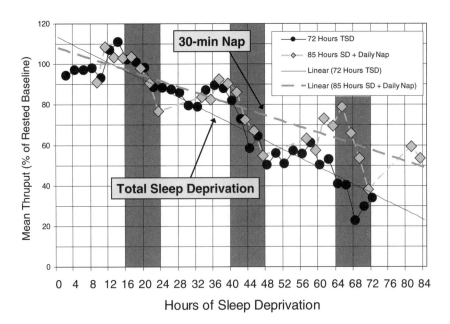

Figure 5.8
Effects of Three Nights of Total Sleep Deprivation (TSD) on Speed of Cognitive Operations (Shaded areas represent nighttime periods [approximate] during which volunteers would otherwise be sleeping.)

opportunities to sleep whenever they can to accumulate the optimum 8 hours sleep per 24-hour period (i.e., sleep does not have to be taken as one continuous 8-hour period; see Wesensten et al., 1999; 2000). Promoting sleep (naps or otherwise) under operational conditions can be enhanced by applying factors that contribute to the likelihood that sleep will occur. These factors are reviewed next.

Sleep Environment

As most individuals know implicitly, the sleep environment itself largely determines whether sleep occurs. As noted above, sleep can be disrupted by environmental factors (e.g., noise), effectively reducing total sleep time. Simple and straightforward fixes are readily available to deal with some environmental disturbances: ear plugs can be used to block ambient noise, and sleep masks or eye patches can be used to block ambient light. Constant white noise can also be used to block intermittent, ambient noises (the latter are more disruptive than a continuous, monotonic noise). Another factor, environmental temperature (extreme heat or extreme cold), is often more difficult to deal with under operational conditions. However, even if these conditions cannot be controlled, an awareness that sleep will be reduced—and subsequent cognitive performance degraded—will be useful to consider as part of operational planning.

Timing of Sleep

The timing of the sleep period (whether the main sleep period or a nap) plays a crucial role regarding the likelihood that an individual will actually be able to sleep. When possible, sleep periods should be timed for the early morning (preferably before 1000 hours) or early afternoon (circa 1500 hours) since at these times of day, sleep is most likely to occur. Certain times of day have even been identified as forbidden zones for sleep, meaning that even totally sleep-deprived individuals have difficulty falling asleep (and remaining asleep) in the midmorning or early evening hours (Lavie, 1986).

Other Factors

Common wisdom is to avoid substances that fragment sleep (that is, increase amounts of wake and stage 1). As noted above, stimulants, including caffeine but also nicotine, ephedrine (found in weight loss and purported physical endurance-enhancing products), and theobromine (found in chocolate) disrupt sleep. Even some sedatives (most notably alcohol) fragment sleep; for example, alcohol increases feelings of drowsiness and may hasten sleep onset, but alcohol also increases wake time and light sleep (Roehrs & Roth, 2001).

Despite the fact that stimulants as well as alcohol disrupt sleep, most of us use these substances on a regular basis. Two observations may account for this apparently counterproductive behavior. First, individuals may be unaware that sleep is being disrupted—brief awakenings and arousals to light sleep are not remembered the next day, leading to the perception that sleep was not disrupted. Second, *withdrawal* from substances such as nicotine may actually disrupt sleep more than the substance itself.

Finally, there is no objective evidence that particular dietary constituents in otherwise normal, healthy individuals objectively improve sleep (although again such substances may make the individual feel as though he/she slept more soundly). There is some evidence that the hormone melatonin (which is produced endogenously by the pineal hormone) improves daytime sleep (Wesensten, Killgore & Balkin, 2005), but melatonin's effects on nighttime sleep appear to be restricted to individuals with inadequate levels of this hormone. In these individuals, taking synthetic forms of melatonin merely serves to return endogenous levels to normal (Monti & Cardinali, 2000).

Pharmacological Strategies for Promoting Sleep

Even when sleep time is available, sleep may be unlikely. For example, the period available for sleep may be in the midmorning when it is unlikely that the person will be able to sleep. Also, under operational conditions, the quality of the sleep environment is often poor: it may be loud, brightly lit, too hot or cold, and/or the individual may be trying to sleep in an uncomfortable bunk or in a plane. Under these conditions, behavioral strategies for promoting sleep may not be sufficient, and improving sleep using a sleep-inducing agent may be a solution. As with prescription stimulants, prescription sleep-inducing agents are currently available, but mainly to certain military groups such as aviators (under guidance of a flight surgeon); such agents are not widely available in operational settings.

The ideal sleep-inducing agent would increase recuperative sleep time, possess a rapid onset of action, and possibly also a short duration of action (if the sleep period were of limited duration). Most important (and possibly the reason why individuals hesitate to use sleep-inducing agents), the ideal sleep-inducing agent would not impair performance after awakening. All currently available prescription sleep-inducing agents impair learning and memory in a dose-dependent fashion if individuals are required to perform while the drug is still present in the body. The sleep-inducing agents zolpidem (Ambien®) and temazepam (Restoril®) have been tested extensively both in the laboratory and in the field. They have the same mechanism of action (inducing sleep by binding to the benzodiazepine receptor in the brain). They differ mainly in terms of their pharmacokinetic profiles, which translates into duration of action and ultimately into required downtime after ingestion: zolpidem reaches peak blood concentrations within approximately 90 minutes of oral administration, and displays a 2- to 4-hour elimination half-life. Temazepam possesses a similar profile, but is eliminated more slowly (half-life = 6–8 hours).

Results from field studies have highlighted additional potential contraindications for use of sleep-inducing agents during deployment. In one such study, triazolam (Halcion®) was evaluated in a field study at Fort Lewis. In this study, nine ranger rifle platoons were evaluated during exercises in which they were sleeping in the cold but otherwise experienced no disruptions requiring action on their part. Volunteers were given triazolam 0.5 mg (twice the recommended dosage at the time the study was conducted), triazolam 0.25 mg, or a placebo just before a four-hour nighttime sleep period (approximately 0200 to 0600 hours). Sleep/wake amounts were determined from wrist-worn actigraphy. Complex mental operations were tested immediately upon awakening, then again 20 hours later (corresponding to 4 and 24 hrs postdrug). Triazolam 0.5 mg substantially improved sleep in the field; however, it also impaired performance measured upon awakening (4 hrs postdose). Triazolam 0.25 mg also substantially improved sleep, but did not impair postsleep performance. Importantly, at 24 hours postdose, soldiers given triazolam 0.25 mg performed significantly better on complex mental tests than the placebo group. This study demonstrated the value of relatively small amounts of sleep (and shows that the benefits derived are long lasting). However, in this field study, triazolam caused some soldiers to fall asleep even before they zipped themselves into their sleeping bags—requiring the study investigators to go from soldier to soldier, securing each in his sleeping bag to protect against the subfreezing temperatures. This field study thus highlighted a contraindication for the use of sleep-inducing medications (i.e., in harsh environments), especially if soldiers cannot be closely monitored.

Transmeridian travel is another situation under which individuals may not be able to sleep. The reason for sleep difficulties is that transmeridian travel leads to desynchrony between external time cues at the new time zone and the individual's internal timing (circadian) system, which is located in the suprachiasmatic nucleus of the brain (and which responds to day/night). This desynchrony, or "jet lag," is characterized by (among other things) difficulty initiating and maintaining sleep for several nights until the circadian system adapts to the new time zone. Shift work causes many of the same symptoms as jet lag because individuals are attempting to remain awake at times when the circadian system is synchronized for sleep.

The most critical component of the jet lag syndrome may be sleep deprivation. Indeed, many of the symptoms of jet lag (e.g., degradation in performance, alertness, and mood) mimic those of sleep deprivation, suggesting that sleep loss is one of the main factors contributing to jet lag symptoms (Wesensten, Comperatore, Balkin & Belenky, 2003). Therefore, short-term (several nights) use of sleep-inducing agents following transmeridian travel may improve next-day performance and alertness (Nicholson, 1990)

Summary: Sleep Management

Factors that cannot be measured and quantified cannot be managed or predicted. In the operational setting, managing cognitive performance requires the ability to measure sleep/wake amounts and predict operationally relevant performance. The above-outlined system for managing sleep to sustain performance and thereby enhance safety and productivity through optimal application of appropriate interventions (e.g., on-the-fly schedule changes and optimally timed administration of pharmacologic agents) has broad applicability. Applications can be envisioned for virtually any operational setting in which the possibility exists that operator performance could be impacted by sleep loss—including military operations, long-haul trucking, shift work in the manufacturing industries, power plant operations, and police and firefighting operations.

Conclusions: An Example From Future History

Sleep sustains the cognitive capacities that underlie operational effectiveness. Inadequate sleep causes cognitive degradation that initially translates into decreased productivity but can ultimately translate into accidents and friendly fire incidents. Tools are available to allow the operator to treat sleep as a consumable to be measured and managed. The following notional scenario serves as a practical example of the operational benefits of treating sleep as an item of logistic resupply.

It is August 2014. An American expeditionary force is deploying to a foreign country to contain aggression by a disciplined, technologically sophisticated, motivated and well-led force.

All soldiers in the American force are equipped with a wristwatch-replacement biomedical monitoring system (BMS) which includes sensors to record actigraphy (for determining sleep/wake amounts), body temperature, hydration status, caloric expenditure, and so on. The BMS is linked through the individual soldier computer and communication system to the U.S. Department of Defense Global Information Grid. All soldiers wear this device at all times—in garrison, during training exercises, and during operations. Embedded in the BMS is software to predict each individual soldier's cognitive effectiveness from his sleep/wake history. These running predictions are telemetered up the soldier's chain of command for purposes of operational planning. At the unit level, autonomous agent software models predict unit-level effectiveness (an emergent property) based on predictions of individual cognitive effectiveness, giving commanders the information they need to optimize sleep scheduling to sustain operational readiness. Software modules recommend behavioral and pharmacological countermeasures and predict their effects when implemented.

The Americans are deploying by air after five days of preparation, during which there has been little opportunity for sleep. The BMS indicates that soldiers have had only four hours of sleep during the past five days, and that even with countermeasures (e.g., caffeine), unit effectiveness is degraded. On the basis of current intelligence, commanders are anticipating immediate engagement with enemy upon insertion into the theater of operations. Given mission requirements, optimum performance is essential to a successful outcome.

Lead elements are now several hours from takeoff. The optimization software recommends that all planning activities cease once the planes are "wheels-up" and that a sleep-inducer be used to ensure that all personnel throughout the hierarchy of command and control sleep at least eight hours on the plane. Racks and stacks on the troop transport planes ensure that all soldiers can sleep lying down. Once airborne, all soldiers take the sleep-inducer. Light levels, noise and commotion are kept to a minimum during the sleep period. After 9 hours of "time in rack," the soldiers are awakened. They are refreshed from their sleep. Their thinking is clear and rapid. Their motivation is high. They are ready for combat. The BMS indicates that soldiers averaged 8.5 hours of sleep during the flight. Performance prediction modeling indicates that performance at both the individual and unit level will be optimal.

The initial insertion into the combat zone goes well. Enemy resistance is suppressed. The buildup in theater is rapid and U.S. forces rapidly expand their area of control. Because sleep/wake amounts are measured continuously via the BMS, performance prediction for all personnel is up to date, allowing real-time optimization of sleep scheduling to sustain operational performance. Shortened nocturnal sleep is supplemented with daytime naps in order to sustain 24-hour-a-day operations. Forty-eight hours into the operation, the expeditionary force comes under pressure as the enemy launches all its forces in a coordinated, combined-arms counterattack. Commanders anticipate a short period of intense operations in which the opportunity for sleep will be slim to nonexistent. The optimization software recommends the implementation of a stimulant drug to sustain operational performance without sleep for the next 12 hours. The counterattack is repulsed with the enemy taking heavy casualties. The operation proceeds as planned. Two weeks into the operation, organized enemy action ceases. This first phase of the operation concludes successfully with minimal casualties from enemy action and no losses from error, accident, or friendly fire.

References

Balkin, T. (2000). *Effects of sleep schedules on commercial motor vehicle driver performance.* Washington, DC: U.S. Dept. of Transportation, Federal Motor Carrier Safety Administration.

Balkin, T., Badia, P., Harsh, J., & Klempert, A. (1985). Behavioral responsivity during recovery sleep. *Biological Psychology, 20*(1), 17–20.

Balkin, T. J., Bliese, P. D., Belenky, G., Sing, H., Thorne, D. R., Thomas, M., et al. (2004). Comparative utility of instruments for monitoring sleepiness-related performance decrements in the operational environment. *Journal of Sleep Research, 13*(3), 219–227.

Balkin, T. J., Braun, A. R., Wesensten, N. J., Jeffries, K., Varga, M., Baldwin, P., et al. (2002). The process of awakening: a PET study of regional brain activity patterns mediating the reestablishment of alertness and consciousness. *Brain, 125*(Pt. 10), 2308–2319.

Belenky, G., Martin J. A., & Marcy, S. C. (1996). After-action critical incident stress debriefing and battle reconstruction following combat. In J. A. Martin, L. R. Sparacino, and G. Belenky (Eds.), *The Gulf War and mental health: A comprehensive guide* (pp. 105–113). Westport, CT: Praeger.

Belenky, G., Wesensten, N. J., Thorne, D. R., Thomas, M. L., Sing, H. C., Redmond, D. P., et al. (2003). Patterns of performance degradation and restoration during sleep restriction and subsequent recovery: a sleep dose-response study. *Journal of Sleep Research, 12*(1), 1–12.

Bonnet, M. H., Balkin, T. J., Dinges, D. F., Roehrs, T., Rogers, N. L., Wesensten, N. J. (2005). The use of stimulants to modify performance during sleep loss. A review by the Sleep Deprivation and Stimulant Task Force of the American Academy of Sleep Medicine. *Sleep, 28*, 1163–1187.

Braun, A. R., Balkin, T. J., Wesenten, N. J., Carson, R. E., Varga, M., Baldwin, P., et al. (1997). Regional cerebral blood flow throughout the sleep-wake cycle. An H2(15)O PET study. *Brain, 120*(Pt. 7), 1173–1197.

Comperatore, C. A. (1996). The crew rest system. In C. A. Comperatore, J. Caldwell & L. Caldwell (Eds.), *Leader's guide for crew endurance* (pp. 21–25). Fort Rucker, AL: U.S. Army Safety Center.

Dinges, D.F., & Mallis, M. M. (1998). Managing fatigue by drowsiness detection: Can technological promises be realised? In L. R. Hartley (Ed.), *Managing fatigue in transportation. Proceedings of the third international conference on fatigue and transportation* (pp. 209–229). Fremantle, Western Australia. Oxford, UK: Elsevier Science.

Harrison, Y., & Horne, J. A. (1998). Sleep loss impairs short and novel language tasks having a prefrontal focus. *Journal of Sleep Research, 7*(2), 95–100.

Harrison, Y., & Horne, J. A. (1999). One night of sleep loss impairs innovative thinking and flexible decision making. *Organizational Behavior and Human Decision Processes, 78*(2), 128–145.

Haslam, D.R., & Abraham, P. (1987). Sleep loss and military performance. In G. Belenky (Ed.), *Contemporary studies in combat psychiatry* (pp. 167–184). Westport, CT: Greenwood Press.

Killgore, W. D. S., Balkin, T. J., & Wesensten, N. J. (2005). Impaired decision-making following 49 hours of sleep deprivation. Manuscript submitted for publication.

Lavie, P. (1986). Ultrashort sleep-waking schedule. III. 'Gates' and 'forbidden zones' for sleep. *Electroencephalography and Clinical Neurophysiology, 63*(5), 414–425.

Lumley, M., Roehrs, T., Zorick, F., Lamphere, J., & Roth, T. (1986). The alerting effects of naps in sleep-deprived subjects. *Psychophysiology, 23*(4), 403–408.

McLellan, T. M., Kamimori, G. H., Bell, D. G., Smith, I. F., Johnson, D., & Belenky, G. (2005). Caffeine maintains vigilance and marksmanship in simulated urban operations with sleep deprivation. *Aviation, Space, and Environmental Medicine, 76*(1), 39–45.

Monti, J. M., & Cardinali, D. P. (2000). A critical assessment of the melatonin effect on sleep in humans. *Biological Signals and Receptors, 9*(6), 328–339.

Newhouse P., et al. (1992). Stimulant drug effects on performance and behavior after prolonged sleep deprivation: A comparison of amphetamine, nicotine, and deprenyl. *Military Psychology, 4*, 207–233.

Nicholson, A. N. (1990). Hypnotics and occupational medicine. *Journal of Occupational Medicine, 32*(4), 335–341.

Penetar, D., McCann, U., Thorne, D., Kamimori, G., Galinski, C., Sing, H., et al. (1993). Caffeine reversal of sleep deprivation effects on alertness and mood. *Psychopharmacology (Berl), 112*(2–3), 359–365.

Pigeau, R., Naitoh, P., Buguet, C. et al. (1995). Modafinil, d-amphetamine, and placebo during 64 hours of sustained mental work. I. Effects on mood, fatigue, cognitive performance and body temperature. *J. Sleep Res., 4*, 212–228.

Reyner, L. A., & Horne, J. A. (1998). Evaluation of "in-car" countermeasures to sleepiness: Cold air and radio. *Sleep, 21*(1), 46–50.

Roehrs, T., & Roth, T. (2001). Sleep, sleepiness, and alcohol use. *Alcohol Research & Health, 25*(2), 101–109.

Thomas, M., Sing, H., Belenky, G., Holcomb, H., Mayberg, H., Dannals, R., et al. (2000). Neural basis of alertness and cognitive performance impairments during sleepiness. I. Effects of 24 h of sleep deprivation on waking human regional brain activity. *Journal of Sleep Research, 9*(4), 335–352.

Van Dongen, H. P., Maislin, G., Mullington, J. M., & Dinges, D. F. (2003). The cumulative cost of additional wakefulness: dose-response effects on neurobehavioral functions and sleep physiology from chronic sleep restriction and total sleep deprivation. *Sleep, 26*(2), 117–126.

Wesensten, N. J., Balkin, T. J., & Belenky, G. (1999). Does sleep fragmentation impact recuperation? A review and reanalysis. *Journal of Sleep Research, 8*(4), 237–245.

Wesensten, N. J., Balkin, T. J., & Belenky, G. (2000). Reply to comments by Dr. Michael Bonnet: Does sleep fragmentation impact recuperation? A review and reanalysis. *Journal of Sleep Research, 9*, 403–406.

Wesensten, N. J., Belenky, G., & Balkin, T. J. (2005). Cognitive readiness in network-centric operations. *Parameters, 35*, 94–105.

Wesensten N. J., Comperatore C. C., Balkin T. J., & Belenky, G. (2003). Jet lag and sleep deprivation. In P. W. Kelley (Ed.), *Military preventive medicine: Mobilization and deployment. Volume 1. Textbooks of military medicine* (pp. 287–300). Washington, DC: Office of the Surgeon General at TMM Publications.

Wesensten, N. J., Killgore, W. D. S., & Balkin, T. J. (2005). Performance and alertness effects of caffeine, dextroamphetamine, and modafinil during sleep deprivation. *Journal of Sleep Research, 14*(3), 255–256.

CHAPTER 6

Augmented Cognition: Aiding the Soldier in High and Low Workload Environments through Closed-Loop Human-Machine Interactions

Eric R. Muth, Amy A. Kruse, Adam Hoover,
and Dylan Schmorrow

The Problem

The complex battlefield environment demands that war fighters perform simultaneous, complex tasks in extreme environments with little room for error. Typically the tasks, when performed in isolation, may not require all the war fighter's cognitive resources. Tasks performed simultaneously under operational conditions and mounting time constraints, however, multiply the demand on cognitive resources, thereby quickly using up a soldier's available mental processing for even the most mundane tasks. As anyone knows from experience, performing several tasks simultaneously is often more difficult than performing a single task because the demands of the separate tasks can, and often do, interfere with one another. In the military, this is further complicated by degradation in cognitive performance caused by the challenging situations in which war fighters operate.

Dual/Multitask Interference

The psychological literature is rich with studies on task interference in the laboratory environment. Tasks are typically broken down into single tasks, dual tasks, and multitasks. Research has shown that once an individual has to perform more than a single task, performance on the secondary task can interfere with performance on

The views expressed in this chapter are those of the authors and do not reflect the official policy or position of the U.S. Department of Defense or the U.S. Government.

the primary task. Within the literature there are three main types of models of dual/ multitask interference: capacity sharing, bottleneck or task-switching, and crosstalk (Pashler, 1994).

The capacity-sharing models (Kahneman, 1973; Navon & Gopher, 1979; Wickens, 1980) state that individuals have a certain amount of processing capability. This processing capability is shared in parallel among tasks. The more tasks an individual performs, the less processing he or she can dedicate to any given task. At some point, a task or tasks may consume all the processing capability available, making performance on other tasks degrade or fail. Most of us can relate to the idea of a capacity-sharing model, as during our daily lives when we are bombarded with more and more things to do, we inevitably forget to do something, only later to remember that we forgot to do it. We simply off-loaded the task to failure because we did not have enough processing to handle the tasks at hand.

The bottleneck or task-switching models (Pashler, 1984) affirm that certain tasks require the dedication of certain resources, and therefore parallel processing is not possible. Hence, only a single task can be processed until that resource bottleneck is cleared. For example, if a war fighter is performing a visually demanding task such as aiming a weapon, he cannot also accurately drive a vehicle, as both tasks demand visual attention and a visual bottleneck is created.

The cross-talk models (Kinsbourne, 1981) assert that interference may be a result of the information being processed, not the processing functions themselves, as with the capacity sharing and bottleneck/task-switching models. For example, a soldier having to remember three numerical navigational way points while simultaneously utilizing several distances to calculate targeting information may mix up the numbers for the two separate tasks. This happens to all of us on occasion when we are counting objects and listening to someone else counting simultaneously.

Regardless of the model used to explain the interference, war fighters are faced with a multitasking work environment. In a multitask environment, performance on individual tasks will likely be degraded compared to performance on any of the tasks alone due to task interference. While training can mitigate some of these effects (Morey & Cowen, 2004), it will not eliminate the problem entirely, especially in light of the environmental extremes war fighters operate in (Committee on Human Factors, 1997).

Cognitive Effects of Extreme Environments

War fighters are not limited to ground combat; they are found in planes at high altitudes and hypobaric conditions (lower than normal pressure; in this case, air pressure) and in submarines with negative altitudes and hyperbaric conditions (higher than normal pressure; in this case, water pressure). In the course of one mission, war fighters might encounter sandy deserts with burning temperatures and mountainous terrains with freezing temperatures. In these physically demanding environments, war fighters are asked to do arguably one of the most difficult and complex cognitive tasks a human faces: choose whether or not to take another human life—

a decision most of us would have trouble making from the extreme comfort of our living room easy chair. The war fighter's ability to make this difficult decision, as well as simpler decisions, is undeniably degraded by the environmental extremes in which he operates.

In terms of general military operations, it has been shown that even simulated combat conditions during a combat training period can impact short-term and long-term memory (Pierard et al., 2004). Most military operations involve sustained operations and sustained sleep deprivation. Sleep loss associated with real or simulated military operations has been shown to degrade general cognitive performance (Haslam, 1985); visual vigilance and memory for words (Englund, Ryman, Naitoh, & Hodgdon, 1985); situational awareness and reaction time (Caldwell, Caldwell, Brown, & Smith, 2004); and mood (Angus & Heslegrave, 1985). It is also common for soldiers to operate under thermal stress. Heat has been shown to negatively affect time estimation (Curley & Hawkins, 1983) and map reading (Fine & Kobrick, 1987) in military- relevant situations.

In cases specific to certain military jobs, cognitive performance has also been shown to be affected. In aviators who have experienced gravity-induced loss of consciousness (G-LOC), it takes approximately one minute before full psychomotor performance is recovered (Forster & Cammarota, 1993). In soldiers exposed to simulated high-altitude conditions, the speed and accuracy at which card-sorting tasks were performed was degraded, with the complex decision-making card-sorting tasks more impaired then the simple card-sorting tasks (Cahoon, 1972). Soldiers being asked to work on embedded systems, such as flying a flight simulator aboard a ship, have been shown to have visual impairments (Muth & Lawson, 2003) and cognitive deficits (Muth, 2004). The effects of embedded systems are likely to be found in more common tasks, such as operating a remote vehicle from inside a moving vehicle or viewing a command and control station in a fixed or moving vehicle (e.g., Cowings, Toscano, DeRoshia & Tauson, 2000).

A Proposed Solution

Improved or additional technology is often proposed as the solution to the extreme conditions and multitask environments that war fighters face. However, as the war fighter is issued more technology, the operation of this technology becomes yet an additional task for the user. As we know from the review of task interference, this additional technology task load can lead to further cognitive-related performance decrements rather than improvements. Technology alone cannot be the solution. We suggest a new way of thinking about technology called *augmented cognition* as a potential remediation for these cognitive challenges.

The field of augmented cognition centers on the development of revolutionary human–computer interactions (HCI), where the awkward and nonintuitive interface between humans and their computational devices is eliminated. In its place is an interface that allows humans and computers to interact in a natural way that expands, enhances, and extends the human's mental resources (Card, Moran &

Newell, 1983). Although adaptive user interfaces exist, they rely primarily on key-strokes, mouse clicks, and other observable actions to estimate or model the user's state. The intent of augmented cognition systems is to sense the user status *seconds to minutes* before overt behavioral measures might pick it up.

An Overview of Augmented Cognition

Fundamental to the field of augmented cognition is the mounting evidence that humans are the limiting variable in the advanced war fighting equation. As outlined above, humans suffer from a host of intrinsic limitations in information processing, including restricted memory, attention, wakefulness, and sensory inputs that are compounded in extreme environments. These information bottlenecks cannot be overcome by simply improving human computer interface design, since the problems are deep within the human cognitive resources, not just manifested in behavior. These bottlenecks are intimately tied to cognition and human information processing and are truly part of the fabric of the human mind. Thus, overcoming these bottlenecks requires something as dramatic as sensing the functioning of the brain in real time. Only by accessing the core of information processing is there hope of overcoming these bottlenecks and expanding the processing capability of the human brain.

Most technology barely understands who is using it, let alone the user's state and his or her current information processing load. What augmented cognition attempts to do is assess that type of human information and turn it into something actionable which computational systems can use to improve the user's performance. Figure 6.1 outlines the novel approach to human-technology interactions augmented cognition presents.

In engineering, it is typical to have a database of knowledge about the machine system and sense real-time data regarding the machine system. As shown in Figure 6.1, this includes information about the task, specifications (specs), and status of the machine system. The task refers to the global mission, the current mission being performed, and the goals of those missions. The specs refer to the operating limits and operating parameters of the machine system; basically, an on-line operating manual for the machine system. The status refers to the current state of the system, including its location, hardware and software integrity, and so on.

In computational systems it is practically unheard of to have a database of knowledge about the human system. As shown in Figure 6.1, this database would include knowledge about the task, person, and situation. The task, as with the machine system, refers to the global and current missions and the goals for those missions. The person entails the traits, personality, current physiological status, behaviors, and so on, at both a state and trait level for the individual user. The situation refers to the place, time, environment, social context, and so on, in which the person is operating.

The key to augmented cognition is that both machine and human system information is sensed and collected and then integrated by an augmentation unit (as seen in Figure 6.1). In essence, the augmentation unit performs two functions, one related

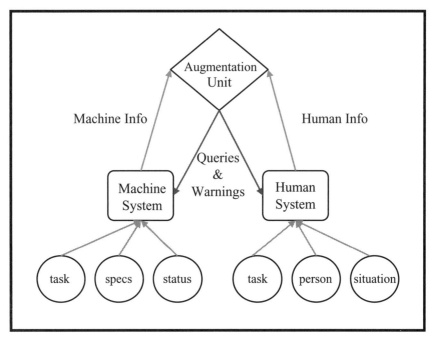

Figure 6.1
A Novel Approach to Human–Computer Interaction Involving Augmented Cognition

to input, and the other to output. On the input side, the augmentation unit has algorithms that assess the states of the human and machine systems based on the sensor data coming from those systems. On the output side, the augmentation unit acts as a task manager, offering queries and warnings to the human and machine systems based on the integration of the information coming from these systems. The augmentation unit can off-load repetitive or memory tasks, aid in decision making, and manage the presentation of tasks and task workload to minimize or avoid the task interference described above. It is important to note that the augmentation unit is not intended to make mission critical decisions for the human system. Rather, it is intended to maximize the information flow between the human and machine systems in a way that manages noncritical, but important task workload and frees the individual to complete mission critical tasks when necessary with the cognitive resources and information he needs. For example, consider a soldier and his weapon. Information can be sent to the augmentation unit regarding how many rounds are left in the weapon. As the number of rounds gets low, but before the weapon is totally empty, the augmentation unit can recommend to the soldier that he reload or warn him that the weapon is getting empty. This warning can be given at an appropriate time based on information the augmentation unit has received regarding the human—i.e., he is relaxed and not performing other cognitive tasks. In this way, a simple task like loading a weapon can be optimized to be done at a time when needed (the weapon is getting low on ammunition) and when appropriate (the human is waiting to perform a task).

Developing Augmented Cognition-Based Systems

Augmented cognition systems must have two main capabilities: (a) the individual's cognitive state must be monitored in real time, and (b) cognitive state information must be used to modify some task or interface with the benefit of improved performance, thus "closing the loop." Each step represents a milestone in the ultimate development of this symbiotic human computer system.

In Part A, the focus is on assessment of war fighter status and on the detectors and sensors for assessing both cognitive and physiological function. For example, one can use heart- rate variability to assess human physiological arousal, as described later in this chapter. In Part B, the goal is manipulation of the task environment in a manner that is suitably matched to the current state of the user. For example, when human arousal is low and a user is falling asleep when he should be alert and vigilantly monitoring his computer screen, the augmented cognition system can give the user additional tasks to do or recommend the user intake a caffeinated beverage. The ultimate goal of Part B is improvement of war fighter performance, particularly under the realistic operational conditions of stress and fatigue. This implementation relies heavily on the lessons learned from the initial steps to design manipulation schemes that are effective in operational environments.

The First Step: Sensing Cognitive State

The first step, correctly determining the user's cognitive state in real time, is not an insignificant challenge. This step is filled with issues of its own, the first of which is the meaning of *cognitive state*. This is an enormous concept that academic scholars have debated for years and will continue to do so! The field of augmented cognition uses a working definition of cognitive state, rather than a purely abstract or academic one. Cognitive state is frequently described using the example of good health. One could argue that there is not an absolute definition of health. Nonetheless, on a daily basis, physicians are able to classify their patients as being in good health. How can this be? Physicians take a patient's temperature, blood pressure, listen to his or her vital organs, and perhaps administer blood tests. Individually, each of these observations cannot describe *health*. It is only when taken together that a picture of the state of health begins to emerge. Cognitive state can be viewed in the same manner. Scientists have many individual tools that can be used to assess specific cognitive functions. When combined together and evaluated in the context of the user, these tools can yield a holistic picture of cognitive state. Thus, cognition does not have to be abstractly defined in order to make advancements in human performance, any more than what fundamentally constitutes health has to be known in order to cure someone of disease. What is essential is that there is a series of measures that correlate well with cognitive function, and that by monitoring these measures and feeding that information into computational systems, human performance ultimately improves.

The next issue in determining cognitive state is deciding which cognitive functions should be measured to assess cognitive function relative to performance. Since each potential application of augmented cognition is different—command and control, dismounted operations, unmanned aircraft interface, vehicle systems, etc.—there are certain cognitive functions that are more critical to one context versus another. However, researchers generally work on a common list considered applicable to many systems; these include, but are not limited to: autonomic arousal, attention, verbal working memory, spatial working memory, error detection, stress, and cognitive workload (Balaban et al., 2004; Berka et al., 2004; Duta, Alford, Wilson & Tarassenko, 2004; Hoover & Muth, 2004; Izzetoglu, Bunce, Onaral, Pourrezaei & Chance, 2004; Schmorrow & McBride, 2004; St. John, Kobus, Morrison & Schmorrow, 2004; Young, Clegg & Smith, 2004). There is no shortage of cognitive functions described in the literature for controlled laboratory settings. The challenge, however, is in correctly classifying these states and functions in operational conditions. This is a crucial endeavor, as sensors often suffer degraded performance in a freely moving human system in a constantly changing environment (NATO-RTO, 2004).

The final issue in detecting cognitive state is perhaps the most critical. Given a working definition of cognitive state, the challenges of operational settings and the various observable cognitive functions, can cognitive state even be measured in real time? The scientific literature is filled with studies describing the measurable, involuntary changes in human physiology as a result of mental workload and cognitive effort. Initially, work focused on the autonomic nervous system and changes in peripheral organ systems, such as the heart, pupil, and sweat glands (e.g., Hess & Polt, 1964; Humphrey & Kramer, 1994; Just & Carpenter, 1993). More recently, technology has enabled research to focus directly on the central nervous system and brain through the use of modern techniques like functional magnetic resonance imaging (fMRI), magnetoencephalography (MEG), electroencephalography (EEG), and optical recording methods (e.g., Gevins & Smith, 2000; Gundel & Wilson, 1992). Unfortunately, a relatively small portion of these studies has been made in real time. In addition, most observations have been made using hospital and laboratory-grade devices, like fMRI and MEG, whose size, weight, and expense make their use in operational environments out of the question. Since the explicit goal of augmented cognition is to identify cognitive state shifts in real time (on the order of seconds) in order for computational systems to adapt, significant advances must occur in both sensor miniaturization and signal processing. The further need for the cognitive-state detection devices to be operationally deployed in harsh conditions far from the laboratory places additional pressure on researchers to create rugged, portable, and wireless (or minimally wired) technologies.

Research teams, including neuroscientists and biomedical engineers, are developing devices to meet these stringent criteria. Scientists in the augmented cognition field are engaged in the testing of portable EEG devices, eye-tracking/pupillometric devices (Marshall, 2000) and near-infrared (NIR) optical imaging equipment

(Gratton & Fabiani, 2001), as well as new electrode designs, EEG caps/nets, and wireless/portable imaging devices (Ferree, Luu, Russell & Tucker, 2001; Gevins et al., 1995). One of the technologies that shows great promise is a wearable, optically based brain-imaging device. Optical imaging makes possible the continuous, noninvasive, and portable monitoring of the brain's neuronal (event-related optical signal, or EROS) and hemodynamic (near-infrared spectroscopy, or NIRS) responses (Gratton & Fabiani, 1998; Gratton, Goodman-Wood & Fabiani, 2001; Villringer & Chance, 1997). Using near-infrared light (700–1000 nm), it is possible to image changes in the oxygenation of particular regions of the brain (correlated to activity) by measuring changes in light scattering. In these experiments, a source/detector array is placed on the subject's head and near-infrared light is transmitted harmlessly through the skull. Corresponding reflected light from the upper surface of the brain cortex is measured and reconstructed into a map of activation (Gratton & Fabiani, 2001; Villringer & Chance, 1997). This technique is particularly promising since it allows for the measurement of hemodynamic and neuronal activity from the same volume of brain tissue on the order of seconds. The current resolution of this technology is on the order of a cm^3, but efforts are being made to extract signals from deeper levels of tissue than just the cortex (Kruse, Gorski & Schmorrow, 2003). Hemodynamic changes (e.g., changes in the level of oxygenated blood over particular regions) are the same type of signals detected by fMRI, but the optical equipment is a fraction of the size and cost.

When conducting applied research in operational domains, it is critical to use observations of cognitive state already described in the literature as a springboard for more advanced and prototype devices. Since brain-imaging technologies like fMRI are the gold standard for studying the spatial localization of human cognitive function, researchers can validate their new observations against old standards to see how they correlate with and confirm or contradict previous observations. Studies demonstrating co-localization of fMRI and optical data add weight to the argument that these newer devices can be used with confidence in operational environments. Likewise, EEG has been used for over 50 years to document the temporal aspects of brain function. The simultaneous measurement and correlation of EEG and evoked response potential (ERP) signals and EROS data gives further credence to this technique. When available, correlations between old and new techniques advance the goal of a comprehensive picture of brain state.

Cross-validation in the laboratory does not allow the scientist to overlook field validation. The operational environment is not like the laboratory—and it may be impossible to completely validate observations using comparisons, for instance, of fMRI and MEG. This is not to say that validation work will not continue, but that results from these comparisons should be evaluated knowing that context and environment have enormous impact on the behavior of the human brain. Research into validation between the laboratory and field continues, but several efforts have chosen a unique approach using neural networks to classify cognitive state. In this method, researchers use a training condition of a known difficulty or workload to establish what sensor output during these conditions might look like. A computer program, known as a neural network, is trained to recognize these patterns and responses and then triggers the appropriate categorization of cognitive state based on the sensor output. In this way, the cognitive state does not have to be compared or validated against a laboratory standard—but is instead compared to a standard within the context of the user's environment (Wilson, 2001; Wilson, Lambert & Russell, 1999).

An additional challenge facing the deployment of these devices in operational environments is the need for data-analysis methods and signal-processing algorithms to enable real-time analysis of data. Without question, techniques like EEG and ERP are the fastest measurements of brain function available. They record the collective firing of neurons throughout the brain on the order of milliseconds. The processing of these data is complex, however, often requiring hundreds of trials to isolate a signal. This data processing does not typically occur in real time. Researchers are working on new methods for the real-time analysis of EEG data, including methods for the subtraction of artifacts and the isolation of signals of interest in one trial (as compared to hundreds). Several research groups are making good progress with the advanced signal-processing methods needed to make this happen (Ferree, Eriksen & Tucker, 2000; Parra et al., 2002). Looking ahead, new processes must be developed to turn standard analysis output into information that can be used in a closed-loop system.

Although described in detail, near-infrared devices represent only a small portion of the technologies currently used in augmented cognition research to analyze and assess cognitive state and are primarily useful for monitoring verbal and spatial workload. A more comprehensive list includes the following:

- EEG—electroencephalography (Gevins, Smith, McEvoy, & Yu, 1997): for monitoring verbal and spatial working memory;
- ERP—event-related potential (Fabiani, 2000): for detecting errors and monitoring attention;
- NIRS—near infrared spectroscopy & EROS—event-related optical signals (Gratton & Fabiani, 2001; Villringer & Chance, 1997): for monitoring verbal and spatial working memory;
- Pupillary reflexes and eye tracking—(Just & Carpenter, 1993; Marshall, 2000): for monitoring attention and general cognitive workload;
- Physiological—measures of parasympathetic and sympathetic activity, temperature, galvanic skin response, blood pressure, heart rate (Hoover & Muth, 2004): for monitoring arousal, attention, stress and general cognitive workload;
- Behavioral Measures—voice stress, mouse pressure, error rates, task performance (Ark, Dryer & Lu, 1999): for monitoring arousal, attention, stress and general cognitive workload.

The Next Step: Closing the Loop

In the development of augmented cognition systems, it is not sufficient just to detect cognitive state. As system development moves from Step 1 to Step 2, the focus of research must shift from detection to the means by which state data can be classified and turned into actionable information which computational systems can interpret and use to make meaningful adaptations to benefit the user. Thus, in this next step we move away from individual measures and sensors to a combined output that yields a complete picture of cognitive state. The ultimate goal of closing the loop depends heavily on the transition between Step 1 and Step 2. Without this transition, we will have merely characterized the state of the user in real time, not an insignificant achievement, but also not the ultimate goal. The ultimate goal is to have cognitively aware computational systems that use this cognitive state information to adapt to and improve the performance of their users. As mentioned previously, there is a body of literature describing adaptive computer systems. These types of systems have been a goal of human–computer interaction (HCI) researchers for some time; however, they have lacked the sophisticated cognitive assessment tools under development by augmented cognition researchers (Parasuraman, 1990; Parasuraman, Mouloua & Molloy, 1996; Scerbo, Freeman & Mikulka, 2003). Advanced cognitive state detection and adaptive interfaces currently exist but only independently. The challenge in this second step is to bring these disparate fields together for substantial improvement in performance.

An Example of a State Sensor: The Arousal Meter

Background Theory

The autonomic nervous system (ANS) regulates internal states by acting as a feedforward and feedback system from the central nervous system (CNS) to the periphery and from the periphery to the CNS. The parasympathetic nervous system (PNS) is the branch of the ANS that is often associated with homeostatic functions, i.e., returning the organism to rest. The sympathetic nervous system (SNS) is often associated with fight or flight, arousing the organism. PNS and SNS interactions are complex in that the PNS and SNS can act independently, coactively, or reciprocally (Bernston, Cacioppo & Quigley, 1991). Internal organs such as the heart and stomach respond to PNS and SNS interactions. Typically, during arousal, there is PNS withdrawal and SNS activation; heart rate increases, and stomach activity decreases.

Respiratory sinus arrhythmia (RSA) is a well established, noninvasive, cardiovascular index that can be used to objectively assess the parasympathetic activity of the autonomic nervous system (Grossman, 1992). When cardiac variability, most of which occurs between 0.0–1.0 Hz. (Mezzacappa, Kindlon & Earls, 1994), is plotted as a continuous function against time, three periodic fluctuations can be observed. These include a low-frequency (LF) peak between .04–.08 Hz, a mid-frequency peak (MF) centered around .1 Hz, and a high-frequency (HF) peak between .15–.5 Hz. The physiological basis for the HF component, a measure of RSA, is well known and many studies have validated the use of various RSA measures as indices of parasympathetic nervous system activity (e.g., Eckberg, 1983; Grossman, Karemaker & Wieling, 1991; Katona & Jih, 1975). Arousal is inversely related to RSA. Hence,

RSA can be used as a measure of arousal, which is indirectly related to attention and workload.

Algorithm Implementation/Design

The Arousal Meter (AM) consists of two components: a heart rate sensor and analysis software. The AM has been implemented in both a desktop and wearable version. The wearable unit contains both the sensor and analysis software and transmits the data wirelessly using the 802.11b wireless standard. The wearable unit currently measures 12.7 cm × 17.8 cm × 3.8 cm. It is expected that as processing components get smaller, the size of the wearable unit will be reduced. In both the desktop and wearable units, the operator is monitored via three electrode leads: one on the person's right side just below the collar bone, one on the left side just below the left breast, and one on the right side just below the last stationary rib.

Interbeat intervals (IBIs) are derived by monitoring the raw electrocardiogram (ECG) and recording the time interval between successive R-spikes of the cardiac QRS interval (as shown in Figure 6.2). The analysis software reads 64 seconds of IBI data and processes a data window that moves forward in time every 250 msec using the Fast-Fourier-Transform (the mathematical equivalent of passing light through a prism and breaking it into its component frequencies). Power is derived and plotted across frequencies to determine the high frequency (HF) peak associated with PNS activity (between 9 and 30 cycles per minute). This HF peak is then plotted over time. The mean and standard deviation of the HF peak are continually recalculated. The log power of the HF peak is calculated and a standardized arousal score is derived on the log HF power as $[-(x-\mu/\sigma)]$. Based on the moving analysis window, arousal data are available up to 4 Hz.

One of the research problems facing augmented cognition systems can be highlighted here. Although IBI analysis is a common clinical procedure, it has never previously been applied in a completely closed-loop system, i.e., with no human oversight. Even in the most carefully controlled environment with the most sophisticated equipment, the detection of individual heartbeats is prone to some level of error. The

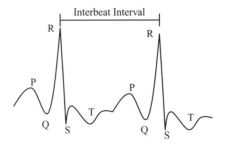

Figure 6.2
Theoretical Electrocardiogram Drawing Indicating the Interbeat Interval

current practice is to have a human expert go over the data off-line, after it has all been acquired, and fix any errors (Bernston, Quigley, Jang & Boysen, 1990). This of course is not possible in an augmented cognition system. Therefore, new methods must be developed that detect and correct raw sensor errors, or alternatively, new analyses methods developed that are robust to raw sensor errors. For example, imagine if the ECG leads on a soldier become loose, or are worn in suboptimal positions, or simply wear and become less reliable. The augmented cognition system of the future must recognize these events and respond accordingly to be useful in the field. It is analogous to the difference between an old-fashioned stereo turntable and a modern MP3 player. Although they both play music, only one of them can be worn during jogging. The current wearable unit has some sensor error detection and correction software built in, and improvements are being studied and implemented.

Another research challenge is to personalize these measures, making them applicable to the individual. In classic clinical studies, results are almost always organized according to groups. Usually the intent is to prove, or disprove that an experimental condition has some effect compared to a control condition. In contrast, an augmented cognition system must respond to an individual person's changes in cognitive state. Thus, the methods should include calibration periods (where data collected from the individual to be monitored are used to set up the system) and equations that include metrics that can be tuned to the individual. In the arousal meter, this is accomplished by the standardization described above. However, this is only a first attempt, and more research is necessary to apply these methods to individuals in the field.

Measuring the Cognitive State of Workload via Arousal

A study was conducted to confirm that the arousal meter was sensitive to manipulations in task difficulty. In this study, subjects completed six tasks. The first three tasks for all subjects were variations of the Gauges Task, a dual-attention task developed by Select International and used with permission for this research. The goal in the task is to calculate the values of two arithmetic expressions on the right of the screen and to determine if they are identical, responding with the "same" and "different" buttons under the expressions. At the same time, it is necessary to monitor six gauges on the left of the display and to reverse the direction of the needle as it approaches the red area. The needle of each gauge moves slowly and steadily in either direction. Small buttons to the right of each gauge reverse the direction. The three versions of the task varied in difficulty: Level 1—slow gauges, easy math; Level 2—fast gauges, easy math; and Level 3—fast gauges, hard math. The order of presentation of the levels was counterbalanced so that each one appeared equally often as first, second, or third. The fourth task for all subjects was a five-minute rest period, required for physiological comparison. The subject was asked to sit quietly and rest. The fifth task for all subjects was a two-minute effort to maintain pressure on a handgrip device. Each subject was first asked to squeeze the device as hard as he or she could. Once the maximum effort was determined, the subject was then instructed to maintain 25 percent of maximum effort for two minutes. A researcher monitored the level and verbally instructed the subject to increase or decrease effort as needed. The sixth and final task for all subjects was a dual-attention task, in which the subject was required to fix attention on a spatial shape that moved about the screen and at the same time to count down from 200 to 0 by three's. The screen at all times showed a blue circle and a red square. Every three seconds, these two shapes changed location. The subject was instructed to keep his or her eyes on the blue circle while counting.

As can be seen inFigure 6.3, as we expected, the handgrip task was significantly more arousing than the rest task (t[14]=1.810, p<0.05). In fact, if you consider zero the break in state between relaxation (positive numbers) and arousal (negative numbers), the arousal measure actually shows a state shift between the rest and the handgrip task. These data confirm that the measure of arousal used in this experiment is sensitive to manipulations that cause physiological arousal (parasympathetic withdrawal). Figure 6.4 shows the arousal-by gauge task. Statistical comparisons were made to the rest task. Further, the 0 point can roughly be thought of as a point of state change between relaxation and arousal. As can be seen, during the gauges 1 (easy) and gauges 2 (moderate) tasks, the arousal measure is close to zero, but during the gauges 3 (difficult) task, the arousal measure indicates a state shift toward arousal. In fact, statistically, there is no difference between gauges 1 and gauges 2 compared to rest (t[14]=1.24, p>0.05 and t[14]=1.12, p>0.05, respectively). However, there is significantly more arousal during the gauges 3 task compared to rest (t[14]=2.35, p<0.05). The likely explanation here is that cognitive workload was low during the easy and moderate tasks and arousal stayed relatively constant. However, during

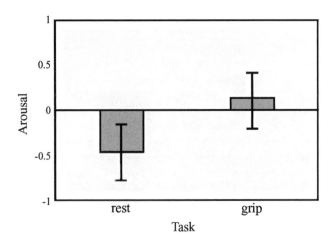

Figure 6.3
Arousal During the Rest and Grip Tasks (Results shown are mean +/− standard error of the mean. Arousal scale is in standard deviation units.)

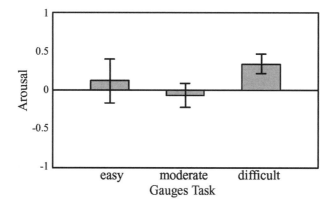

Figure 6.4
**Arousal During the Three Levels of the Gauges Task (Results shown are mean +/− stand-
ard error of the mean. Arousal scale is in standard deviation units.)**

gauges 3, cognitive load became a challenge for subjects, and a level of arousal com-
parable to that observed during the physiological challenge of handgrip was
observed.

This study confirmed that the algorithms previously validated in the literature and
incorporated into the arousal meter are capable of detecting state shifts. Participants
were exposed to low, moderate, and high workload tasks. During low and moderate
workload, arousal stayed close to zero. During high workload, arousal increased
significantly and an arousal state shift, defined as arousal moving from negative to
positive, was detected.

While this confirmation that the arousal meter works according to the predictions of the literature may seem trivial, it must be considered in light of having a wireless, wearable version of the AM available. When soldiers are involved in
battle, they typically can tell which of their comrades is overaroused and underperforming simply through direct observation. The individual soldier who is overaroused and underperforming, however, may not appreciate his own predicament.
Further, at even small distances from that individual, this information is not available
to others.

Imagine a battlefield on which all soldiers were wearing arousal meters. The system could be beneficial at both local and global levels. At the local level, the AM
could essentially be giving the individual automated biofeedback. Via the augmentation unit, the individual could be given guidance on task-switching that might help
him manage his workload. For example, if the AM senses underarousal, implying
that task load is low, the augmentation unit might give the soldier additional tasks
to do to keep him alert and engaged. At the global level, commanders could have
workload information about large groups of individuals. These group data could
indicate units that are overwhelmed or underwhelmed, and commanders could

switch tasks between units at a global level to manage the workload. It is easily seen how having even simple cognitive gauges made rugged and operational in the battle-field could lead to almost endless ideas for how the information could be capitilized on to provide operational superiority. Current efforts are underway to apply the AM in a closed-loop paradigm to see if during a dual task when a bottleneck occurs (as described above), task-switching guidance can be automated in a way that results in improved performance, thus supporting the premise of the potential applications as just described.

Final Thoughts on Augmented Cognition and Closed-Loop Systems

The understanding of cognitive functions and their neural substrates provides a valuable insight into the working of the human brain. The application of these dis-coveries to the complex problems facing our military represents a significant advancement in the types of tools that can be used in operational environments. The monitoring of cognitive state in real time will allow us to build sensing devices and cognitive systems that can optimize the display of critical information and enhance our knowledge of the world around us, hopefully reducing if not eliminat-ing the problem of dual-task interference and allowing humans to accomplish more in less time with fewer errors. The success of augmented cognition will improve the way twenty-first century warriors interact with computational systems, advance the field of human systems integration, and fundamentally reengineer the decision-mak-ing processes using a cognitive-systems approach.

Although still developing, this field is already yielding results. For example, two different systems to enhance the search for certain targets among a field of numerous distracters are being developed. One of these systems uses eye tracking to sense and guide visual attention to areas that have not yet been searched (Araujo, Kowler & Pavel, 2001; Pavel, Wang & Li, 2003). Coupled with a helmet-mounted display with overlay technology (information can be displayed in a three-dimensional manner such that it appears to exist out in the environment), this system could be useful in an operational environment where a soldier has to constantly scan for enemies. As the soldier is scanning the environment, it could mark target errors with a code that indicates how long it has been since he looked in that area, and an augmentation unit could provide alerts when an area has been ignored for a long time. This type of sys-tem could also mitigate the visual-attention bottleneck when a soldier has to do sev-eral demanding visual tasks. For example, if the individual has to scan as described above and also look down at a map, the system could aid in task-switching (time spent looking at the map versus time spent looking in the environment) by monitor-ing the times spent on each task and having the augmentation unit offer reminders and guidance when too much time is spent on one task.

The second of these systems measures a person's brain activity while a computer flashes pictures at a rate that appears beyond visual recognition. Even though the human cannot consciously distinguish between the pictures, the computer can sense through brain activity which pictures evoke a response, and then sort the pictures based on the response to present the most important pictures first, thus targeting the search (Parra, Spence, Gerson & Sajda, 2003). This type of system could be used at security checkpoints. Soldiers at security checkpoints have to quickly look at individuals and identification photographs of individuals and make quick decisions regarding how invasive a search to do, while simultaneously completing numerous other secondary tasks. A soldier outfitted with this type of device could be sent a message through the augmentation unit when the soldier has a response to a face or identification card that he or she is viewing, warning the soldier that he or she may want to examine this individual a little more closely. While this unit clearly could not be the sole means of detecting suspicious individuals, it has the potential to aid an individual who has an impossible task, yet is often pointed to when we ask, "How did the terrorist with the bomb make it through the checkpoint?"

We have only begun to evaluate the Augmented-Cognition approach for application to the war fighting systems under development today. As the field progresses, we expect it not only to impact operations, but also military training, education, and the design of new interfaces and technologies. While augmented cognition is surely not the answer to all the technology, task management, workload or error problems that exist, it is an attempt to redefine human–computer interaction. As with any change in direction, the path must be taken cautiously and proceeded down methodically for it to be successful. For example, issues such as gender, race, and ethnicity and their effects on Augmented-Cognition systems have not been considered up to this point from either the perspective of how they cause systems to fail or how they could be used to benefit systems. Further, the appropriateness of the various models of dual-task interference and their ability to account for data observed in closed-loop type experiments must be evaluated. Currently, the bottleneck model is most often cited when discussing augmented cognition systems. To maximize the war fighter's benefit, these issues among others, must be examined as augmented cognition becomes the human–computer interaction of the twenty-first century.

References

Angus, R. G., & Heslegrave, R. J. (1985). Effects of sleep loss on sustained cognitive performance during a command and control simulations. *Behavior Research Methods, Instruments and Computers, 17*(1), 55–67.

Araujo, C., Kowler, E., & Pavel, M. (2001). Eye movements during visual search: the costs of choosing the optimal path. *Vision Research, 41*, 3613–25.

Ark, W., Dryer, D., & Lu, D. (1999). The emotion mouse. In H. J. Bullinger and J. Ziegler (Eds.), *Human-computer interaction: Ergonomics and user interfaces* (pp. 818–823). London: Erlbaum.

Balaban, C. D., Cohn, J., Redfern, M. S., Prinkey, J., Stripling, R., & Hoffer, M. (2004). Postural control as a probe for cognitive state: Exploiting human information processing to enhance performance. *International Journal of Human-Computer Interaction, 17*(2), 275–287.

Berka, C., Levendowski, D. J., Cvetinovic, M. M., Petrovic, M. M., Davis, G., Lumicao, M. N., Zivkovic, V.T., Popovic, M.V., & Olmstead, R. (2004). Real-time analysis of EEG indexes of alertness, cognition, and memory acquired with a wireless EEG headset. *International Journal of Human-Computer Interaction, 17* (2), 151–170.

Berntson, G. G., Cacioppo, J. T., & Quigley, K. S. (1991). Autonomic determinism: The modes of autonomic control, the doctrine of autonomic space, and the laws of autonomic constraint. *Psychological Review , 98*, 459–487.

Bernston, G. G., Quigley, K. S., Jang, J. F., & Boysen, S. T. (1990). An approach to artifact identification: Application to heart period data. *Psychophysiology, 27*, 586–98.

Cahoon, R. L. (1972). Simple decision making at high altitude. *Ergonomics, 15*(2), 157–164.

Caldwell, J. A., Caldwell, J. L., Brown, D. L., & Smith, J. K. (2004). The effects of 37 hours of continuous wakefulness on the physiological arousal, cognitive performance, self-reported mood, and simulator flight performance of F-117A pilots. *Military Psychology, 16*(3), 163–181.

Card, S. K., Moran, T. P., & Newell, A. (1983). *The psychology of human-computer interaction*. Mahwah, NJ: Lawrence Erlbaum.

Committee on Human Factors (1997). Stress and cognitive workload. In *Tactical display for soldiers: Human factors considerations* (pp. 130–163). Panel on Human Factors in the Design of Tactical Display Systems for the Individual Soldier. National Research Council. Washington, DC: National Academy Press.

Cowings, P. S., Toscano, W. B., DeRoshia, C., & Tauson, R. (2000). *Effects of command and control vehicle (CV2) operational environment on soldier health and performance*. Washington, DC: National Aeronautics and Space Administration; NASA/TM–1999–208786.

Curley, M. D., & Hawkins, R. N. (1983). Cognitive performance during a heat acclimatization regimen. *Aviation, Space and Environmental Medicine, 54*(8), 709–713.

Duta, M., Alford, C., Wilson, S., & Tarassenko, L. (2004). Neural network analysis of the mastoid EEG for the assessment of vigilance. *International Journal of Human-Computer Interaction, 17*(2), 171–199.

Eckberg, D. L. (1983).Human sinus arrhythmia as an index of vagal cardiac outflow. *Journal of Applied Physiology, 54*, 961–966.

Englund, C. E., Ryman, D. H., Naitoh, P., & Hodgdon, J. A. (1985). Cognitive performance during successive sustained physical work episodes. *Behavioral Research Methods, Instruments and Computers, 17*(1), 75–85.

Fabiani, M. (2000). Event-related brain potentials. In J. T. Cacioppo (Ed.), *Handbook of psychophysiology* (pp. 53–84). Cambridge, UK: Cambridge University Press.

Ferree, T. C., Eriksen, K. J., & Tucker, D. M. (2000). Regional head tissue conductivity estimation for improved EEG analysis. *IEEE Transactions on Biomedical Engineering, 47*(12), 1584–1592.

Ferree, T. C., Luu, P., Russell, G. S., & Tucker, D. M. (2001). Scalp electrode impedance, infection risk, and EEG data quality. *Journal of Clinical Neurophysiology, 112*(3), 536–544.

Fine, B. J., & Kobrick, J. L. (1987). Effect of heat and chemical protective clothing on cognitive performance. *Aviation, Space and Environmental Medicine, 58*(2), 149–154.

Forster, E. M., & Cammarota, J. P. (1993). The effect of G–LOC on psychomoter performance and behavior. *Aviation, Space and Environmental Medicine, 64*(2), 132–138.

Gevins, A., & Smith, M. E. (2000). Neurophysiological measures of working memory and individual differences in cognitive ability and cognitive style. *Cerebral Cortex, 10*(9), 829–839.

Gevins, A., Leong, H., Du, R., Smith, M. E., Le, J., DuRousseau, D., Zhang, J., & Libove, J. (1995). Toward measurement of brain function in operational environments. *Biological Psychology, 40*, 169–186.

Gevins, A., Smith, M. E., McEvoy, L., & Yu, D. (1997). High resolution EEG mapping of cortical activation related to working memory: Effects of task difficulty, type of processing, and practice. *Cerebral Cortex, 7*(4), 374–385.

Gratton, G., & Fabiani, M. (1998). Dynamic brain imaging: Event-related optical signal (EROS) measures of the time course and localization of cognitive-related activity. *Psychonomic Bulletin & Review, 5*(4), 535–563.

Gratton, G., & Fabiani, M. (2001). The event-related optical signal: A new tool for studying brain function. *International Journal of Psychophysiology, 10*(2), 109–121.

Gratton, G., Goodman-Wood, M. R., & Fabiani, M. (2001). Comparison of neuronal and hemodynamic measures of the brain response to visual stimulation: An optical imaging study. *Human Brain Mapping, 13*, 13–25.

Grossman, P. (1992). Respiratory and cardiac rhythms as windows to central and autonomic biobehavioral regulation: Selection of window frames, keeping the panes clean and viewing the neural topography. *Biological Psychology, 34*, 131–161.

Grossman, P., Karemaker, J., & Wieling, W. (1991). Prediction of tonic parasympathetic cardiac control using respiratory sinus arrhythmia: The need for respiratory control. *Psychophysiology, 28*, 201–216.

Gundel, A., & Wilson, G. F. (1992). Topographical changes in the ongoing EEG related to the difficulty of mental tasks. *Brain Topography, 5*(1), 17–25.

Haslam, D. R. (1985). Sustained operations and military performance. *Behavioral Research Methods, Instruments and Computers, 17*(1), 90–95.

Hess, E. H., & Polt, J. M. (1964). Pupil size in relation to mental activity during simple problem solving. *Science, 143*, 1190–1192.

Hoover, A., & Muth, E. (2004). A real-time index of vagal activity. *International Journal of Human-Computer Interaction, 17*(2), 197–209.

Humphrey, D. G., & Kramer, A. F. (1994). Toward a psychophysiological assessment of dynamic changes in mental workload. *Human Factors, 36*(1), 3–26.

Izzetoglu, K., Bunce, S., Onaral, B., Pourrezaei, K., & Chance, B. (2004). Functional optical brain imaging using near-infrared during cognitive tasks. *International Journal of Human-Computer Interaction, 17*(2), 211–231.

Just, M. A., & Carpenter, P. A. (1993). The intensity dimension of thought: Pupillometric indices of sentence processing. *Canadian Journal of Experimental Psychology, 47*(2), 310–339.

Kahneman, D. (1973). *Attention and effort.* Englewood Cliffs, NJ: Prentice Hall.

Katona, P. G., & Jih, F. (1975). Respiratory sinus arrhythmia: noninvasive measure of parasympathetic cardiac control. *Journal of Applied Physiology, 39*, 801–805.

Kinsbourne, M. (1981). Single channel theory. In D. Holding (Ed.), *Human skills* (pp. 65–89). New York: Wiley.

Kruse, A. A., Gorski, S., & Schmorrow, D. D. (2003). *Non-invasive optical techniques for biomedical imaging.* Paper presented at 7th World Multiconference on Systemics, Cybernetics and Informatics, Orlando, FL.

Marshall, S. P. (2000). *Method and apparatus for eye tracking and monitoring pupil dilation to evaluate cognitive activity.* U.S. Patent 6,090,051.

Mezzacappa, E., Kindlon, D., & Earls, F. (1994). The utility of spectral analytic techniques in the study of the autonomic regulation of beat-to-beat heart rate variability. *International Journal of Methods in Psychiatric Research, 4,* 29–44.

Morey, C. C., & Cowen, N. (2004). When visual and verbal memories compete: Evidence of cross-domain limits in working memory. *Psychonomic Bulletin and Review, 11*(2), 296–301.

Muth, E. R. (2004). Using flight simulators aboard ships II: Human side effects of a less than optimal scenario. Unpublished manuscript.

Muth, E. R., & Lawson, B. (2003). Using flight simulators aboard ships: Human side effects of an optimal scenario with smooth seas. *Aviation, Space and Environmental Medicine, 74,* 497–505.

Navon, D., & Gopher, D. (1979). On the economy of the human processing system. *Psychological Review, 86,* 254–284.

North Atlantic Treaty Organization Research and Technical Organization (NATO-RTO). (2004). *Operator functional state assessment* (RTO Technical Report TR-HFM-104). RTO/NATO ISBN 92-837-1111-4.

Parasuraman, R. (1990). Event-related brain potentials and human factors research. In R. Rohrbaugh, R. Parasuraman, and R. J. Johnson (Eds.), *Event-related brain potentials* (pp. 279–300). New York: Oxford University Press.

Parasuraman, R. M., Mouloua, M., & Molloy, R. (1996). Effects of adaptive task allocation on monitoring of automated systems. *Human Factors, 38,* 665–679.

Parra, L. C., Alvino, C., Tang, A., Pearlmutter, B., Yeung, N., Osman, A., & Sajdal, P. (2002). Linear spatial integration for single trial detection in encephalography. *Neuroimage, 17,* 223–30.

Parra, L. C., Spence, C. D., Gerson, A. D., & Sajda, P. (2003). Response error correction—a demonstration of improved human-machine performance using real-time EEG monitoring. *IEEE Transactions on Neural Systems and Rehabilitation Engineering, 11*(2), 173–7.

Pashler, H. (1984). Processing stages in overlapping tasks: Evidence for a central bottleneck. *Journal of Experimental Psychology: Human Perception and Performance, 19,* 1292–1312.

Pashler, H. (1994). Dual-task interference in simple tasks: Data and theory. *Psychological Bulletin, 116*(2), 220–224.

Pavel, M., Wang, G., & Li, K. (2003). *Augmented cognition: Allocation of attention* (abstract). 36th Annual Hawaii International Conference on System Sciences, 128.

Pierard, C., Peres, M., Jouanin, J. C., Liscia, P., Satabin, P., Martin, S., Testylier, G., Guezennec, C. Y., & Beaumont, M. (2004). Declarative memory impairments following a military combat course: Parallel neuropsychological and biochemical investigations. *Neuropsychology, 49*(4), 210–217.

Scerbo, M., Freeman, F., & Mikulka, P. (2003). A Brain-based system for adaptive automation. *Theoretical Issues in Ergonomic Science, 4*(2), 200–219.

Schmorrow, D., & McBride, D. (2004). Introduction. *International Journal of Human-Computer Interaction, 17*(2), 127–130.

St. John, M., Kobus, D. A., Morrison, J. G., & Schmorrow, D. (2004). Overview of the DARPA augmented cognition technical integration experiment. *International Journal of Human-Computer Interaction, 17*(2), 131–149.

Villringer, A., & Chance, B. (1997). Non-invasive optical spectroscopy and imaging of human brain function. *Trends in Neuroscience, 20*(10), 435–442.

Wickens, C. D. (1980). The structure of attentional resources. In R. Nickerson (Ed.), *Attention and performance VIII* (pp. 239–257). Hillsdale, NJ: Erlbaum.

Wilson, G. F. (2001). Real-time adaptive aiding using psychophysiological operator state assessment. In D. Harris (Ed.), *Engineering psychology and cognitive ergonomics* (Vol. 6, pp. 175–182). Aldershot, UK: Ashgate.

Wilson, G. F., Lambert, J. D., & Russell, C. A. (1999). Performance enhancement with real-time physiologically controlled adaptive aiding. *Proceedings of the Human Factors and Ergonomics Society 44th Annual Meeting*, 3-61 to 3-64.

Young, P. M., Clegg, B. A., & Smith, C. A. P. (2004). Dynamic models of augmented cognition. *International Journal of Human-Computer Interaction, 17*(2), 259–275.

CHAPTER 7

DECISION MAKING AND PERFORMANCE UNDER STRESS

James E. Driskell, Eduardo Salas, and Joan H. Johnston

One of the authors recently observed a firefighting drill aboard a U.S. Navy ship. The simulated event was a fire in the main propulsion space of the ship, and various teams were dispatched to locate, identify, and fight the fire. This task is one that, if not performed successfully, has serious consequences for the ship's integrity and for the lives of shipboard personnel. Granted this was just an exercise—not the real thing—but even in this simulation, we observed the elements of a high-stress situation. These include:

- Sudden and unexpected demands that disrupt normal procedures. High-stress events unfold quickly and demand an immediate response.
- The consequences of poor performance are immediate and severe.
- The task environment is complex and unpredictable. The causes of the event may be unclear, the required response is outside standard operating procedures, and events are dynamic and variable.
- Personnel must perform multiple tasks under conditions of high time pressure, noise, heat, smoke, darkness, and other stressors.

Although to the casual observer, a naval firefighting drill may seem like a near-riot, the teams observed in this exercise performed admirably. However, while discussing the results of this exercise with the ship's commanding officer, he noted: "Oh, this is nothing—the real concern is when we have to fight five of these at one time."

The topic of *stress and military performance* is a critical one because the military environment is so demanding. Although there are specific military tasks such as bomb disposal (Rachman, 1983), diving (Radloff & Helmreich, 1968), and parachuting (Burke, 1980) that are uniquely high-stress endeavors, even standard military operations are characterized by high risk and high demand (Driskell & Olmstead, 1989). In fact, there are very few settings outside the military that impose such a high demand on personnel and in which there is such a substantial potential for risk, harm, or error. The magnitude of this problem has been recognized for some time. For example, stress effects during the Normandy campaign in World War II were such that "the soldier was slow-witted; he was slow to comprehend orders, directions, and techniques.... Memory defects became so extreme that he could not be counted upon to relay a verbal order" (see Siegel et al., 1981, p. 13).

Stress is also so important in the military environment because failure to prepare for its effects exacts such a high price. The effects of stress on performance are most likely to occur when they can be least tolerated: during critical combat situations. Moreover, the modern military is a high-technology environment that places greatly increased demands on personnel. For example, in the combat information center of a modern naval ship, the amount and complexity of information which must be processed in a short period of time once a potential target has been detected is enormous. Therefore, although modern military systems have greatly extended the military's capabilities, they have increased not only the demands under which personnel must perform but also the potential for catastrophic errors.

The 1988 downing of an Iranian commercial aircraft by the USS *Vincennes* is a prime example of the detrimental effects of increased informational complexity, task load, and time pressure on performance (Klein, 1996). On July 3, 1998, the USS *Vincennes* was patrolling in the Persian Gulf during the height of the Iran–Iraq war. An Iranian commercial airliner, Iran Air Flight 655, took off from a joint military/civilian airport at Bandar Abbas at 0947 local time, on a flight plan that took it directly over the *Vincennes*. Approximately seven minutes later, the aircraft was shot down by the *Vincennes*, killing all 290 persons aboard. Although the various factors that contributed to this accident are covered in detail by Klein (1996), our interest at this point is on the environment in which the *Vincennes* operated. The demands faced by the *Vincennes* crew included:

- *Threat* : The *Vincennes* was operating in a wartime environment. Iranian F-14s operated out of the Bandar Abbas airport, and during the previous month, U.S. Navy ships had issued 150 challenges to potentially threatening aircraft (Klein, 1996). In fact, a year earlier, the USS *Stark* had been struck by two Iraqi antiship missiles, killing 37 sailors.

- *Time pressure*: The unknown aircraft was picked up by the *Vincennes* radar at 0947 and shot down at 0954, a period of about seven minutes. Between the time the aircraft became tactically significant, or perceived as a possible threat to the *Vincennes,* until it was shot down was approximately three minutes.

- *Task load*: During the time the Iranian airliner was airborne, the *Vincennes* was actively engaged in a surface battle with Iranian gunboats.

- *Environmental stressors*: The *Vincennes* was conducting high-speed maneuvering, and firing its 5-inch guns at the Iranian gunboats, accompanied by high noise, flickering lights, and falling gear.

During this scenario, a number of errors were made: The aircraft was misidentified as an F-14, and was erroneously perceived to be descending toward the *Vincennes* and increasing speed. In fact, it was this key, but incorrect, data that along with other factors led to the decision to launch the *Vincennes'* missiles and shoot down the aircraft. This very brief discussion of the *Vincennes* incident is useful for two reasons. First, it provides a context for what we mean by high stress or high demand in a military environment. In fact, this landmark event stimulated a substantial amount of research on performance under stress by the military services (see Cannon-Bowers & Salas, 1998; Driskell & Salas, 1996). Second, it provides a context for the present discussion of decision making and performance under stress. Although the *Vincennes* incident has been studied as an example of decision making under stress, clearly individuals on the *Vincennes* were involved not only in decision making, but also in monitoring displays, tracking targets, communicating with other personnel, or carrying out procedures. In fact, the major errors that occurred involved behaviors such as identification, communication, and coordination, and many argue that the captain of the *Vincennes* made a reasonable decision given the information available. Our approach in this chapter is to discuss decision making, not exclusively, but in the broader context of performance.

Thus, in general terms, what do we mean by stress? Stress occurs in a high-demand, high-threat situation that disrupts performance. Stress builds when events occur suddenly and often unexpectedly, quick and effective task performance is critical, and consequences of poor performance are immediate and often catastrophic. This topic is clearly relevant to the military, but also to many applied settings that share the commonalities of high-demand, high-risk performance conditions (see Driskell & Salas, 1996). In this chapter, our focus is on task performance under stress and on the development of strategies to overcome the detrimental effects of stress on performance. We first attempt to define the concept of stress more precisely, narrowing our emphasis to the topic of stress and performance. We describe stress effects in terms of an input→process→output stress model, and then work through that model by examining types of stressors, stress effects, and different types of stress interventions, including selection, training, and design approaches.

Defining Stress

Military leaders are often ambivalent about the concept of stress. They readily discuss the pressures, the pace, the hours, and the demanding conditions under which they must perform their mission. They are more hesitant to discuss stress *per se*, however, for several reasons. First, military personnel operate in a concrete, practical, real-world environment. They willingly discuss time pressure, noise, threat or danger. They seem less comfortable discussing a diffuse concept such as stress, because it is not as real to them in a day-to-day sense as more specific constructs such as noise. In fact, a ship commander informed one of the authors in no uncertain terms that there would be no stress on his ship because he would not allow it. My guess is that this may not have been exactly the case, but I was not about to disagree. Nevertheless, the concern that the concept of stress is too broad and ambiguous is an important one, and one that is shared by many stress researchers. Hogan and Hogan (1982) noted that the stress literature is "awash in a sea of terminology" (p. 153), and Driskell, Salas, and Johnston (2001) concluded that the concept of stress has been used so broadly as to mean almost anything.

A second problem with the general concept of stress stems from the traditional emphasis on a medical/psychoanalytic perspective as the dominant paradigm for studying stress, as evidenced in the work of Janis, Lazarus, and others. This perspective views people as chronically stressed, and posits that those who are able to deal with stress more effectively possess better coping mechanisms. This view has led to a preoccupation with illness, with the goal of discovering which coping mechanisms distressed persons lack. Thus, the bulk of stress research over the past several decades has emphasized disordered behavior, coping, and treatment, and has almost ignored the effects of stress on performance, effectiveness, and productivity in real-world task environments.

It is useful to define more clearly what we mean by stress. The term *stress* comes from the Latin *stringere*, to draw tight (or to strain, to exert or tax). Thus, from the early Latin, we have a strong hint of what stress means—it taxes, it strains, and it restricts. One of the earliest stress researchers was Selye, a physician, who provided the early direction for stress research by defining stress as the "nonspecific result of any demand upon the body" (1980, p. vii). Thus, Selye provided the first generally accepted conceptualization of stress as a reaction to noxious events, which he termed stressors. Stress reactions were studied *in situ* during World War II by military researchers concerned with the effects of combat on soldier performance. Grinker and Spiegel (1945) studied Air Force crews, noting that "never in the history of the study of human behavior has it been so important to understand the psychological mechanisms of 'normal' individuals in situations of stress" (p. vii). Janis (1951) examined emotional reactions to air raid attacks, and other applied research began to document effects of stress on performance. Gradually, stress research came out from under the purview of medicine and into the field of psychology.

Stress definitions vary in the extent to which they emphasize the *stimulus* environment, the *response* of the individual, or the *relationship* between the person and environment. A stimulus-based definition is couched in terms of the environmental events that impact the individual: "[Stress is] any change in the environment that induces a high degree of unpleasant emotion...and affects normal patterns of information processing" (Janis & Mann, 1977, p. 50). A response-based definition emphasizes the response of the individual to stress: "[Stress is] an adaptive response...that is a consequence of any external action, situation, or event that places special physical and/or psychological demands upon a person" (Ivancevich & Matteson, 1980, p. 8). A relational definition of stress emphasizes the relation between environmental demands and individual responses: "Psychological stress is a particular relationship between the person and the environment that is appraised by the person as taxing or exceeding his or her resources and endangering his or her well-being" (Lazarus & Folkman, 1984, p. 19).

Explicitly examining stress and performance, Salas, Driskell, and Hughes (1996) adopted a relational perspective, defining stress as *a process by which certain environmental demands (e.g., noise, threat, time pressure) evoke an appraisal process in which perceived demand exceeds resources, and that results in undesirable physiological, psychological, behavioral, or social outcomes.* Salas et al. further attempted to qualify their focus on stress and performance more precisely by noting certain limiting characteristics of this approach.

First, interest is restricted primarily to *acute stress*—stress that is sudden, novel, or unexpected, and of relatively short duration. Acute stress is represented by the prototypical emergency situation. An in-flight emergency on an aircraft, or almost any combat or even intense training situation are examples. This approach sets aside chronic stressors that impact the individual over time (e.g., job stress, family stress), stressful life events (e.g., marriage, divorce, illness), and daily hassles. Clearly, these issues are important, and certainly cumulative effects of chronic stressors can lead to degraded performance over time; however these types of stressors differ substantially from emergency or acute stress conditions.

Second, interest is restricted primarily to the *negative* consequences of stress. In some instances, stress can facilitate performance. For example, if the individual is underaroused or understimulated, stress may energize the person to achieve a more optimal level of arousal. This is a variant of the inverted U hypothesis, which holds that there is an optimal level of stress required for effective functioning. However, the primary interest in examining stress and performance is on the downward part of the inverted U, which represents the effect of high arousal on degrading performance.

Third, it is useful to distinguish between *overload* conditions and stressors that increase arousal versus *underload* conditions and stressors that decrease arousal. Stressors such as danger, threat, noise, and time pressure serve to arouse the individual, whereas stressors such as boredom, sleep loss, or fatigue serve to reduce arousal. Although both noise and sleep loss may degrade performance, they have opposing effects on arousal, and subsequently, the interaction of these different types of stressors is complex. Thus, although both types of stressors are relevant to the military environment, it is worthwhile to acknowledge that they differ in some important respects.

This attempt to describe stress in more precise terms accomplishes two things. It defines stress more clearly in a manner that is relevant to discussing military performance. Furthermore, the definition of stress provided by Salas et al. (1996) lends itself to further elaboration in the form of a simple input→process→output model.

Figure 7.1 illustrates a simple three-stage model of stress and performance. The input factors in this model include stressors such as noise, time pressure, task load, threat, or performance pressure. These stressors become salient and lead to the activation and operation of the appraisal process, which mediates the effects of stress on behavior and performance. Briefly, appraisal is an evaluation of whether the potential danger exceeds one's resources to respond. Individuals evaluate an event

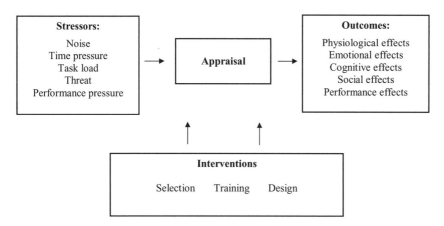

Figure 7.1
An Input→Process→Output Model of Stress Effects

as threatening when the perceived danger exceeds the capacity to respond. Individuals evaluate an event as nonthreatening when the perception of available resources meets or exceeds the perceived threat. The outcome of this process includes a number of physiological, cognitive, emotional, and social effects. It is worthwhile to note that stressors can have direct effects as well as indirect or mediated effects via the appraisal process. For example, noise can directly mask sounds that are task-relevant, such as speech, leading to impaired performance. This direct effect occurs whether or not the noise is appraised as inconsequential or as threatening. However, the indirect (or psychological) effect of noise or time pressure is typically what is studied by stress researchers. Finally, in Figure 7.1, we consider several moderators or factors that can increase or decrease the effects of stress on performance outcomes. Three primary types of interventions to minimize the effects of stress include selection, training, and design. In the remaining sections of the chapter, we will work through this model by examining each separate component: (a) types of stressors, (b) appraisal, (c) types of outcomes, and (d) intervention to counter these outcomes.

Types of Stressors

Noise

Noise is unwanted sound—sound that is unwanted by the listener because it is unpleasant, bothersome, interferes with task activity, or is perceived as potentially harmful (see Kryter, 1970; Moore & Von Gierke, 1991). Noise has also been defined as an auditory stimulus that bears no task-related information (McCormick & Sanders, 1982). According to this definition, sound that carries specific task information is not noise (however, it can in this case increase task load).

The noise of the combat battlefield can be debilitating and may serve as a major source of combat stress. In World War II, research indicated that the fear of enemy weapons was often disproportionate to the actual dangerousness of the weapon; soldiers often feared the *sound* of a weapon more so than its effectiveness. For example, although the 88 mm gun was unquestionably a dangerous and effective weapon, the majority of soldiers reported that they feared it because of "the sounds it produces—when it goes off and when the shell is traveling through the air" (Stouffer et al., 1949, p. 237).

There are several approaches to explaining noise effects. The classic arousal perspective argues that stress results in heightened arousal, and that arousal leads to a narrowing of attention (see Broadbent, 1971; Easterbrook, 1959). As attention narrows, peripheral (less relevant) task cues are first ignored, followed by further restriction of central or task-relevant cues. Poulton (1978) argued that the effects of noise on performance are often related to distraction, or to the effects of noise on masking thought, or inner speech (i.e., noise effects are such that we literally "can't hear ourselves think"). Distraction-arousal theory holds that noise has two primary effects; it can distract the task performer or it can increase the level of arousal (Teichner, Arees, & Reilly, 1963). For example, Teichner et al. found that research subjects performed more poorly when a baseline (81dB) level of noise was either increased *or* decreased, suggesting that the change in the stimulus itself was distracting to the performers.

Most research has shown that noise degrades performance accuracy. Villoldo and Tarno (1984) examined the performance of explosive ordnance disposal personnel and found that stressors such as battlefield and detonation noises led personnel to work more quickly but with decreased accuracy in rendering simulated explosives safe. Other research has also documented evidence of a speed/accuracy tradeoff under noise stress, in that task performers often maintain speed of performance but make more errors (Hockey, 1986). Studies have also documented a narrowing of attentional focus under noise stress. For example, Hockey and Hamilton (1970) found that on a memory recall task, subjects under noise stress were able to recall words accurately, but were not able to accurately recall the location of the words in the word list. This suggests that under noise stress, attention is focused on the primary part of a task, to the detriment of more peripheral cues. Research further suggests that noise may have significant effects on social behavior. Mathews and Canon (1975) found that under high noise conditions, individuals were less likely to come to the aid of others. Some have explained this and related results by noting that stress results in a narrowing of attention, including attention to social cues, so that individuals under stress may be less likely to attend to the interpersonal demands of others (Driskell, Salas & Johnston, 1999).

Time Pressure

Time pressure is defined as a restriction in time required to perform a task. Certainly, the approximately three minutes allotted the crew of the *Vincennes* to evaluate the tactical significance of an unidentified aircraft, gather information, communicate with other parties, evaluate options and take action is a vivid, although not necessarily atypical, example of performance demands under time pressure. Research suggests that time pressure may degrade performance because of the cognitive demands, or information overload, imposed by the requirement to process a given amount of information in a limited amount of time (Wright, 1974). Under the demand of time pressure, individuals may resort to several types of strategies to meet this challenge. The first strategy is an attempt to accelerate performance, increasing information processing to try to match the speed with which information is being presented. A second approach alters the information processing strategy. For example, if an individual is evaluating each available alternative sequentially before attempting a task solution, he or she may adopt a strategy in which all alternatives are considered by a single criterion. A third strategy reflects the general tendency for individuals to restrict information processing under stress by filtering or reducing the amount of information to be processed.

Research indicates that under time pressure, people tend to maintain or increase performance speed, but performance accuracy declines. In a study of pilot performance, Wickens, Stokes, Barnett, and Hyman (1988) found that under the stress of noise, time pressure, and threat, pilot judgments became less accurate, but not necessarily slower. This speed–accuracy tradeoff is similar to that observed for noise stress.

A number of studies have examined the impact of time pressure on decision making. Janis and Mann (1977) presented a model of decision making in which they distinguished between vigilant and hypervigilant decision making. Vigilant decision making is characterized by a systematic information search, thorough consideration of all available alternatives, evaluation of each alternative, and the cautious review of data before making a decision. This type of normative or analytical decision making process makes efficient use of the resources at the individual's disposal and can result in well-informed decisions. A hypervigilant pattern of decision making is characterized by nonsystematic or selective information search, consideration of limited alternatives, rapid evaluation of data, and selection of a solution without extensive review or reappraisal. Hypervigilant decision making has been typically viewed as an impulsive, disorganized process that generally results in poor quality judgments. However, Payne, Bettman, and Johnson (1988) and Klein (1996) have emphasized the contingent nature of decision making, arguing that under certain task conditions, such as increased time pressure, adopting a less analytic decision strategy may be adaptive. Payne et al. (1988) found that time pressure led to the use of simpler, less analytic decision strategies, and that this type of decision making resulted in a better outcome than the use of a truncated normative procedure. Thus, the typical characteristics of hypervigilant decision making, including the narrowing of attention, filtering of information, the use of heuristics to speed information processing, and rapid closure, may under stress represent an efficacious response to task demands.

Johnston, Driskell, and Salas (1997) tested this claim by examining the performance of naval personnel in a computer-based command-and-control simulation. Personnel were required to monitor a radar screen and identify contacts as to (a) type of craft: aircraft, surface craft, or subsurface; (b) status: military or civilian; and (c) intentions: hostile or peaceful, based on information gathered from a series of information fields (e.g., climb rate, speed, etc.). Johnston et al. found that, on this naturalistic task simulation, subjects employing a hypervigilant decision strategy performed better than those employing a vigilant strategy. Furthermore, subjects employing a vigilant strategy performed more poorly under high-demand conditions (increased task load, time pressure and auditory distraction) than under no-stress conditions, whereas the effectiveness of a hypervigilant strategy did not degrade under stress. These results provide empirical evidence that under high-demand conditions such as time pressure, a hypervigilant decision style can be an adaptive and effective strategy.

Task Load

Task load is defined as performing two or more tasks concurrently. It is important to distinguish the concept of task load as a stressor from that of workload, which generally refers to the subjective load or demand stemming from increased task load and time pressure. Real-world examples of the effects of task load on performance abound. One classic example is the 1972 aviation accident involving Eastern Airlines Flight 401. On approach to the Miami airport, the captain noticed that a landing gear indicator light was out. The crew became preoccupied with fixing the indicator light, to the detriment of flying the plane, and the plane lost altitude and crashed into the Everglades, resulting in 99 fatalities. The National Transportation Safety Board (NSTB) accident report indicated that the crash was not related to any structural or equipment failure, other than the errant bulb (NTSB, 1973).

Capacity theories typically examine how an individual's performance trades off between two tasks as task demands change. As one task (e.g., troubleshooting a malfunctioning light bulb) demands more of a person's resources, fewer resources are available for a concurrent task (e.g., flying a plane), and performance on the latter task will be disrupted. Thus, capacity theories maintain that attentional capacity is allocated in graded quantity between separate activities.

Most studies of dual task performance indicate that the addition of a second, concurrent task tends to impair performance on the primary task (Neisser & Becklan, 1975). Research further suggests that the negative effect of task load on performance is greater when the tasks performed are similar (e.g., they have similar processing or response demands) and when the tasks are novel, unfamiliar, or difficult (Eysenck, 1984). Interestingly, research suggests that highly practiced tasks can be performed jointly with little interference (Hirst, Spelke, Reaves, Caharack & Neisser, 1980). More specifically, some draw a distinction between automatic and controlled processing. Automatic processing occurs in well-practiced, consistent tasks and is characterized as fast, parallel, and relatively effortless. Conversely, controlled processing usually occurs in novel or poorly learned tasks and is characterized as slow, effortful, and capacity limited. Research suggests that automatic processing allows a person to carry out a task in an essentially resource-free fashion, lessening interference from concurrent tasks.

Threat

Threat refers to the anticipation or fear of physical or psychological harm (Salas et al., 1996). Certainly, no other factor more clearly defines the combat environment. Military researchers in World War II concluded that the central fact of combat was danger to life and limb (Williams, 1984). In addition to high risk, threat is often defined by other characteristics (Lazarus & Folkman, 1984). *Novelty* refers to events that are unique or unanticipated. *Predictability* refers to the extent to which an event or task sequence can be predicted or anticipated. *Control* refers to the capability of the individual to alter or modify the environment. *Temporal uncertainty* refers to not knowing when an event is going to happen. *Durational uncertainty* refers to uncertainty over how long an aversive event will last. *Ambiguity* refers to a lack of situational clarity induced by task stimuli which are difficult to distinguish, events that disconfirm expectancies, or conflicting information. Thus, in general, an event is more likely to be perceived as threatening if it is high-risk, novel, consequential, unpredictable, uncontrollable, ambiguous, and highly uncertain with respect to time of onset and duration. It is no surprise that most military combat situations can be defined in these terms.

Research on the threat of dangerous or novel environments has been conducted in field settings and in laboratory environments. Berkun, Bialek, Kern, and Yagi (1962) developed a realistic series of stress studies for the Army, all of which involved contrived emergencies and were designed to make subjects feel they were in danger of losing their lives or injuring others. In one scenario, trainees were taken up in a DC-3 aircraft, an in-flight emergency was declared, and the trainees were then given several tasks to perform. Berkun et al. found that the experimental (threat) group showed greater subjective stress and performed more poorly on the performance measures than did controls. Hammerton and Tickner (1969) found that novice military parachutists showed a decrement in tracking performance immediately before and after their descent from a balloon. Burke (1980) examined Army jumpmaster training in order to search for variables predictive of ability to perform under threat. He found a strong negative correlation between jumping performance and perceived stress.

The most common laboratory manipulation of threat is the threat of shock. Research indicates that the threat of shock results in a significant increase in subjective stress and decrease in task performance. Further studies on shock indicate that control can reduce the aversiveness of a threatening event (see Thompson, 1981). People tend to experience less stress in a situation in which they believe they have some degree of control over the threatening event (i.e., they can terminate or avoid the shock).

Performance Pressure

One factor that is prominent in the military operational environment is the concept of performance pressure or command pressure. *Performance pressure* refers to the increased consequences for error in a stress environment. This concern is particularly salient in the military environment because failure on critical military tasks often results in severe consequences and harm to self and others. Military team members are concerned about letting the other team members down. Also inherent in the military environment is concern about evaluation from superiors, or *command pressure*. Not only is the individual performing a critical task with potentially severe consequences, but in a situation where his actions are often under the scrutiny of senior personnel or other evaluative observers.

Some research suggests that the presence of other observers in a task situation tends to impair performance on difficult tasks (Schmitt, Gilovich, Goore & Joseph, 1986). These results are consistent with Zajonc's (1965) drive-arousal model of social facilitation, which addresses the arousal-enhancing effects of the presence of others. The underlying mechanism for this increase in arousal may stem from the increased readiness to accommodate interactions, social monitoring, evaluation apprehension, or attentional conflict (Mullen, Bryant & Driskell, 1997). In a meta-analytic review of the effects of the presence of others on arousal, Mullen et al. (1997) concluded that the effect of *audience others* (persons who are monitoring or observing the performer) was to increase arousal under aversive conditions. However, the presence of *coacting others* (persons who are working with the performer) tends to decrease arousal in aversive situations. Thus, teammates may provide social or task support to reduce arousal in stressful situations, but evaluative others may only tend to increase evaluation apprehension and attentional conflict.

Appraisal

Lazarus and Folkman (1984) have distinguished between primary and secondary appraisal. Primary appraisal involves evaluation of demand, or the extent of threat that an event poses. Secondary appraisal is an evaluation of perceived capacity or resources to meet this threat. Traditional models of stress presume that appraisal is a function of the degree of discrepancy between demand and capacity. In the model presented in Figure 7.1, environmental stimuli become salient, and through the appraisal process, become evaluated as positive (and seen as a challenge) or negative (and seen as a threat). The appraisal process leads to the formation of performance expectations—feelings of self-efficacy or mastery. If the perception of available resources exceeds the perceived threat, positive performance expectations result. If demands exceed perceived resources, negative performance expectations are formed. The development of positive performance expectations is a crucial factor in preparing personnel to operate under stress conditions. Research on hazardous duty training given to British military bomb disposal experts showed that those who developed positive performance expectations reported relatively little fear during operations (Rachman, 1983).

Outcomes of Stress

Finally, stress may result in a number of outcomes of interest, including physiological reactions, emotional reactions, cognitive effects, social behavior, and performance outcomes.

Physiological Effects

Research indicates that stress may result in physiological changes such as increased heartbeat, labored breathing, and trembling (Rachman, 1983). Physiological reactions to stress have been assessed by a host of measures, including skin conductance, pulse rate, heart rate, systolic and diastolic blood pressure, and catecholamine (e.g., adrenaline and noradrenaline) output. Although the relationship of physiological state to performance is unclear, novel physiological reactions are, at the least, a source of distraction to the task performer. Individuals under stress may often overinterpret or assign heightened importance to novel bodily sensations (see Clark, 1988), and this attentional conflict may impair task performance. In fact, Worchel and Yohai (1979) found that individuals who were able to label or identify novel physiological reactions (i.e., individuals who were able to attribute their physiological reactions to some reasonable cause) were less distressed or aroused by those reactions.

Emotional Effects

Emotional reactions to stress may include subjective feelings of fear or anxiety, annoyance, tension, frustration, and increased concern for the well-being of self and others. Marshall (1947) described emotional responses on the combat battlefields of WWII:

> In an attack, half of the men on a firing line are in terror and the other half are unnerved. When the infantryman's mind is gripped by fear, his body is captured by inertia. [Combat failure] is the result of paralysis which comes from varying fears. (p. 71)

Cognitive Effects

Cognitive effects of stress include narrowing of attention or perceptual tunneling (Easterbrook, 1959), reduced working memory (Huey & Wickens, 1993), and performance rigidity (Staw, Sandelands & Dutton, 1981). The claim that attentional focus narrows or is reduced under stress is one of the most well-documented findings in the stress literature (Wickens, 1996). For complex tasks, in which the individual must attend to a relatively larger number of salient task cues, this narrowing of attention may result in the elimination of relevant task information, and task performance will suffer.

Research has also documented other stress-induced cognitive changes. Stress tends to restrict information retrieved from long-term memory to that information which is most dominant or well learned (Eysenck, 1984). Cohen (1952) found that stressful conditions led to greater problem-solving rigidity, a tendency to persist with a set method of problem solving when it ceased to provide a direct task solution. Dorner (1990) found that individuals under stress were prone to "ballistic" decision making —making decisions without checking the consequences of their decision.

Social Effects

Social effects of stress may include a reduction in the tendency to assist others, increased interpersonal aggression, neglect of social or interpersonal cues, and less cooperative behavior among team members. Although considerable research has examined individual reactions to stress, comparatively little work has examined the effects of stress on team performance (see Driskell & Salas, 1991; Kanki, 1996).

We have noted that one of the most well-established findings in the stress literature is that as stress or arousal increases, the individual's breadth of attention narrows (Easterbrook, 1959). Perhaps the earliest statement of this phenomenon was William James's (1890) belief that the individual's field of view varied, from a broader perspective under normal conditions to a narrower, more restricted focus under stress. Driskell et al. (1999) extended this research to the group level of analysis by arguing that as stress restricts attentional focus, the resulting "tunnel vision" may include a restriction of social stimuli as well. Thus, team members may adopt a narrower, more individual perspective of task activity, impairing team behavior. Driskell et al. (1999) conducted a study in which three-person teams of naval enlisted personnel performed a target identification task under normal or high-stress conditions. Results indicated that stress resulted in a narrowing of team perspective. Team members in high-stress conditions were less likely to adopt a team-level task perspective or develop a strong team identity and more likely to describe task activities in individual versus team terms. Furthermore, team perspective was found to be a significant predictor of task performance. These results indicate that stress can impact team performance by narrowing or weakening the team-level perspective required for effective team functioning.

Performance Effects

Specific performance effects vary according to the nature of the task; however, research indicates that under certain conditions, stress may increase errors on operational procedures threefold (Villoldo & Tarno, 1984). Performance outcomes typically examined in the stress-research literature include performance accuracy (usually assessed by the number of errors incurred on a task), performance speed (the time required to perform a task), and performance variability (variability in accuracy or speed). One general pattern reported in many studies is that of a speed/accuracy tradeoff under stress (Hockey, 1986). That is, under stress, individuals tend to maintain speed of performance, but with a corresponding decrease in performance accuracy. This tendency may be particularly detrimental for those tasks in which effective performance is primarily determined by accuracy.

Interventions

Stress interventions fall into three broad categories: selection, training, and design. In the military environment, all personnel must be prepared to perform their tasks under high-demand, emergency, or combat conditions. In this sense, selection is often not an option. However, some jobs are more demanding than others, and one goal of a selection strategy is to determine those individuals most suited to performing in high-stress environments. A second approach, training, focuses on the objective of training personnel to perform more effectively under stressful conditions. Finally, design strategies focus on designing the task environment to buffer the negative effects of stress.

Selection

Acts of exceptional courage have always served as rallying points for combat personnel. In the recent Iraq War, Sgt. First Class Paul Smith was lauded by fellow soldiers and nominated for the Medal of Honor for exceptional bravery and valor for manning a machine gun, holding off a Republican Guard counterattack, and saving dozens of lives until he was killed (Zentkovich, 2003). Courage, self-sacrifice, and commitment are hallmarks of bravery and performance under stress. In the military, the *Warrior Ethos* construct encapsulates the attitudes and characteristics that define the exceptional soldier. The Warrior Ethos is not only relevant to acts of extraordinary bravery, but also to acts of *ordinary* bravery. U.S. Army Field Manual 22-100 notes that the Warrior Ethos

> fuels the fire to fight through those conditions to victory no matter how long it takes, no matter how much effort is required...it drives the bone-tired medic continually to put others first. It pushes the sweat-soaked gunner near muscle fatigue to keep up the fire. It drives the heavily loaded infantryman into an icy wind, steadily uphill to the objective. (Department of the Army [DA], 1999, pp. 2–21)

Marshall (1947) presents a perspective on combat consistent with this view. Marshall reported that on the WWII battlefield, the number of men in a company who actually engaged the enemy with fire was less than 25 percent. However, Marshall also noted that one characteristic of most battlefield victories was that they pivoted on the action of a few men (p. 96). Moreover, he noted that those men who led the attack on Monday would carry the attack when fight was renewed on Wednesday, and that the hand that pulled the trigger was the same hand that was most likely to be found tossing a grenade. Marshall stated, "The same names continued to reappear as having taken the initiative…. [This man would] probably keep going until he was dead" (p. 59).

Although the military environment offers compelling examples of bravery, courage, and performance under stress, researchers have struggled to develop sound procedures to select personnel that are most suited to operating under stress conditions. Rachman and colleagues conducted research to examine determinants of courageous military performance by studying British military bomb disposal operators during a 19-week tour of duty in Northern Ireland (Rachman, 1983). The majority of personnel reported some degree of fear during their tour of duty, especially early in the tour. Although researchers found that decorated personnel were somewhat calmer and reported less hypochondria than the average soldier, there were few factors identified that predicted courageous behavior. More recently, Bartone (1999) has developed a measure of hardiness that has been shown to be valuable in predicting resilience to stress effects.

Hogan and Lesser (1996) have adopted a comprehensive perspective on selection of personnel for hazardous duty. They propose that selecting personnel for hazardous duty requires attention to four factors. The first is *job suitability*. They argue that those who perform most effectively under stress conditions are those who are most well suited for the job or task that they are engaged in. A second factor is *technical competence*. Because many high-stress environments are technically demanding and require continuous retraining to maintain proficiency, those who are technically competent are most likely to excel under high-demand conditions. A third factor is *physical capability*. Because many high-stress tasks are physically demanding, those who will excel under stress conditions must possess the strength, endurance, and coordination required to perform the task. A final factor is *psychological suitability*.

The Big-Five personality models (see Sinclair & Sommers, this volume) provide an approach to defining the psychological traits of persons that may be more resistant to stress effects. Although there is some divergence on how personality traits should be labeled and organized, personality theorists generally agree on the nature of the structure of personality. Most theorists propose a hierarchical model, with broad, higher-order factors or traits that subsume and organize more specific lower-level facets (cf. Saucier & Ostendorf, 1999). The Big Five trait dimensions are typically described as extraversion, emotional stability, agreeableness, conscientiousness, and openness to experience. These traits are in turn composed of more specific facets. For example, the broad trait of conscientiousness has been associated with a number of facets, including competence, dependability, achievement striving, and dutifulness (Moon, 2001).

We would expect the facet of *dependability* to be relevant to performance under stress. Those that are dependable are responsible, organized, careful, and trustworthy. Those who are undependable or have poor impulse control put themselves and others in jeopardy, especially in high-demand situations. Marshall (1947) noted that initiative is important on the combat battlefield, but it must be tempered with responsibility:

We can put it down as an axiom that initiative is a desirable characteristic in a soldier only when its effect is concentric rather than eccentric: The rifleman who plunges ahead and seizes a point of high ground which common sense says cannot be held can bring greater jeopardy to a company than any mere malingerer. (p. 132)

In the team-oriented military environment, the facet of *sociability* or *affiliation* is important to effective performance under stress. In a series of classic studies conducted in World War II, Stouffer et al. (1949) found that what kept soldiers going in extremely hostile conditions was not political ideals or hatred of the enemy, but primary group obligations. Marshall (1947) concurred: "I hold it to be one of the simplest truths of war that the thing that enables an infantry soldier to keep going with his weapons is the near presence or presumed presence of a comrade" (p.42). Marshall further noted, "In battle, you may draw a small circle around a soldier, including within it only those persons and objects which he sees or which he believes will influence his immediate fortunes. These primarily will determine whether he rallies or fails, advances or falls back" (p. 154).

Finally, the facet of *adjustment* has been defined as freedom from anxiety, depression, and somatic complaints. Gunthert, Cohen, and Armeli (1999) describe maladjusted or neurotic individuals as "caught in a web of negative behaviors, cognitions, and moods....They seem to experience (perhaps generate) more interpersonal stressors, their perceptions of daily events are more negative, and their coping choices are maladaptive" (p. 1099). Although the preceding discussion is a very brief overview of the topic of selection for stress environments, research suggests that important dimensions to consider include job suitability, technical competence, physical capability, and psychological suitability.

Training

It is important that we distinguish between *training* and *stress training*. The primary goal of training is skill acquisition and retention. Therefore, most training takes place under conditions designed to maximize learning, such as in a quiet classroom and under predictable and uniform conditions. However, some tasks must be performed in conditions quite unlike those encountered in the training classroom. For example, high-stress environments include specific task conditions (such as time pressure) and require specific responses (such as the flexibility to adapt to novel events) that differ from those found in the normal task environment. Research has shown that, for some tasks, normal training procedures (training conducted under normal nonstress conditions) often do not improve task performance when that task has to be performed under stress conditions (Zakay & Wooler, 1984).

In brief, the primary purpose of *training* is to ensure the acquisition of required knowledge, skills, and abilities. The primary purpose of *stress training* is to prepare the individual to maintain effective performance in a high-stress environment. Therefore, stress training is defined as an intervention designed to enhance familiarity and teach skills necessary to maintain effective task performance under stress conditions.

There have been numerous attempts to implement different types of stress train-ing techniques (see Lipsey & Wilson, 1993 for an overview of the effectiveness of various psychological interventions). However, most studies have examined the effec-tiveness of isolated training techniques, such as overlearning (Driskell, Willis, & Copper, 1992). Although the emphasis on specific techniques is important, what has been missing is a comprehensive, systematic approach to stress training. Driskell and Johnston (1998) developed an integrated stress training approach, termed *stress exposure training* (SET), which provides a structure for designing, developing, and implementing stress training (see also Johnston & Cannon-Bowers, 1996; Saunders, Driskell, Johnston & Salas, 1996). According to Driskell and Johnston (1998), an integrated stress training approach must achieve three objectives:

- *Enhance familiarity.* Training must provide trainees with basic information on stress, stress symptoms, and likely stress effects in the performance setting.
- *Impart high-performance skills.* Training must incorporate specialized skills training to pro-vide the skills that are required to maintain effective performance in the stress environment.
- *Practice skills and build confidence.* Training must allow gradual exposure to the high-stress environment to promote practice of skills under realistic conditions and build trainee con-fidence to perform.

The SET approach is defined by a three-stage training intervention. The first stage is *information provision*: an initial stage in which information is provided regarding stress, stress symptoms, and likely stress effects in the performance setting. The sec-ond stage is *skills acquisition*: a skills training phase in which specific cognitive and behavioral skills are taught and practiced. These are called *high-performance* skills, representing those skills required to maintain effective performance in the stress envi-ronment. The third stage is *application and practice*: the application and practice of these skills in a graduated manner under conditions that increasingly approximate the criterion environment. In the following, we elaborate the stress exposure training approach by examining the activities that comprise each stage.

Phase 1: Information Provision

Clausewitz (1832/1976) wrote,

> It is immensely important that no soldier, whatever his rank, should wait for war to expose him to those aspects of active service that amaze and confuse him when he first comes across them. If he has met them even once before, they will begin to be familiar to him. (p. 122)

Phase 1 of SET includes two primary components: (a) indoctrination, or discus-sion of why stress training is important; and (b) preparatory information on stress effects.

The first component of Phase 1 is trainee indoctrination. Trainees need to know the objectives of training and why stress training is important. Indoctrination is aimed at increasing trainee attention and motivation. Indoctrination often emphasizes the rewards and costs of effective and ineffective performance in the stress environment, and may be provided by discussing operational incidents or case histories in which stress had a significant impact on performance. The second component of Phase 1 is the provision of preparatory information. A National Research Council study on enhancing military performance concluded that "stress is reduced by giving an individual as much knowledge and understanding as possible regarding future events" (Druckman & Swets, 1988, p. 21). They also note, however, that this approach often runs counter to military practice, which is to give the individual the least amount of information necessary for a given situation.

It is likely that preparatory information mitigates negative reactions to stress in several different ways. First, by providing a preview of the stress environment, preparatory information renders the task less novel and unfamiliar. Second, knowledge regarding an upcoming event increases predictability, which can decrease the attentional demands and distraction of having to monitor and interpret novel events in real time. Third, preparatory information may enhance the sense of behavioral or cognitive control over an aversive event by providing the individual with an instrumental means to respond to the stress.

A comprehensive preparatory information strategy should provide: what to expect in the stress environment; typical physiological, emotional, and cognitive reactions to stress; indications of how stress is likely to affect performance; and information on how the person may adapt to these changes. Driskell and Johnston (1998) define three types of preparatory information: (a) *sensory information* is information regarding how the individual is likely to feel when under stress, including typical physiological and emotional responses to stress; (b) *procedural information* describes the events that are likely to occur in the stress environment, including a description of the setting, the types of stressors that may be encountered, and performance effects the stressors may have; and (c) *instrumental information* describes what to do to counter the undesirable consequences of stress. This type of information has instrumental value in that it provides the individual with a means to resolve the problems posed by the stress environment.

Inzana, Driskell, Salas, and Johnston (1996) tested the effectiveness of preparatory information, examining the performance of naval personnel on a command-and-control decision-making task under high- and low-stress conditions. The preparatory information intervention included sensory information (e.g., "Stressors such as high task load may cause you to feel distracted or hurried."); procedural information (e.g., "These are normal reactions, but may lead you to misinterpret specific data fields."); and instrumental information (e.g., "Try to match the pace of the task, but pay close attention to the information in those fields."). Inzana et al. found that the personnel who received preparatory information prior to performing under high-stress conditions reported less anxiety, were more confident in their ability to perform the task, and made fewer performance errors than those who received no preparatory information.

Phase 2: Skills Acquisition

The second phase of stress training focuses on the acquisition of skills required to counter negative stress effects. The goal of training at this stage is to build the high-performance skills required to maintain effective performance under stress. Specific stress training techniques may include:

1. *Cognitive control techniques.* The term *cognitive control* subsumes a number of training approaches which attempt to train individuals to recognize task-irrelevant thoughts and emotions that degrade task performance and to replace them with task-focused cognitions. The primary emphasis of cognitive control techniques is to train the individual to regulate emotions (e.g., worry and frustration), regulate distracting thoughts (self-oriented cognitions), and maintain task orientation. As Wine (1971) noted, "Performance may be improved by directing attention to task-relevant variables, and away from self-evaluative rumination" (p. 100). An attentional-training approach proposed by Singer, Cauraugh, Murphey, Chen, and Lidor (1991) attempts to train individuals to maintain attentional focus on task-relevant stimuli in the face of external distractions. Singer et al. examined whether attention-focusing skills could be directly trained, and found that attentional training resulted in improved task performance when subjects worked under noise stress. This approach included training to describe when, why, and how attention may be distracted during task performance, and practice in performing the task under stress, focusing attention, and refocusing attention after distraction. The results indicated that training which concentrates directly on enhancing attentional focus may overcome the distraction and perceptual narrowing that occurs in stress environments.

2. *Physiological control techniques.* Physiological control techniques attempt to provide the trainee with control over negative physiological reactions to stress. These approaches attempt to train the responses that are characteristic of effective performance: being calm, relaxed, and under control. Training may include relaxation training (awareness and control of muscle tension, breathing, etc.), biofeedback, and autogenic-feedback training, which has been used successfully in alleviating space motion sickness (Cowings & Toscano, 1982). All these techniques have in common an effort to increase the extent to which the individual's physiological reactions are under conscious control.

3. *Overlearning.* The term *overlearning* refers to deliberate overtraining of a performance skill beyond the level of initial proficiency (Driskell et al., 1992). For example, Schendel and Hagman (1982) examined the effects of overlearning on retention of a military procedural task (disassembly/assembly of an M60 machine gun). They found that the overtrained group achieved 65 percent fewer errors than a control group when retested after eight weeks. Overlearning (drilling, drilling, and more drilling) is a common component of military training, and is a useful training procedure for stress environments. Given that one effect of stress is to reduce or narrow attentional capacity, behaviors that are more automatic should be less resistant to degradation. Tasks that are overlearned become more routinized or more

automatic, require less active attentional capacity, and are less subject to disruption by increased attentional demands.

4. *Mental practice.* Mental practice refers to the cognitive rehearsal of a task in the absence of overt physical movement (Driskell, Copper, & Moran, 1994). In a meta-analysis of research on the effects of mental practice, Driskell et al. (1994) found that mental practice was an effective means of enhancing performance, although somewhat less effective than physical practice. However, Driskell et al. concluded that mental practice may be a particularly effective technique for training complex cognitive tasks, for rehearsing tasks that are dangerous to train physically, or for training tasks such as emergency procedures where the opportunity for actual practice occurs very seldom.

5. *Decision-making training.* Formal, analytic decision making approaches require the decision maker to carry out an elaborate and exhaustive procedure characterized by a systematic, organized information search, thorough consideration of all available alternatives, evaluation of each alternative, and reexamination and review of data before making a decision. Although this procedure is often taught as the decision making ideal, some researchers have argued that under high task demands, decision makers do not have the luxury to adopt a time-consuming analytic strategy. Moreover, encouraging the decision maker to adopt an analytic model could undermine behavior that may more adequately fit the requirements of the task situation (see Cannon-Bowers & Salas, 1998). Johnston et al. (1997) found that on a time-pressured, realistic military task, those who were trained to use a less analytic decision-making strategy performed more effectively than those who used a formal, analytic decision strategy. These results emphasize the importance of adaptability and flexibility in decision making. Johnston et al. suggest that training should not encourage the adoption of a complex analytic strategy under the conditions that characterize many high-demand task environments. Thus, one goal of decision-making training for stressful environments is to emphasize the use of simplifying heuristics to manage effort and accuracy, and to improve the capability of the decision maker to adapt decision-making strategies to high-demand conditions.

6. *Enhancing flexibility.* Research indicates that stress leads to greater problem-solving rigidity (Cohen, 1952). Rigidity refers to the tendency to approach a problem with a restricted attentional focus and an expectance that there is a single solution that does not vary. High-stress environments, however, require flexibility to respond to novel and varied task contingencies. Certain training procedures can enhance flexible behavior. Gick and Holyoak (1987) found that positive transfer (i.e., the extent to which training results transfer from the training setting to the real-world setting) is more likely when a variety of different examples were provided during training. Schmidt and Bjork (1992) refer to this technique as practice variability, noting that intentional variation during skills practice can enhance the transfer of training. Thus, presenting training material or training activities in various contexts, from different perspectives, and with diverse examples can result in more flexible use of a skill under novel and variable task conditions.

Phase 3: Application and Practice

Effective performance requires that the skills learned in training are transferred to the operational setting. The novelty of performing even a well-learned task in a high-stress real-world environment can cause severe degradation in performance. Therefore, the final phase of stress training requires the application and practice of skills learned in training under conditions that approximate the operational environment. Allowing skills practice in a graduated manner across increasing levels of stress (from moderate stress scenarios or exercises to higher stress exercises) allows preexposure to the conditions that are likely to be faced in a high-stress or emergency situation.

Military operational personnel often want training scenarios to look just like the real-world environment. However, it is not necessarily true that higher fidelity always leads to better training, and many training strategies reduce fidelity early in training to reduce complexity. Based on the assumption that a high degree of complexity in the training environment may interfere with initial skill acquisition, graduated training is an approach to maximize training effectiveness by partitioning training into separate phases: During initial training, trainees practice skills in a relatively low-fidelity or low-complexity environment; latter stages of training incorporate greater degrees of complexity or realism.

Friedland and Keinan (1992) note that for military tasks which require the performance of complex skills, training that incorporates either no stress or constant high-intensity stress are both likely to be counterproductive. They argue that phased training—allowing skills practice in a graduated manner across increasing levels of stress—satisfies three important requirements: (a) it allows the individual to become more familiar with relevant stressors without being overwhelmed; (b) it enhances a sense of individual control and builds confidence; and (c) it is less likely to interfere with the acquisition and practice of task skills than would immediate exposure to intense stress (Keinan & Friedland, 1996).

It is important to note that SET is a model for stress training rather than a specific training technique. The SET model describes three stages of training, each with a specific overall objective. The specific content of each stage, however, will vary according to the specific training requirements. Both the type of stressors and the skills required for effective performance depend on the specific task setting. Therefore, stress training must be context-specific, and a careful needs analysis is required to define the specific tasks to be trained, determine the types of stress in the task environment, and develop training content.

Design

A human-factors approach to stress reduction focuses on the design of the task environment in an attempt to reduce demands on the individual (see Wickens, 1996). Huey and Wickens (1993) propose that design solutions should be developed in the context of what we know regarding stress effects. Thus, to the extent that perceptual narrowing is one likely outcome of stress, reducing the amount of unnecessary information presented to the individual and increasing its organization should help buffer stress effects. Other ways to address this problem include integrating separate information displays into a single display and providing graphical rather than numeric displays. Yates, Klatzky, and Young (1995) suggest that, given the effects of the narrowing of attention under stress, we should not expect individuals to perform complex or lengthy cognitive procedures unaided. One way to counter these effects is to construct checklists to force individuals to acknowledge performing critical task steps.

Huey and Wickens (1993) also note that stress reduces working memory capacity, and that design solutions can minimize the need to maintain information in working memory. For example, emergency procedures should be provided that are clear and simply phrased. When possible, emergency instructions should be presented in both voice and print and phrased in direct statements of actions that should be taken, rather than actions to avoid. For example, voice alerts in aircraft ("pull up") are direct commands of actions required in an emergency. Another approach to reduce demands on working memory is to minimize the number of steps to be taken in an emergency procedure.

Stress seems to limit retrieval of information from long-term memory to those habits or responses that are well learned or dominant. To the extent that this bias is imposed by stress, systems should be designed so that emergency task procedures are as consistent as possible with normal task procedures. Huey and Wickens (1993) state that if step A follows step B under normal circumstances, ideally this should be the same procedure in an emergency. This consistency may not be possible to achieve, especially if the high-demand task conditions or the contingencies of a novel task environment have rendered the previous procedures ineffective. It is important to note, however, that any changes to normal procedures should be made prominent and easily discernable.

Research suggests that stress is likely to alter patterns of interaction and communication among team members. For example, research indicates that team leaders may become overloaded under stress conditions (Driskell & Salas, 1991) and that the narrowing of attention induced by stress may result in a shift in perspective from a broad team perspective to a narrower self-focus (Driskell et al., 1999). Tasks should be designed so that teams function properly even under high-stress conditions. Thus, given a task that requires a high level of interdependence, one approach to counter the effects of stress in narrowing team perspective is to structure the task to enhance or at least maintain interdependence among team members.

In brief, designing task environments to compensate for the effects of stress on individuals and teams is an important but difficult task. Huey and Wickens (1993) conclude that a clear understanding of stress effects and adherence to fundamental principles of design is the best approach to minimizing the negative effects of stress.

Future Directions

The nature of stress events is that they disrupt normal procedures, unfold quickly, and demand an immediate response. Quick and effective task performance is critical, and consequences of poor performance are immediate and often catastrophic. These emergency or high-stress events are, by definition, relatively rare in comparison to standard working conditions. In high-demand settings such as the military, however, a practical understanding of stress effects is critical. Huey and Wilkens (1993) suggest that, in one sense, interventions related to emergency conditions should be afforded an even higher priority than normal operations. In practice, however, this is usually not the case; attention is focused on day-to-day concerns until high-profile events such as the *Vincennes* incident force us to pay attention to the pressures and demands that emergency conditions place on military personnel.

Moreover, there is every indication that these pressures and demands are increasing rather than decreasing. Complex, high-technology systems pervade the military. The desire to design even more sophisticated, complex, and demanding technological systems shows no signs of abating. Moreover, as Salas et al. (1996) have noted, technological advances tend not to reduce demands on the operator, but at best often serve to maintain a balance between system demands and operator capabilities. They note that the practical impact of a heads-up display, which projects aircraft information onto the cockpit windshield, is not to make the pilot's job any *easier*, but to allow the pilot to maintain control of aircraft that are becoming faster and more complex, and to fly them under more demanding conditions. In fact, Perrow (1999) advanced the paradoxical thesis that advanced technologies involved in many high-technology industries are becoming so complex that accidents must be considered a normal feature of their operation. This is a compelling claim: High-demand conditions are becoming so inevitable that emergencies should be considered normal. In fact, the USS *Vincennes* incident can be viewed in this light. In conditions in which one operates under extreme time pressure, high task load, in a threat situation which has not been anticipated, and with complex and highly automated equipment, the possibility of human error should be expected—a sobering thought, but one that should serve as a clarion call to those concerned with stress and performance.

References

Bartone, P. T. (1999). Hardiness protects against war-related stress in Army Reserve forces. *Consulting Psychology Journal: Practice and Research, 51*, 72–82.

Berkun, M., Bialek, H., Kern, R., & Yagi, K. (1962). Experimental studies of psychological stress in man. *Psychological Monographs, 76*(15), 1–39.

Broadbent, D. E. (1971). *Decision and stress*. New York: Academic Press.

Burke, W. P. (1980). *Development of predictors of performance under stress in Jumpmaster training*. (Research Report No. 1352). Ft. Benning, GA: U.S. Army Research Institute.

Cannon-Bowers, J. A., & Salas, E. (Eds.). (1998). *Making decisions under stress: Implications for individual and team training*. Washington, DC: American Psychological Association.

Clark, D. M. (1988). A cognitive model of panic attacks. In S. Rachman & J. D. Maser (Eds.), *Panic: Psychological perspectives* (pp. 71–89). Hillsdale, NJ: Erlbaum.

Clausewitz, C. von (1976). *On war* (M. Howard & P. Paret, Trans.). Princeton, NJ: Princeton University Press. (Original work published 1832).

Cohen, E. L. (1952). The influence of varying degrees of psychological stress on problem-solving rigidity. *Journal of Abnormal and Social Psychology, 47*, 512–519.

Cowings, P. S., & Toscano, W. B. (1982). The relationship of motion sickness susceptibility to learned autonomic control for symptom suppression. *Aviation, Space, and Environmental Medicine, 53*, 570–575.

Department of the Army (1999). *Army leadership* (Field Manual 22–100), Washington, DC.

Dorner, D. (1990). The logic of failure. In D. E. Broadbent, J. Reason, & A. Baddeley (Eds.), *Human factors in hazardous situations* (pp. 463–473). Oxford, UK: Clarendon Press.

Driskell, J. E., & Johnston, J. H. (1998). Stress exposure training. In J. A. Cannon-Bowers & E. Salas (Eds.), *Making decisions under stress: Implications for individual and team training* (pp. 191–217). Washington, DC: American Psychological Association.

Driskell, J. E., & Olmstead, B. (1989). Psychology and the military: Research applications and trends. *American Psychologist, 44*, 43–54.

Driskell, J. E., & Salas, E. (1991). Group decision making under stress. *Journal of Applied Psychology, 76*, 473–478.

Driskell, J. E., & Salas, E. (Eds.). (1996). *Stress and human performance*. Hillsdale, NJ: Erlbaum.

Driskell, J. E., Copper, C., & Moran, A. (1994). Does mental practice enhance performance? *Journal of Applied Psychology, 79*, 481–492.

Driskell, J. E., Salas, E., & Johnston, J. H. (1999). Does stress lead to a loss of team perspective? *Group Dynamics, 3*, 1–12.

Driskell, J. E., Salas, E., & Johnston, J. (2001). Stress management: Individual and team training. In E. Salas, C. A. Bowers, & E. Edens (Eds.), *Improving teamwork in organizations: Applications of resource management training* (pp. 55–72). Mahwah, NJ: Erlbaum.

Driskell, J. E., Willis, R., & Copper, C. (1992). Effect of overlearning on retention. *Journal of Applied Psychology, 77*, 615–622.

Druckman, D., & Swets, J. (1988). *Enhancing human performance: Issues, theories, and techniques*. Washington, DC: National Academies Press.

Easterbrook, J. A. (1959). The effect of emotion on cue utilization and the organization of behavior. *Psychological Review, 66*, 183–201.

Eysenck, M. W. (1984). *A handbook of cognitive psychology*. Hillsdale, NJ: Erlbaum.

Friedland, N., & Keinan, G. (1992). Training effective performance in stressful situations: Three approaches and implications for combat training. *Military Psychology, 4*, 157–174.

Gick, M. L., & Holyoak, K. J. (1987). The cognitive basis of knowledge transfer. In S. M. Cormier & J. D. Hagman (Eds.), *Transfer of training: Contemporary research and applications* (pp. 9–46). New York: Academic Press.

Grinker, R. R., & Spiegel, J. P. (1945). *Men under stress*. Philadelphia: Blakiston.

Gunthert, K. C., Cohen, L. H., & Armeli, S. (1999). The role of neuroticism in daily stress and coping. *Journal of Personality and Social Psychology, 77*, 1087–1100.

Hammerton, M., & Tickner, A. H. (1969). An investigation into the effects of stress upon skilled performance. *Ergonomics, 12*, 851–855.

Hirst, W., Spelke, E. S., Reaves, C. C., Caharack, G., & Neisser, U. (1980). Dividing attention without alternation or automaticity. *Journal of Experimental Psychology: General, 109,* 98–117.

Hockey, G. R. J. (1986). Changes in operator efficiency as a function of stress, fatigue, and circadian rhythms. In K. R. Boff, L. Kaufman, & J. P. Thomas (Eds.), *Handbook of perception and human performance* (pp. 44.1–44.49). New York: Wiley.

Hockey, G. R. J., & Hamilton, P. (1970). Arousal and information selection in short-term memory. *Nature, 226,* 866–867.

Hogan, J., & Lesser, P. (1996). Selection of personnel for hazardous performance. In J. E. Driskell & E. Salas (Eds.), *Stress and human performance* (pp. 195–222). Mahwah, NJ: Erlbaum.

Hogan, R., & Hogan, J. C. (1982). Subjective correlates of stress and human performance. In E. A. Alluisi & E. A. Fleishman (Eds.), *Human performance and productivity: Stress and performance effectiveness* (pp. 141–163). Hillsdale, NJ: Erlbaum.

Huey, B. M., & Wickens, C. D. (Eds.) (1993). *Workload transition: Implications for individual and team performance.* Washington, DC: National Academies Press.

Inzana, C. M., Driskell, J. E., Salas, E., & Johnston, J. (1996). Effects of preparatory information on enhancing performance under stress. *Journal of Applied Psychology, 81,* 429–435.

Ivancevich, J. M., & Matteson, M. T. (1980). *Stress and work: A managerial perspective.* Glenview, IL: Scott, Foresman.

James, W. (1890). *The principles of psychology* (Vol. 1). New York: Holt.

Janis, I. L. (1951). *Air war and emotional stress.* New York: McGraw-Hill.

Janis, I. L., & Mann, L. (1977). *Decision making: A psychological analysis of conflict, choice, and commitment.* New York: Free Press.

Johnston, J. H., & Cannon-Bowers, J. A. (1996). Training for stress exposure. In J. E. Driskell & E. Salas (Eds.), *Stress and human performance* (pp. 223–256). Mahwah, NJ: Erlbaum.

Johnston, J., Driskell, J. E., & Salas, E. (1997). Vigilant and hypervigilant decision making. *Journal of Applied Psychology, 82,* 614–622.

Kanki, B. G. (1996). Stress and aircrew performance: A team-level perspective. In J. E. Driskell & E. Salas, (Eds.), *Stress and human performance* (pp. 127–162). Hillsdale, NJ: Erlbaum.

Keinan, G., & Friedland, N. (1996). Training effective performance under stress: Queries, dilemmas and possible solutions. In. J. E. Driskell & E. Salas, (Eds.), *Stress and human performance* (pp. 257–277). Mahwah, NJ: Erlbaum.

Klein, G. (1996). The effect of acute stressors on decision making. In J. E. Driskell & E. Salas (Eds.), *Stress and human performance* (pp. 49–88). Mahwah, NJ: Erlbaum.

Kryter, K. D. (1970). *The effects of noise on man.* New York: Academic Press.

Lazarus, R. S., & Folkman, S. (1984). *Stress, appraisal, and coping.* New York: Springer.

Lipsey, M. W., & Wilson, D. B. (1993). The efficacy of psychological, educational, and behavioral treatment: Confirmation from meta-analysis. *American Psychologist, 48,* 1181–1209.

Marshall, S. L. A. (1947). *Men Against fire: The problem of battle command in future war.* Gloucester, MA: Peter Smith.

Mathews, K. E., & Canon, L. K. (1975). Environmental noise level as a determinant of helping behavior. *Journal of Personality and Social Psychology, 32,* 571–577.

McCormick, E. J., & Sanders, M. S. (1982). *Human factors in engineering and design.* New York: McGraw Hill.

Moon, H. (2001). The two faces of conscientiousness: Duty and achievement-striving within escalation of commitment dilemmas. *Journal of Applied Psychology*, 86, 533–540.

Moore, T. J., & Von Gierke, H. E. (1991) Military performance in acoustic noise environments. In R. Gal & A. Mangelsdorff (Eds.), *Handbook of military psychology* (pp. 295–311). London: Wiley.

Mullen, B., Bryant, B., & Driskell, J. E. (1997). The presence of others and arousal: An integration. *Group Dynamics, 1*, 52–64.

National Transportation Safety Board. (1973). *Aircraft accident report: Eastern Airlines, Inc. L-1011, N310EA Miami Florida* (NTSB/AAR-73/14). Washington, DC.

Neisser, U., & Becklan, R. (1975). Selective looking: Attending to visually significant events. *Cognitive Psychology, 7*, 480–494.

Payne, J. W., Bettman, J. R., & Johnson, E. J. (1988). Adaptive strategy selection in decision making. *Journal of Experimental Psychology: Learning, Memory, and Cognition, 14*, 534–552.

Perrow, C. (1999). *Normal accidents: Living with high-risk technologies.* Princeton, NJ: Princeton University Press.

Poulton, E. C. (1978). A new look at the effects of noise: A rejoinder. *Psychological Bulletin, 85*, 1068–1079.

Rachman, S. (Ed.) . (1983). Fear and courage among military bomb-disposal operators [Special issue]. *Advances in Behaviour Research and Therapy, 4*(3), 175.

Radloff, R., & Helmreich, R. (1968). *Groups under stress: Psychological research in Sealab II.* New York: Appleton-Century-Crofts.

Salas, E., Driskell, J. E., and Hughes, S. (1996). Introduction: The study of stress and human performance. In J. E. Driskell & E. Salas, (Eds.), *Stress and human performance* (pp. 1–45). Hillsdale, NJ: Erlbaum.

Saucier, G., & Ostendorf, F. (1999). Hierarchical subcomponents of the Big Five personality factors: A cross-cultural replication. *Journal of Personality and Social Psychology, 76*, 613–627.

Saunders, T. Driskell, J. E., Johnston, J., & Salas, E. (1996). The effect of stress inoculation training on anxiety and performance. *Journal of Occupational Health Psychology, 1*, 170–186.

Schendel, J. D., & Hagman, J. D. (1982). On sustaining procedural skills over a prolonged retention interval. *Journal of Applied Psychology, 67*, 605–610.

Schmidt, R. A., & Bjork, R. A. (1992). New conceptualizations of practice: Common principles in three paradigms suggest new concepts for training. *Psychological Science, 3*(4), 207–217.

Schmitt, B. H., Gilovich, T., Goore, N., & Joseph, L. (1986). Mere presence and social facilitation: One more time. *Journal of Experimental Social Psychology, 22*, 242–248.

Selye, H. (1980). The stress concept today. In I. L. Kutash & L. B. Schlesinger (Eds.), *Handbook on stress and anxiety: Contemporary knowledge, theory, and treatment* (pp. 127–143). San Francisco: Jossey-Bass.

Siegel, A. I., Kopstein, F. F., Federmen, P. J., Ozkaptan, H., Slifer, W. E., Hegge, F. W., & Marlowe, D. H. (1981). *Management of stress in Army operations* (Research Product No. 81–19). Alexandria, VA: U.S. Army Research Institute for the Behavioral and Social Sciences.

Singer, R. N., Cauraugh, J. H., Murphey, M., Chen, D., & Lidor, R. (1991). Attentional control, distractors, and motor performance. *Human Performance, 4*, 55–69.

Staw, R. M., Sandelands, L. E., & Dutton, J. E. (1981). Threat-rigidity effects in organization-al behavior: A multi-level analysis. *Administrative Science Quarterly, 26*, 501–524.

Stouffer, S. A., Lumsdaine, A. A., Lumsdaine, M. H., Williams, R. M., Smith, M. B., Janis, I. L., Star, S. A., & Cottrell, L. S. (1949). *The American soldier: Combat and its after-math*. Princeton, NJ: Princeton University Press.

Star, S. A., & Cottrell, L. S. (1949). *The American soldier: Combat and its aftermath*. Princeton, NJ: Princeton University Press.

Teichner, W. H., Arees, E., & Reilly, R. (1963). Noise and human performance: A psycholog-ical approach. *Ergonomics, 6*, 83–97.

Thompson, S. C. (1981). Will it hurt less if I can control it? A complex answer to a simple question. *Psychological Bulletin, 90*, 89–101.

Villoldo, A., & Tarno, R. L. (1984). *Measuring the performance of EOD equipment and opera-tors under stress.*(Technical Report No. 270). Indian Head, MD: Naval Explosive Ordnance Disposal Technical Center.

Wickens, C. D. (1996). Designing for stress. In J. E. Driskell & E. Salas (Eds.), *Stress and human performance* (pp. 279–295). Hillsdale, NJ: Erlbaum.

Wickens, C. D., Stokes, A. F., Barnett, B., & Hyman, F. (1988). *Stress and pilot judgment: An empirical study using MIDIS, a microcomputer-based simulation*. Proceedings of the 32nd annual meeting of the Human Factors Society. Santa Monica, CA: Human Factors Society.

Williams, R. M. (1984). Field observations and surveys in combat zones. *Social Psychology Quarterly, 47*, 186–192.

Wine, J. (1971). Test anxiety and direction of attention. *Psychological Bulletin, 76*, 92–104.

Worchel, S., & Yohai, S. M. L. (1979). The role of attribution in the experience of crowding. *Journal of Experimental Social Psychology, 15*, 91–104.

Wright, P. (1974). The harassed decision maker: Time pressures, distractions, and the use of evidence. *Journal of Marketing Research, 44*, 429–443.

Yates, J. F., Klatzky, R. L., & Young, C. A. (1995). Cognitive performance under stress. In R. S. Nickerson (Ed.), *Emerging needs and opportunities for human factors research* (pp. 262–290). Washington, DC: National Academy Press.

Zajonc, R. B. (1965). Social facilitation. *Science, 149*, 269–274.

Zakay, D., & Wooler, S. (1984). Time pressure, training and decision effectiveness. *Ergonomics, 27*, 273–284.

Zeltkovich, C. (2003). A great generation, too. *Liberator*. 3rd Infantry Division (Mech.) Public Affairs Office. Retrieved June 15, 2005, from http://www.centcom.mil/Operations/Iraqi_Freedom/Liberator/Lib2.pdf

PART IV

SOCIAL AND PERSONALITY DIMENSIONS OF MILITARY OPERATIONS

CHAPTER 8

MORALE DURING MILITARY OPERATIONS: A POSITIVE PSYCHOLOGY APPROACH

Thomas W. Britt and James M. Dickinson

Military leaders and scholars of military psychology have long recognized the importance of morale as a critical determinant of performance during different types of military operations (see *Army Leadership*, 1999; Kellett, 1982; Manning, 1991). In addition, media reports frequently question leaders and policy makers about the morale of troops deployed to various locations across the globe, with the assumption that high levels of morale will lead to a variety of benefits, including an increased probability of mission success and reduced levels of psychological difficulties and hardships. The assumption appears to be that when morale is high, good things will happen, and that therefore understanding what leads to high morale should be one of the primary goals of theory and research in military psychology.

Given the hypothesized importance of morale, it is surprising that relatively little empirical research has been conducted on the determinants and consequences of morale during actual military operations. In fact, psychological theory and research on morale in general has not received a great deal of research attention, especially recently (military morale was studied more frequently in the years following World War I and World War II; see Boring, 1945). In order to obtain a quantitative indicator of the level of recent research on morale, we conducted a search for any journal article dealing with military morale, and compared the number of citations to the number of citations for posttraumatic stress disorder (PTSD) among service

The preparation of this manuscript was facilitated by a contract from the Medical Research and Material Command to Thomas W. Britt (Contract #DAJA02-01-P-1694). The views expressed in this chapter are those of the authors and do not reflect the official policy or position of the U.S. Department of Defense or the U.S. Government.

members. We focused only on the past 20 years (1984–2004) because PTSD as a phrase was not coined until 1984. We used a variety of search terms such as "military," "army," "navy," and "soldier" in order to capture all studies in a military context. We then performed two searches (one for "morale" and one for "PTSD") for articles that contained those words and at least one of these four military key words.

Figure 8.1 presents a graph based on the number of references to military morale and military PTSD as a function of year of publication. One can immediately see that interest in morale from a psychological perspective has been consistently and substantially lower than interest in PTSD. The amount of research devoted to the maladaptive psychological response pattern of PTSD is much larger than that devoted to the more adaptive phenomenon of morale. We do not mean to suggest that too much research has been devoted to PTSD, but rather point out that research in military psychology has been focused more on understanding what causes a minority of service members to develop psychological disorders than on what causes a larger number of service members to have high levels of personal morale.

This type of imbalance in research between maladaptive and adaptive responses is exactly the type of concern that has spawned the recent movement of "positive psychology." The field of positive psychology arose because of a perception that psychology was too focused on pathology and repairing damage, and not focused enough on developing an understanding of the characteristics of positive psychological health, such as happiness, satisfaction, and having a sense of purpose (Seligman & Csikszentmihalyi, 2000). One important point made by proponents of this approach is that maladaptive problems and adaptive functioning are usually

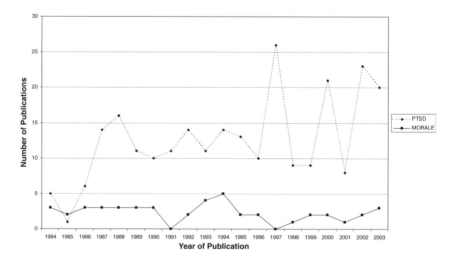

Figure 8.1
Number of Citations Dealing with Morale and Posttraumatic Stress Disorder (PTSD) as a Function of Year of Publication

two separate constructs rather than opposing ends of a single dimension. Therefore, simply extrapolating from the predictors of dysfunctional patterns of behavior to understand what contributes to positive psychological functioning is not appropriate. The determinants of positive psychological responses are likely to be different from those of dysfunctional responses (see Hart & Cooper, 2001). As discussed in more detail below, we view morale as a positive motivational state that should be related to superior performance under stress, adaptive responding to operational demands, and positive job attitudes.

The present chapter has three goals. One is to introduce a definition and model of military morale, drawing from recent theory and research on positive psychology (see Seligman & Csikszentmihalyi, 2000; Snyder & Lopez, 2002). A second purpose is to review the research that has been conducted on morale in the context of our framework, with a critical emphasis on how issues with conceptualization and measurement have influenced our understanding of morale. A final goal of the chapter is to summarize the results of an investigation of morale during the U.S. peacekeeping operation in Kosovo, and to provide some suggestions for future research examining the determinants and consequences of morale. Ultimately, we hope the present chapter will lay the groundwork for research that will empirically illustrate the importance of morale in military operations, both in terms of mission success and psychological benefits for the service members performing the mission.

A Theoretical Framework of Morale: Definition, Antecedents, and Consequences

In developing a theoretical framework for understanding military morale, we were faced with three major tasks. The first was to arrive at a definition and conceptualization of morale that was informed by past conceptualizations and was specific enough to clearly differentiate the construct from other variables (e.g., unit cohesion, well-being). We devote some time to addressing our definition of morale, because this conceptual definition informed our second major task, which was to understand those factors that predict high versus low levels of morale. Finally, our third task was to consider the hypothesized consequences of morale, which also follow from how morale is conceptualized. Our theoretical framework is presented in Figure 8.2, and will guide our discussion of defining and measuring morale, as well as our understanding of the antecedents and consequences of morale. In addition, we review past research and theory on morale within the context of the various components of our theoretical model.

Defining and Measuring Morale

Manning (1991) provided an authoritative review of research and theory on morale that included a number of definitions offered by prior authors. Manning's (1991) own definition of morale was "the enthusiasm and persistence with which a member of a group engages in the prescribed activities of that group" (p. 455). In

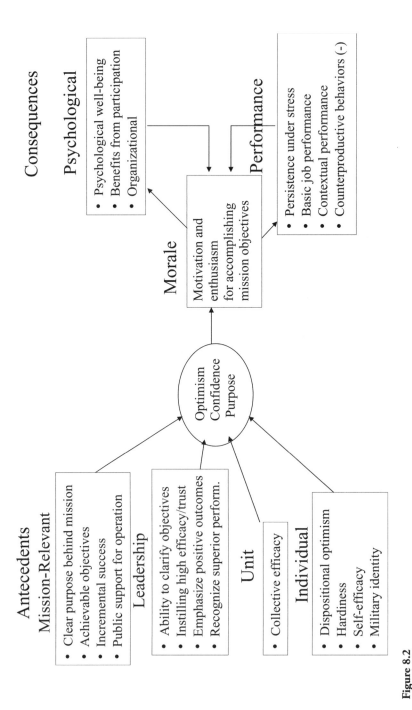

Figure 8.2
A Model of Morale During Military Operations

discussing the experiences of Australian soldiers in Vietnam, Smith (1985) defined morale as "a forward-looking and confident state of mind relevant to a shared and vital purpose" (p. 53). Ingraham and Manning (1981) defined morale as "a psychological state of mind, characterized by a sense of well-being based on confidence in the self and in primary groups" (p. 6). Dziewulski (1996), examining morale among Polish service members, defined the construct as human energy that is engaged in action. These definitions emphasize the motivational nature of the morale construct.

In contrast to these relatively succinct definitions of morale, others have tended to view morale as subsuming multiple dimensions. For example, Manning notes that the field manual *Army Leadership* (FM 22-100) defines morale as "the mental, emotional, and spiritual state of the individual. It is how he feels—happy, hopeful, confident, appreciated, worthless, sad, unrecognized, or depressed" (p. 228). In addition, Baynes (1967) devotes a great deal of effort to reviewing prior definitions of morale, and ends up defining morale as the possession of a confident, self-sacrificing, and courageous attitude toward group tasks. Motowidlo and Borman (1978) also consider morale to be a multidimensional construct, including teamwork, pride in unit, and military discipline in their assessment. Although the latter definitions contain some important aspects of what morale is hypothesized to entail, including all of the descriptors in the definition would lead to morale being a catch-all term for virtually any positive subjective state of the service member.

Given the diverse theoretical conceptualizations of morale, it is not surprising that authors have measured morale differently. The most popular single-item indicators of morale typically ask soldiers to simply rate their level of personal morale and/or morale in their unit (Bliese & Britt, 2001; Gal, 1986; Schumm, Gade, & Bell, 2003). Obviously, single-item measures of morale are not ideal from a psychometric perspective and do not likely capture the content domain of the construct. It is our opinion, however, that these measures of personal morale are often used because researchers are unsure of how else to question service members about their level of morale. At the very least, the use of a single item asking service members to rate their morale has a high level of face validity and assesses morale in a direct manner.

Other authors have measured morale multidimensionally with a diverse set of items (Gal & Manning, 1987; Motowidlo & Borman, 1978; Rosen, Moghadam, & Vaitkus, 1989). An example of a multidimensional assessment of morale comes from Rosen et al. (1989), who measured morale with items assessing self-efficacy, confidence, worth, and pride with respect to the soldier's military role. As another example, Motowidlo and Borman (1978) assessed the morale of units at the company and platoon level through the use of behaviorally anchored rating scales assessing community relations, teamwork and cooperation, reactions to adversity, superior–subordinate relations, performance and effort of soldiers at work, military discipline and appearance, pride in unit, Army, and country, and the quality of how time was used when soldiers were off duty. Needless to say, inconsistency in the measurement of morale has hindered research progress in understanding the importance of the construct. A quote from Motowidlo et al. (1976) remains applicable today:

Unless further theoretical and conceptual work defines the aspects of morale in more manageable terms, the investigator is not likely to develop a practical, self-report measure of what military people mean by "morale" by trying to measure its subcomponents. (p. 116)

In examining how to define and measure morale, we felt it was critical to define morale in a way that clearly places the construct in the nomological network (Cronbach & Meehl, 1955) of human dimensions relevant to service members as they do their work. This entails defining morale with enough specificity that it does not become an umbrella term for a number of different variables. When examining the various definitions of morale offered by prior authors, relatively common aspects include a sense of enthusiasm, persistence, confidence, and purpose. Considering prior definitions and the current model we are proposing, we define morale as "a service member's level of motivation and enthusiasm for accomplishing mission objectives." This definition of morale is highlighted in Figure 8.2.

Three characteristics of this definition warrant further elaboration. First, we conceive of morale as a motivational variable driven by an enthusiastic orientation to the mission. We do not view morale as primarily an emotional state, such as subjective well-being, positive affect, lack of depression, or a cognitive state of mind, such as being satisfied with work. We view morale as a variable that is capable of energizing a service member's efforts in ways that will lead to improved performance under stressful conditions.

The second characteristic of the definition inherent in the conceptualization of morale as the level of energy and enthusiasm possessed by service members is that morale is a state that will be determined by both environmental and dispositional factors. As we will discuss in more detail when describing the antecedents of morale, we view morale as a variable that has the capacity to fluctuate depending on changes in an operational environment. Consider a situation in which soldiers on a peacekeeping mission are suddenly required to adopt a combat orientation because of a violation of the peace accord among one of the parties involved. Or consider a combat mission that starts out as an attempt to quell a small uprising, but turns out to involve a major confrontation. Depending on leadership and other factors discussed below, morale may change rather drastically as a result of such changes in the mission. For these reasons, we believe morale needs to be assessed multiple times during a military operation if researchers are interested in understanding what leads to enhanced versus reduced levels of morale both within and between operations.

The third characteristic of the definition that is more implicit addresses the point of whether morale is best defined at the level of the individual service member or at the unit level. Our view of morale is consistent with Manning's (1991) analysis that morale is an individual-level phenomenon that takes place in the context of a unit. It is meaningful to speak of unit morale, but high morale in a unit would simply be a function of a unit containing a number of service members with high morale. That being said, in past theory and research this question has been framed in "either/or" terms, with some authors focusing on the unit level of analysis in examining morale (Grinker & Spiegel, 1945; Leighton, 1943; Motowidlo & Borman, 1978), and other authors arguing for the study of morale as an individual-level phenomenon that occurs within a group context (Manning, 1991). However, recent developments in multilevel modeling have made it possible to consider the determinants and consequences of morale at both the individual and unit levels (Bliese, 2002; Bliese & Jex, 2002).

For example, consider the association between morale and performance during a military mission. Given that data are collected among individuals within groups, morale at the individual level can be related to performance, and then the ability of average unit-level morale to predict performance can be examined. In addition, the amount of variance in service members' morale based on unit membership can be assessed empirically by examining the intraclass correlation coefficient among a given sample (see Bliese, 2002). A sizeable unit-level influence on individual reports of morale would likely reflect the operation of an environmental characteristic affecting all members of a given unit (e.g., leader behaviors). However, even given significant unit-level influences of morale, it is still possible that individual-level sources of morale will be important to examine, because individuals within the same unit may react differently to the same unit-level influences.

It is worth noting that the definition of morale as level of motivation and enthusiasm toward achieving mission success shares conceptual similarities to recent civilian definitions of morale. For instance, Hart and his colleagues (Hart, 1994; Hart & Cooper, 2001; Hart, Wearing, Conn, Carter, & Dingle, 2000) have examined the concept of morale in industrial-organizational psychology. Hart and Cooper (2001) defined morale as "the energy, enthusiasm, team spirit, and pride that employees experience as part of their work" (p. 102). Therefore, morale in areas of work outside the military has been defined in terms of energy, drive, and enthusiasm, although we would point out that the definition given by Hart and Cooper (2001) is too broad in the sense that it includes elements of feelings about one's work group and emotional responses to work. Our definition of morale also shares conceptual similarity with the concept of subjective vitality, which is defined as feelings of aliveness and positive energy (sample item, "I feel alive and vital"; Ryan & Frederick, 1997). Similar to the current definition of morale, these authors defined subjective vitality as a state of motivation characterized by enthusiasm.

Having defined morale as level of motivation and enthusiasm for accomplishing mission objectives, it becomes important to address how best to measure morale in a way that captures this definition. A first step in the measurement process was conducted by Britt (1997), who examined how U.S. Army soldiers thought about morale using a prototype analysis developed in cognitive psychology. He asked a small sample of soldiers to indicate what they thought were the key characteristics of morale. Britt (1997) found that soldiers were most likely to indicate the attributes of motivation and drive in their views of morale. On the basis of these responses, Britt developed a four-item measure of morale that simply asked soldiers to rate their level of personal morale, motivation, energy, and drive from very low to very high. Britt and Dawson (2005) reported alphas of .94 and .91 for a large sample of soldiers tested over two time periods. Although this short scale serves as a good assessment of morale as motivation and drive, it does not do a good job of measuring enthusiasm and tying motivation and enthusiasm to mission pursuits. A more complete measure of morale should include items assessing enthusiasm, and the instructions preceding the items should ask service members to respond to the questions thinking about the current mission. A revised military morale scale that considers these issues is presented in Table 8.1. Tying the assessment of morale to the current mission should serve to further separate the construct from more generic measures of depression and well-being. For example, measures of depression frequently include items such as "lack of energy" (Radloff, 1977). The conceptualization and assessment of morale should refer to level of energy in the context of accomplishing mission-relevant objectives, rather than a general sense of zeal or lethargy.

Morale as a Motivational Orientation

In the model of morale presented in Figure 8.2, we identify a number of factors that are hypothesized to influence morale. Before addressing the separate categories of antecedents, it is worth noting that all of the antecedents in some way relate to the service member having a sense of purpose, confidence, and optimism about the mission and whether progress is being made in succeeding at the mission objectives. In this sense, morale can be viewed from the standpoint of positive psychology as a motivational orientation that should be related to adaptive outcomes such as thriving, success, and psychological growth (e.g., deriving benefits from stressful events; Seligman & Csikszentmihalyi, 2000; Snyder & Lopez, 2002). Researchers have shown that possessing an optimistic, hopeful, and confident orientation toward a particular goal or activity is related to more adaptive coping in the face of obstacles (Carver & Scheier, 2002) and an increased determination that results in a greater likelihood of goal achievement (Bandura, 2000; Carver & Scheier, 2002). Also,

Table 8.1
Military Morale Scale

The following items refer to your motivation and enthusiasm for accomplishing mission objectives. Please rate the following items using the scale below.

1	2	3	4	5
Very Low	Low	Medium	High	Very High

_____1. Your level of motivation.

_____2. Your level of morale.

_____3. Your level of energy.

_____4. Your level of drive.

_____5. Your level of enthusiasm.

_____6. Your level of eagerness.

research on dispositional and state hope (the former referring to a more stable individual characteristic, the latter to hope within a specific context) has revealed positive relationships between these constructs and positive appraisal of events (Snyder et al., 1996) as well as performance (Curry, Snyder, Cook, Ruby, & Rehm, 1997).

We believe that a positive psychology framework may serve to integrate and unify those factors that are hypothesized to influence morale. Numerous analysts, and to a lesser extent researchers, have posited multiple factors that predict high versus low morale among soldiers. Unfortunately, much of this work results in a laundry list of antecedents that includes any factor presumed to influence the mood of the service members. In a discussion of the determinants of morale, Boring (1945) cited a diverse list, ranging from water, food, and cleanliness to self-importance, jobs, and group solidarity. The trend to cite multiple and diverse determinants of morale was present in Manning's (1991) conceptualization of morale, in which he also cited factors ranging from the possession of basic physical necessities to self-confidence and the clarity of goals (see also Stouffer et al. 1949).

It is our opinion that one reason for the prevalence of long lists of contributors to morale has to do with the broad definitions that many analysts have offered for the construct. If one conceives of morale as comprising numerous positive states, it is not surprising that virtually any positive reinforcer would be hypothesized to contribute to morale. If morale is going to have any discriminant utility as a human dimension relevant to service members on a military operation, however, the predictors of morale are going to have to be theoretically tied to a clear definition of the variable. In our theoretical model of morale presented in Figure 8.2, the hypothesized antecedents of morale are tied to our conceptualization of morale as motivation and enthusiasm for achieving mission success. This motivation and enthusiasm is presumed to be determined by a service member's sense of purpose, confidence, hope, and optimism regarding the given military operation. Therefore, the antecedents in our model are all hypothesized to influence one or more of these essential proximal determinants of morale. This is indicated in Figure 8.2 by showing that all of the antecedents are hypothesized to lead to one or more of these positive psychological states. We categorize the antecedents of morale into the following areas: mission-relevant factors, leadership, unit attributes, and individual differences (see Figure 8.2).

Antecedents of Morale: Mission-Related Factors

Although it is meaningful to speak of morale in garrison, military morale is a construct that has the most relevance during an actual military operation (Gal & Manning, 1987; Kellett, 1982; Manning, 1991). When service members are deployed in support of a unified military operation, characteristics of that mission have the capacity to affect the morale of soldiers. When service members are in garrison, differences in morale may still be observed, but the factors influencing morale are likely to be diverse and not as centrally focused. Our model specifies four mission-relevant factors that should be related to morale: (a) the service member's belief in a clearly stated purpose behind the mission; (b) the service member's belief that the mission and its objectives are attainable; (c) the soldier's belief that ultimate mission accomplishment is being met through incremental successes; and (d) public support for the importance of the operation.

Mission Has Clear Purpose

Given that morale is seen as a motivational state characterized by enthusiasm toward achieving mission success, factors that cast doubt on whether the mission can succeed or suggest the mission is illegitimate should harm morale. Morale may be reduced when a mission is perceived as illegitimate because service members may not exhibit much motivation or enthusiasm for succeeding on a mission lacking in purpose, even if such success is not difficult. On the other hand, missions with a clear purpose and goals should contribute to increased morale. An important point to make is that missions can change dramatically from having a clear sense of purpose to being perceived as almost meaningless, which is one reason for measuring morale throughout the course of a military operation. Unfortunately, we are aware of no published research that has measured morale at multiple time points during a military operation, which is a point we address later in the chapter.

Smith (1985) took a qualitative approach to analyzing morale based on the experiences of Australian soldiers in Vietnam, and argued that one factor in the prediction of morale among these soldiers was the perceived purpose of the mission. Gal and Manning (1987) also studied the correlates of morale among Israeli and U.S. soldiers stationed in the United States and Europe. These authors noted that the perceived legitimacy of the mission appeared to be a stronger determinant of the morale of U.S. soldiers than Israeli soldiers, perhaps because of the all-volunteer nature of the U.S. force. That is, soldiers who choose to join the Army may be driven more by the purpose and importance of a mission than soldiers who are legally required to serve.

Recent research has also examined how service members view the purpose behind peacekeeping operations, and has found that service members frequently question the importance of such operations. Britt (1998) found that among U.S. service members deployed to Operation Joint Endeavor in Bosnia, only 40 percent agreed with the statement that the U.S. military served an important role by participating in peacekeeping operations. Similar findings were obtained by Halverson and Bliese (1996) in their study of U.S. peacekeepers during Operation Uphold Democracy in Haiti. This mission was initially meant to be a forced insertion to overthrow the existing government, but turned into a peacekeeping mission where service members oversaw an exchange of governments. During this mission, 49 percent of service members did not believe the United States should be involved in the operation, 43 percent did not believe in the value of the operation, and 38 percent did not think the mission was important. Miller and Moskos (1995) studied U.S. service members who had deployed to Operation Restore Hope in Somalia, which was a humanitarian mission to help end the starvation caused by interclan warfare. When asked if the United States was right to send forces into the region, 47 percent agreed, and 48 percent disagreed. Although the relationship between mission purpose and morale was not examined in these studies, our model would predict that those individuals perceiving some purpose in the operation would have higher morale than soldiers not perceiving purpose in the mission.

Mission Has Achievable Objectives

Morale should be higher when clear objectives exist for what should take place during the mission and what should constitute mission success. Clear, achievable objectives should lead not only to a greater sense of purpose, but should also contribute to an increased sense of optimism and confidence that the mission will succeed (see Bandura, 2000; Skinner, 1996). In a qualitative review, Wattendorf (1992) recounts his interviews with American soldiers in Saudi Arabia on the cusp of Operation Desert Storm. The review is a free-flowing analysis of his observations and interactions with American troops, touching on the effects of many variables on soldier morale. Wattendorf notes that the impact of living conditions on the morale of soldiers may have been moderated by President Bush's deadline for Iraqi withdrawal from Kuwait, which removed some of the uncertainty pertaining to when action might come. He also noted that most soldiers believed there was moral justification for the mission. Although the timeline for the mission and belief in the purpose of the mission helped to clarify aspects of the mission for soldiers, Wattendorf (1992) also noted that soldiers were not clear on what would constitute American victory, citing a wide variety of answers when queried.

Britt (1998) has argued that one difficult aspect of peacekeeping operations is that service members face a number of ambiguities concerning what constitutes mission success. Peacekeepers must often perform their work in a chaotic environment where the rules of engagement are unclear and soldiers may have little control over events that cast doubt on whether mission objectives can be achieved. Thomas and Castro (2003) also reviewed evidence for what happens when objectives on a military operation are not met. In the U.S. peacekeeping mission in Kosovo, both the Yugoslavian military and the Kosovo Liberation Army (KLA) agreed to deadlines for ending armed confrontation. The Yugoslavian military was to withdraw from Kosovo immediately, and the KLA was to disarm 90 days later ("K+90" agreement). The Yugoslavian military maintained their part of the agreement, but the KLA did not disarm, and was given repeated extensions by senior U.S. military leaders. This allowed the KLA to roam the area heavily armed, creating a dangerous environment for the peacekeepers to do their work. Thomas and Castro (2003) surveyed peacekeepers regarding their opinions about the violation of the K+90 objective and found that those NCOs who were concerned about the policy reported lower morale and well-being than NCOs who did not have policy concerns.

Mission Is Being Achieved through Incremental Success

In today's military environment, service members can sometimes expect to be deployed in support of a military operation for a year or longer. We expect that over the course of a deployment of such length, morale has the potential to fluctuate markedly. One contributor to morale at any given time should be a sense that steps are being taken toward accomplishing the overall goals of the mission. If soldiers feel that specific milestones are being accomplished, then they should have a greater sense of confidence and optimism that the mission is going well, which is hypothesized to lead to higher levels of morale. Unfortunately we are aware of no longitudinal research that has examined perceptions of mission success as a determinant of morale. As indicated earlier, however, Thomas and Castro (2003) did find a cross-sectional relationship between perceptions that a key milestone of a mission had not been met and reports of morale among NCOs. In the U.S. peacekeeping mission to Kosovo, the failure of members of the KLA to disarm 90 days after the withdrawal of the Yugoslavian military had psychological consequences for the soldiers who were attempting to create a stable atmosphere for a peaceful solution to the conflict. Recall that NCOs who were concerned about the violation of this key milestone were more likely to report lower morale.

Although morale was not assessed multiple times within the Kosovo deployment, we would hypothesize that soldier morale as a whole would have likely been reduced following the repeated violation of this milestone. Such an effect could be hypothesized to occur not only because of doubts created regarding the ability to achieve objectives, but also because soldiers would sense that progress toward mission objectives had not been made. The failure to achieve the intermediate goal of the KLA disarming would likely have cast doubt on the timetable for the rest of the mission objectives, thereby creating a sense of pessimism that could have dampened morale (see Gillham, Shatte, Reivich, & Seligman, 2001). We would argue that the failure to achieve intermediate mission objectives during military operations is one of the most understudied predictors of morale during military operations. Finding support for a link between incremental success toward mission objectives and morale would illustrate the importance of setting and meeting realistic objectives within a military operation. In addition, such a link would support the idea that "winning the war or mission" is a critical determinant of morale.

Mission Has Public Support

The final mission-relevant factor we consider as a predictor of morale is the support of the public for the operation. Although such perceptions are undoubtedly less important than immediate perceptions of purpose and success, it is likely the case that service members are aware in a general sense of how the mission is perceived by their own country's citizens and perhaps even on a global level. It seems reasonable to argue that service members who are involved in a military operation that has strong public support at home will sense a greater purpose for being involved in the operation, and therefore view the operation with a greater degree of enthusiasm.

In his qualitative analysis of interviews with American soldiers on the cusp of Operation Desert Storm, Wattendorf (1992) noted that many soldiers felt public support for their involvement in the operation, but also expressed a concern with losing public support for the operation if soldiers stayed in the country for a long period of time. Although we are aware of no research conducted with service members during the military operation in Afghanistan following the September 11, 2001 attack on the United States, service members participating in the operation likely felt a strong sense of public support for dismantling a regime that was seen as responsible for the attacks. In one of the few studies to specifically examine soldier perceptions of public support for a peacekeeping operation, Halverson and Bliese (1996) found 50 percent of the soldiers reported uncertainty about whether U.S. society supported Operation Uphold Democracy in Haiti. More importantly, soldier perception of public support was one of the biggest predictors of their own level of support for the operation. We would argue that public support for the operation is likely to influence the purpose or importance service members place on a particular operation, which should influence morale.

Antecedents of Morale: Leadership, Unit, and Individual Factors

Leadership Influences on Morale

The qualities of both officers and NCOs play a role in a service member's level of morale, especially during military operations. Researchers have noted a large number of leadership qualities that have the capacity to influence motivation and performance (see Chemers, 2000; House, 1996). Our discussion of leader attributes predictive of morale, however, is again guided by our theoretical conceptualization of morale as motivation and enthusiasm that stems from a sense of optimism, confidence, hope, and purpose regarding mission objectives. Therefore, we consider the following attributes critical for understanding how leaders influence the morale of soldiers: clarifying unit and mission objectives, instilling high efficacy through training and leading by example, creating an atmosphere of trust between leader and subordinates, emphasizing positive outcomes that will result from dedicated skill execution, and recognizing performance by service members.

Other researchers and analysts have emphasized the importance of leadership for morale and motivation (Gal, 1986; Gal & Manning, 1987; Kellett, 1982). Studying Israeli soldiers positioned in the Golan Heights on high alert, Gal (1986) found that one of the strongest predictors of soldier morale was relationships with unit commanders. Gal and Manning (1987) also found that confidence in the soldier's battalion or squadron commander was a significant predictor of personal morale among both Israeli and U.S. soldiers.

In a study that addresses the impact of senior leader decision making, Segal, Rohall, Jones, and Manos (1999) had a unique opportunity to observe two American PATRIOT missile military units on the same assignment at different times. There was important contextual information, however, that they predicted would make the units differ in their levels of morale. The soldiers in the first battalion sent on the assignment (to defend interests in South Korea from possible North Korean missile attacks) had been told they would not be deployed over the next two years.

Because of military cuts, however, they were forced into six-month duty with little warning. The second unit, on the other hand, had much more time to prepare for deployment, which was to last twelve months and begin after the first unit's duty was complete. The authors hypothesized that morale, motivation, perceived performance, intent to remain in the Army, and support from families for continued service would be lower in the first unit. All analysis was done at the individual level with multiple survey questions. On eight out of nine questions having to do with morale, motivation, and performance, members of the second unit scored significantly higher. The authors posited that the violation of trust that occurred at being deployed sooner than promised may have contributed to the reduced morale among soldiers.

Although not specifically dealing with morale, Britt and Bliese (1998) examined whether soldiers' perceptions of the leadership behaviors of clarifying goals/providing structure and considerateness/support would predict how personally engaged (responsible and committed) soldiers reported being in their work. The relationship between perception of leader behaviors and job engagement was tested when soldiers were deployed in support of Operation Joint Guard in Bosnia. Britt and Bliese (1998) found that clarifying goals/providing structure was a stronger predictor of job engagement during the peacekeeping mission than perceptions of a leader's considerate behavior. The authors speculated that during particularly ambiguous military operations, providing clarification and structure to a soldier's work environment may be more important than providing social support and consideration. Leader behaviors that clarify objectives for soldiers and indicate the purpose for their efforts should be especially likely to elevate morale during military operations.

The second attribute of leaders that we believe is important for predicting morale is instilling a high sense of self- and collective efficacy for mission accomplishment. Officers and NCOs who lead by example and work to ensure the development of skills necessary for mission success should enable service members to have a sense of confidence and optimism that they will be able to accomplish their tasks during military operations (*Army Leadership,* 1999). Chen and Bliese (2002) conducted a multilevel investigation examining how the leadership behaviors of NCOs and officers predicted self-efficacy (belief that one can perform one's job) and collective efficacy (a group's belief that they can successfully perform their job) in soldiers participating in the Task Force XXI exercise in 1996 and 1997. The authors found that clarifying and supportive behaviors by NCOs and officers at the unit level were predictive of soldiers' level of self-efficacy, and that such behaviors by officers were especially predictive of the collective efficacy of soldiers. Importantly, self-efficacy and collective efficacy have both been found to buffer soldiers from the negative consequences of work-related stress (Jex & Bliese, 1999). We would also argue that both self-efficacy and collective efficacy (discussed below) should be related to a service member's morale.

The third aspect of leaders that we consider an important antecedent to morale is the ability to emphasize positive outcomes associated with effective performance. Here we do not mean unrealistically rosy images of the future, but rather an emphasis on the positive outcomes that will result from being highly trained and motivated to accomplish the mission. Such an emphasis can be contrasted with an emphasis on the negative outcomes that will result from failing to exert sufficient effort to attain mission objectives. We know from recent research on self-regulation that individuals who approach tasks with a "promotion focus" (where the goal is to try to attain high levels of success) have greater motivation to perform and actually end up performing better than individuals who approach tasks with a "prevention focus" (where the goal is to try to avoid failing; see Higgins & Spiegel, 2004). An emphasis on the positive outcomes of hard work and execution of skills necessary for success can be considered one attribute of charismatic leadership (see Conger, 1999; House, 1996). We know of no research with service members that has examined whether an emphasis on future positive outcomes by leaders is related to higher levels of morale in their subordinates, but our model would predict that a realistically positive emphasis by leaders should result in higher levels of motivation and enthusiasm toward accomplishing mission-relevant objectives.

Finally, leader behaviors that acknowledge the performance of service members through awards, praise, and other sorts of recognition should be related to increased morale. Thomas and Castro (2003) noted that a lack of recognition for sacrifices and performance under stress was a major concern for soldiers deployed in support of the peacekeeping mission to Kosovo. The recognition of job performance by leaders should lead to increased morale in part because it causes service members to experience a greater sense of purpose and efficacy in their work, thereby affecting motivation and enthusiasm.

Unit Influences on Morale

One of the most frequently mentioned correlates of morale in past research is unit cohesion (Gal, 1986; Gal & Manning, 1987; Manning, 1991; Shiron, 1976). Manning (1991) notes that many prior researchers have viewed morale and unit cohesion synonymously, even though unit cohesion and morale represent different constructs. Manning (1991) argued that unit cohesion should be viewed as an important contributor to morale rather than another name for morale. Other researchers have pointed out that there are times when unit cohesion and morale may be unrelated, or even negatively related to one another. Kellett (1982) notes that a high level of cohesion among comrades, depending on the situation, may actually lead to dissent from the mission and goals of the army. This could be an issue of "the dark side of cohesion" in which units become centered on new goals contrary to those of the overarching organization (e.g., procuring desired items illegally). The fact that unit cohesion can be high while morale or commitment to the mission is low further supports the relative independence of unit cohesion and morale as constructs.

We believe that diffuse and broad definitions of morale may have contributed to unit cohesion being theoretically and operationally confused with morale. Our definition of morale as motivation and enthusiasm toward accomplishing mission-relevant objectives leads to hypotheses about specific aspects of unit functioning that should be related to morale. For example, a high level of cohesiveness among unit members *per se* would not be expected to correlate with morale as we define the construct. High cohesiveness (especially social cohesiveness; see Siebold, this volume) by itself would not be expected to be related to a sense of optimism, purpose, or confidence. However, unit cohesiveness that breeds a sense of collective efficacy (a belief that unit members are capable of working together to accomplish tasks; see Chen & Bliese, 2002) and that is centered on goal attainment should be related to an individual's level of morale. When collective efficacy is high, service members should be more confident and optimistic about the likelihood of mission success. Shamir, Brainin, Zakay, and Popper (2000) have also argued that collective efficacy is an important component of morale, supporting our conceptualization of the relationship between these constructs. Although measures of unit cohesion and morale are clearly positively related, we would argue that this relationship is primarily a function of collective efficacy, rather than the interpersonal bonding.

*Individual determinants of morale.*Researchers frequently assume that a service member's level of morale is completely determined by mission characteristics or other external conditions of the operational environment (e.g., living conditions, recreation opportunities). Whether a service member reports high versus low levels of morale on any given occasion, however, is also likely influenced by dispositional factors having nothing to do with the mission or environment. For example, we would argue that the individual's dispositional tendency to approach life with an optimistic orientation should be related to a service member's morale during military operations. A basic definition of an optimistic individual is someone who believes "that the future holds positive opportunities with successful outcomes" (Burke, Joyner, Czech, & Wilson, 2000, p. 129). Given our view that morale is determined in part by the service member having an optimistic view of mission success, it makes sense that a service member's dispositional level of optimism would in part determine his or her level of morale during a military operation.

In addition to dispositional optimism, a service member's level of hardiness should also be related to reports of morale. Hardy individuals are committed to life goals, perceive control over consequences, and enjoy the challenge of demanding situations (see Kobasa, 1979). Bartone (1999) found that soldiers scoring higher on a measure of hardiness were less likely to develop psychological problems after exposure to war-related stressors. In addition, Britt, Adler, and Bartone (2001) found that higher levels of hardiness were related to a greater tendency to perceive a sense of meaning during a peacekeeping mission to Bosnia. Therefore, hardiness would be expected to relate to the determinants of morale dealing with perceiving a sense of purpose and confidence during a military operation.

Two final individual attributes that should be related to morale are dispositional self-efficacy and commitment to a military identity. Self-efficacy refers to confidence in being able to execute the actions necessary to succeed in a given domain (see Bandura, 2000). Service members who are confident in their ability to do their job, especially under difficult conditions, should report higher levels of morale. Commitment to a military identity reflects the extent to which service members consider their role as a service member to be a central part of their identity (Franke, 2003). Prototypical examples of these types of service members include those in elite units such as Special Forces or Rangers (Manning & Fullerton, 1988). Individuals who are more committed to the identity of being a service member should be more likely to report higher levels of morale even under difficult or challenging operational conditions.

Consequences of Morale

One of the reasons military psychologists and leaders are interested in morale is that they assume high levels of morale will translate into superior performance during different types of military operations (Manning, 1991). Although often only implicit in discussions of morale, there is also the assumption that service members with high levels of morale will be less likely to develop psychological problems as a result of participating in the operation. Finally, the assumption exists that high levels of morale will lead to a reduced likelihood of service members leaving the military, therefore leading to a stronger and more experienced force.

The consequences that we hypothesize come from morale are guided by our theoretical conceptualization of morale as motivation and enthusiasm toward achieving mission objectives (see Figure 8.2). We discuss the hypothesized psychological consequences (e.g., well-being, benefits from participating in the operation) and performance consequences related to high versus low levels of morale. One difficulty in analyzing the consequences of morale is the lack of longitudinal research on the construct, especially in the context of a military operation. In order to truly show that psychological attributes or performance were a consequence of morale, morale would need to be measured at one point in time, and psychological attributes and performance measured at a later point in time. Given that the research we review in this section is largely cross-sectional, we cannot be sure that high versus low levels of morale caused differences in psychological functioning or performance. It may be just as possible that service members' level of psychological functioning or performance determined morale (see Figure 8.2). It could be that longitudinal research may show a circular, recursive pattern in these relationships, indicated by the arrows returning from the consequences to morale in Figure 8.2.

Psychological Consequences

As indicated earlier in the chapter, a large amount of research has been devoted to examining the predictors of PTSD and other psychological difficulties among soldiers who have served on different types of military operations (see Orsillo, Roemer, Litz, Ehlich & Friedman, 1998; Weisaeth, 2003). However, there has been substantially less research examining potential positive consequences service members might experience as a result of participation in military operations. It may seem strange to discuss positive consequences coming out of combat, and we certainly do not mean to imply that service members are not exposed to extreme sources of stress that can have dramatic consequences for their psychological and physical health. We would argue, however, that it is just as important to study the determinants of potential benefits coming out of successfully accomplishing a given mission as it is to study the development of psychological problems following such operations.

Service members who evidence high levels of morale throughout a military operation should be in the best position to report high levels of well-being and benefits from participation in the operation. Although we are aware of no longitudinal research linking morale to positive psychological consequences, Britt et al. (2001) did conduct a longitudinal study examining whether engagement in meaningful work during a peacekeeping mission was related to deriving benefits (e.g., increased ability to cope with stress, greater appreciation for life) in the months following participation in the mission. These authors found that soldiers who reported being personally engaged in important work during the mission were more likely to report benefits after the mission was over. We would also predict that morale would reveal a similar pattern, in that exhibiting high levels of motivation and energy throughout the mission as a result of purpose, confidence, and optimism would result in a greater sense that the mission afforded the individual an opportunity to execute skills in a manner that contributed to overall mission success. Furthermore, we would argue that perceiving more benefits as a result of participating in a mission would lead to a higher sense of psychological well-being following the operation. Of course, we should point out that the possibility of deriving benefits from participating in military operations will be lower when the operation is perceived by the service member as unsuccessful.

Although we might also predict that high levels of morale would be negatively related to psychological problems following the operation, past research indicates that seeing something positive in the mission does not necessarily translate into reduced levels of PTSD (see Litz, King, King, Orsillo & Friedman, 1997). This research emphasizes the point that the predictors of positive consequences following military operations are not necessarily the same as those that predict dysfunctional psychological problems. We will be in a better position to understand the differential prediction of positive and negative outcomes following military operations only by conducting longitudinal research (with multiple assessments during a military operation) explicitly comparing the predictors of psychological problems versus benefits.

One final psychological consequence of morale should be increased positive attitudes toward the service member's job and an increased commitment to the army as an organization. Service members who experience high levels of motivation and energy should ultimately experience higher levels of job satisfaction, because they are approaching their work with a determination driven by confidence and purpose. In addition, service members who experience high levels of morale should attribute at least part of their motivation and enthusiasm to the mission-relevant and leadership factors that are hypothesized to give rise to morale. This should result in an increased level of commitment to the unit and the army as a whole (see Meyer & Allen, 1991).

Performance Consequences

Most analysts have operated according to the assumption that higher levels of morale should be related to higher levels of performance among soldiers in garrison and during military operations. Only a small amount of research, however, has been devoted to examining the performance consequences of morale. Before addressing this research, it is important to emphasize that performance is a multifaceted construct that represents more than the ability to carry out the technical aspects of one's specific job within an organization. Campbell (1999; see also Jex, 1998) has argued that performance represents any behavior that contributes to the achievement of organizational goals and objectives. Viewed in this manner, performance can consist of carrying out the technical aspects of one's specific job (basic job performance), as well as engaging in behaviors that benefit the organization, such as helping fellow service members complete a common mission and showing dedication in the face of obstacles. This latter type of performance has often been referred to as contextual performance (Motowidlo & Van Scotter, 1994). In addition, researchers have noted the need to consider not only behaviors that contribute to the organization's goals, but also behaviors that undermine the mission of an organization (e.g., drug abuse, violations of the code of conduct for an organization). These types of behaviors have been referred to as counterproductive work behaviors.

Theoretically, morale should be related to all aspects of performance, because approaching work with increased motivation and enthusiasm driven by optimism and confidence should be associated with the enhanced ability to carry out the basic requirements of one's job, maintain high levels of performance under stress, facilitate the work of others in order to accomplish unit goals, and refrain from engaging in behaviors that undermine the interests of the organization. In one of the few studies to investigate the relationship between morale and objective aspects of performance, Motowidlo and Borman (1987) used a behaviorally anchored rating scale filled out by military leaders at both the platoon and company levels. Although they noted there was some argument regarding the true definition of morale, they concluded that three major elements were commonly viewed as part of the construct: satisfaction, motivation, and group cohesiveness. Also, they held that morale is a group phenomenon, so the ratings were made at the group level. This was done by having the military leaders rate the frequency of eight dimensions of behavior for each unit they observed: community relations; teamwork and cooperation; reactions to adversity; superior–subordinate relations; performance and effort on the job; bearing, appearance, and military discipline; pride in unit, army, and country; and use of time during off-duty hours. Other measures in the study were several self-report surveys taken by unit members (and averaged to create group-level variables) on motivation and satisfaction. In addition, objective measures of performance included number of visits to sick call, awards, and serious incidents. Results showed that morale was correlated with global measures of satisfaction only, and not motivation or subscales of satisfaction with things like pay, supervision, and coworkers. Also, morale was significantly related to congressional inquiries ($r = -.44$) and reenlistments ($r = .53$) and only at the company level. It is worth noting that the way morale was defined and operationalized in the Motowidlo and Borman (1987) study is different from the approach to morale taken in the present chapter.

A Research Example

Despite the assumed importance of morale as a motivational construct critical to mission success, theory and research on morale is characterized by a lack of consensus regarding how morale is defined and assessed. Therefore, it is difficult to arrive at generalizations about the antecedents and consequences of morale based on the research that has been conducted. In the present chapter, we have attempted to provide a definition and conceptualization of morale that sets the construct apart from theoretically related variables, and emphasizes morale as motivation and enthusiasm for achieving mission objectives. In the remainder of this chapter, we present the results of a recent longitudinal investigation on the correlates and consequences of morale, and offer a framework for future research that facilitates an understanding of morale and its consequences.

A Longitudinal Investigation of Morale

Britt and Dickinson (2005) have recently conducted an analysis of the correlates and consequences of morale among soldiers participating in the U.S. peacekeeping mission to Kosovo. The peacekeeping mission in Kosovo represented a challenging operation for U.S. soldiers. The mission directly followed the Kosovo air war against Yugoslavia, with negotiations between the Kosovo Liberation Army (KLA) and the Yugoslavian military still ongoing (see Thomas & Castro, 2003). Both factions were still engaged in hostile actions, which made the mission more dangerous and uncertain than many prior peacekeeping operations in which the United States had been involved.

The data for the study were collected from U.S. Army-Europe soldiers deployed to Kosovo in October of 1999 (three to four months into the operation) in support of a research protocol examining the effects of operations tempo in the U.S. Army (see Castro, Adler, Bienvenu, Huffman, Dolan & Thomas, 1998). In addition, soldiers also completed a survey one to two months following their return from the Kosovo mission (in February of 2000). As noted earlier in the chapter, prior researchers in the field of positive psychology have argued that different variables may predict positive versus negative psychological states (Hart & Cooper, 2001; Nelson & Simmons, 2003). In the context of the peacekeeping mission to Kosovo, Britt and Dickinson (2005) examined whether the correlates and consequences of morale during a deployment were different from the correlates and consequences of depression during the same deployment. Depression is a frequently studied psychological problem during military operations (see Bartone, Adler & Vaitkus, 1998; Britt, 1999).

Predicting Morale Versus Depression during the Operation

Although the Kosovo study was not designed to test the determinants and consequences of morale, a number of variables relevant to the model presented in Figure 8.2 were assessed during the Kosovo deployment. Specifically, soldiers completed measures assessing task significance and clarity of goals for the mission (mission-relevant antecedents in Figure 8.2), the extent to which leaders provided clarifying instructions and soldiers' perceptions of job recognition (leadership antecedents), and unit cohesion and collective efficacy (unit-level antecedents).

In addition, morale was assessed with a 4-item scale described earlier (see Britt & Dawson, 2005). Specifically, participants were instructed to "Rate the following": "Your personal morale," "Your level of motivation," "Your level of energy," and "Your level of drive." Responses were made on a 5-point scale with the response options "Very Low," "Low," "Medium," "High," and "Very High." The internal reliability for the morale scale was .89 when assessed during the deployment, and .92 when assessed at postdeployment. These alphas (which reflect all four items on the scale are assessing a similar variable) are high for a 4-item scale. In addition, the mean on the scale was 3.13, with a standard deviation of .90. This indicates that scores on morale were normally distributed among soldiers during the military operation. It is worth noting that the measure of morale used in the Kosovo survey does not specifically measure motivation and enthusiasm with specific reference to achieving mission-relevant objectives, which would have been desirable given the definition of morale proposed in the present chapter. In future research, this measure of morale could be easily supplemented with items assessing enthusiasm, as well as by having service members respond to the questions with specific reference to achieving mission success (see Table 8.1). Given the model presented in Figure 8.2, our primary hypothesis relevant to the prediction of morale was that each of the theoretically relevant antecedents would predict unique variance in our measure of morale.

In terms of the possibility of different predictors of positive and negative psychological states, it is worth considering what would be expected to predict depression during the Kosovo operation. Britt and Dickinson (2005) examined the predictors of a modified version of the Center for Epidemiological Studies Depression Scale (Radloff, 1977; see Mirowsky, 1996). This depression scale requires participants to indicate how many days (0–7) during the past week they have had different experiences, such as "felt sad" and "felt you couldn't shake the blues." Interestingly, the mean for the depression scale was 1.58 on a 0–7 scale, with a standard deviation of 1.71, reflecting a much more skewed pattern of scores. This skewness emphasizes the importance of measuring positive constructs such as morale in addition to depression, as positive constructs should be relevant to a wider segment of the military population.

Relevant to the prediction of depression, one approach would be to argue that the same variables that predict morale would predict depression, only the signs would be opposite. Such a pattern would support the idea that morale and depression are two opposite ends of the same continuum. A different approach, however, would be to argue that stressors experienced during deployment would be the primary determinants of depression; whereas the positive variables identified earlier would be the primary determinants of morale. In addition to measuring some of the proposed antecedents of morale, the Kosovo survey included measures of how much stress was caused by various factors (e.g., "concerns about accidents," "concerns about disease," "concerns about mines or unexploded ordnance") and whether soldiers had experienced stressful events during the operation (e.g., "being shot at," "being injured").

Britt and Dickinson (2005) found that the theoretically relevant antecedents of morale were consistently more positively correlated with morale than negatively correlated with depression. Conversely, ratings of stressors and the experience of stressful events were stronger predictors of depression than morale. More convincingly, the correlations between morale and the theoretically relevant antecedents remained significant and were not reduced to a large extent when controlling for depression. The correlations between depression and the theoretically relevant antecedents to morale, however, were substantially reduced (often to nonsignificance) when controlling for morale. On the other hand, the correlations between depression and ratings of stressors and reporting of stressful events remained significant and were not substantially reduced when controlling for morale, whereas the correlations between morale and the stressors were reduced to nonsignificance when controlling for depression. This pattern of results suggests that different deployment conditions and variables predicted morale versus depression during a military operation. Such a pattern supports the viewpoint that the determinants of positive psychological states during a military operation are not the same as those that predict negative psychological states, which justifies additional research examining the predictors of thriving during and after military operations.

In a more direct test of whether each of the theoretically relevant antecedents measured is a unique predictor of morale, Britt and Dickinson (2005) conducted a simultaneous regression with morale as the outcome measure, and task significance, clarity of goals, leader clarification, job recognition, unit cohesion, and collective efficacy as predictors. The authors found that all of the predictors, except for unit cohesion, accounted for unique variance in morale. This analysis therefore supports some of the hypothesized connections between antecedents and morale presented in Figure 8.2, and also provides some justification for the emphasis on collective efficacy versus unit cohesiveness *per se* in the prediction of morale. The analysis indicates that soldiers were more likely to report higher levels of morale during the Kosovo operation when they perceived that what they were doing was important, understood the goals of the mission, perceived leaders as providing clarifying instructions, were recognized for their job performance, and had a belief in the collective efficacy of their unit.

Longitudinal Analyses Examining Consequences of Morale

According to the model presented in Figure 8.2, morale should have both psychological and performance consequences. Although no performance measures were available in the Kosovo study, soldiers did complete measures assessing the positive and negative consequences of deploying in the months following the deployment, as well as a measure of PTSD. Given our conceptualization of morale as reflecting a positive motivational state, we predicted that morale would be especially likely to predict positive consequences of the deployment (perceived benefits of the deployment). In contrast, we predicted that depression would be especially likely to predict negative consequences of the deployment (e.g., negative perceptions of deployment, PTSD).

For the analysis involving perceived benefits from the deployment (e.g., "The deployment gave me a chance to use my job skills"), morale emerged as the only unique predictor. Soldiers reporting higher levels of morale during the deployment were more likely to report positive consequences of the deployment months after it was over. Depression did not predict perceived benefits. The next set of analyses focused on two negative consequences of the deployment. The first dealt with negative perceptions of deployments (e.g., "The deployments are too long"), and the second dealt with a self-report measure of posttraumatic stress disorder. The results revealed that depression assessed during the deployment emerged as a significant predictor of negative perceptions following the deployment, whereas morale was not a significant predictor. Similarly, depression emerged as a strong independent predictor of PTSD, whereas morale during the deployment was not a significant predictor. Therefore, depression emerged as a significant longitudinal predictor of negative perceptions outcomes of the operation, whereas morale did not. This pattern of results supports the hypothesis that morale assessed during a military operation should predict outcome measures that are distinct from those predicted by dysfunctional problems that occur during a deployment.

Future Directions

Given the conceptualization advanced in the present chapter, morale should be considered a variable that may be expected to fluctuate during a military operation as a result of mission-relevant characteristics and developments. The extent to which morale is likely to fluctuate on a military operation will depend on the extent to which the antecedents identified in the present chapter vary or remain constant. Morale could remain stable across a military operation if the antecedents remain at a particular level (e.g., if the mission is seen as justifiable and having attainable objectives), or could change markedly if there are frequent changes in the antecedent conditions (e.g., dramatic changes in public support for the operation or in the belief that the mission is succeeding). Therefore, in order to completely examine the determinants and consequences of morale, longitudinal research designs will need to be employed where morale is assessed at multiple points during a military operation. Having multiple assessments of morale throughout the course of a military operation would permit the use of correlational and quasi-experimental designs that could investigate how changes and developments during a given operation contribute to changes in morale. For example, researchers could examine service member morale both before and after a particular successful or unsuccessful phase of the operation, and the impact of developments in particular regions of the operational theater on morale could be examined.

Given the need to measure morale multiple times during a military operation, it would be very helpful to have a brief measure that was simple and easy to complete. We believe the 4-item measure of morale described earlier is a good start for a short assessment tool, but we recommend the 6-item measure included in Table 8.1, because it includes items assessing enthusiasm and contains instructions emphasizing the given military operation.

Two research approaches we see as particularly fruitful for understanding the determinants and consequences of morale are examining the impact of naturally occurring events that should presumably influence morale, and conducting structured diary-type studies to examine within-person variation in the correlates and consequences of morale. As already indicated, the former methodology could be used to examine the impact of a myriad of events that occur during a military operation. Currently, all we have are hypotheses about how various deployment-related events will influence morale, with little data to assess what types of experiences are associated with the greatest reductions or elevations in morale. Intensively studying the morale of service members over time during a military operation could allow us to assess the impact of such events as a notification that the service member's tour length will increase, a presidential visit, or a broadcast of a recent victory in battle. This kind of investigation could begin to illuminate how much influence deployment-related events actually have on service members.

The second research strategy we propose is having service members complete measures assessing morale and theoretically related antecedents and consequences multiple times throughout the course of a military operation, and using the statistical procedure of multilevel modeling to examine the predictors and consequences of morale within service members over time. Recent advances in statistical procedures to model variation within individuals over time makes it relatively simple to assess those factors that are most associated with changes in a given variable (e.g., morale), and which outcome measures (e.g., health, persistence under stress) are most influenced by changes in a given variable (see Nezlek, 2001, 2003). Such a methodology could allow us to assess whether a service member's level of morale over time is especially likely to vary with his or her optimism about the likelihood of mission success, or perhaps the extent to which his or her contribution to the mission is being acknowledged. In conducting this type of future research on morale, it will be useful to examine whether the findings generalize across militaries from different cultures. Such generalization may be expected given the existence of a "supranational" military culture (see Soeters et al., Volume 4 of this set), but cross-cultural research needs to be conducted.

Although morale is frequently referred to by military leaders and the general public, a thorough understanding of the construct has been hampered by different conceptualizations and measurement strategies. By clarifying the definition and building a model, morale can become a useful variable for understanding the parameters of motivation, drive, and positive expectations on military operations. Ultimately, morale could be one of the primary human dimensions used to judge the readiness and potential to perform among service members at various stages of a military operation.

References

Army Leadership (Field Manual 22-100) .(1999). Department of the Army, Washington, DC.

Bandura, A. (2000). Social cognitive theory: An agentic perspective. *Annual Review of Psychology, 52*, 1–26.

Bartone, P. T. (1999). Hardiness protects against war-related stress in Army Reserve Forces. *Consulting Psychology Journal: Practice and Research, 51*, 72–82.

Bartone, P. T., Adler, A. B., & Vaitkus, M. A. (1998). Dimensions of psychological stress in peacekeeping operations. *Military Medicine, 163*, 587–593.

Baynes, J. C. (1967). *Morale.* New York: Praeger.

Bliese, P. D. (2002). Multilevel random coefficient modeling in organizational research: Examples using SAS and S-PLUS. In F. Drasgow and N. Schmitt (Eds.), *Modeling in organizational research: Measuring and analyzing behavior in organizations.* (pp. 401–445). San Francisco: Jossey-Bass.

Bliese, P. D., & Britt, T. W. (2001). Social support, group consensus and stressor-strain relationships: Social context matters. *Journal of Organizational Behavior, 22*, 425–436.

Bliese, P. D., & Jex, S. M. (2002). Incorporating a multilevel perspective into occupational stress research: Theoretical, methodological, and practical implications. *Journal of Occupational Health Psychology, 7*, 265–276.

Boring, E. G. (Ed.) . (1945). *Psychology for the armed services.* Washington, DC: Infantry Journal.

Britt, T. W. (1997). *What do soldiers think of morale, unit cohesion, and esprit de corps?* Research Committee on Armed Forces and Conflict Resolution, International Sociological Association Interim Meeting, Modena, Italy.

Britt, T. W. (1998). Psychological ambiguities in peacekeeping. In H. J. Langholtz (Ed.), *The psychology of peacekeeping* (pp. 111–128). Westport, CT: Praeger.

Britt, T. W. (1999). Engaging the self in the field: Testing the Triangle Model of Responsibility. *Personality and Social Psychology Bulletin, 25*, 696–706.

Britt, T. W., Adler, A. B., & Bartone, P. T. (2001). Deriving benefits from stressful events: The role of engagement in meaningful work and hardiness. *Journal of Occupational Health Psychology, 6*, 53–63.

Britt, T. W., & Bliese, P. (1998). *Leadership, perceptions of work, and the stress-buffering effects of job engagement.* Colloquium presented at the Center for Creative Leadership as winner of the Walter F. Ulmer Applied Research Award.

Britt, T. W., & Dawson, C. R. (2005). Predicting work–family conflict from workload, job attitudes, unit attributes, and health: A longitudinal study. *Military Psychology, 17*, 203–228.

Britt, T. W., & Dickinson, J. M. (2005). [Analysis of morale among soldiers deployed to Kosovo]. Unpublished data analysis.

Burke, K. L., Joyner, A. B., Czech, D. R., & Wilson, M. J. (2000). An investigation of concurrent validity between two optimism/pessimism questionnaires: The Life Orientation Test-Revised and the Optimism/Pessimism Scale. *Current Psychology: Developmental, Learning, Personality, and Social, 19*, 129–136.

Campbell, J. P. (1999). The definition and measurement of performance in the new age. In D. Ilgen & E. D. Pulakos (Eds.), *The changing nature of performance: Implications for staffing, motivation, and development* (pp. 399–429). San Francisco: Jossey-Bass.

Carver, S. C. & Scheier, M. F. (2002). Optimism. In C. R. Snyder & S. J. Lopez (Eds.), *Handbook of positive psychology*. London: Oxford University Press.

Castro, C. A., Adler, A. B., Bienvenu, R. V., Huffman, A. H., Dolan, C. A., & Thomas, J. L. (1998). *Walter Reed Army Institute of Research Protocol #700: A Human Dimensions Assessment of the Impact of OPTEMPO on the Forward-Deployed Soldier.*

Chemers, M. M. (2000). Leadership research and theory: A functional integration. *Leadership Quarterly, 4*, 27–43.

Chen, G., & Bliese, P. D. (2002). The role of different levels of leadership in predicting self- and collective efficacy: Evidence for discontinuity. *Journal of Applied Psychology, 87*, 549–556.

Conger, J. A. (1999). Charismatic and transformational leadership in organizations: An insider's perspective on these developing streams of research. *Leadership Quarterly, 10*, 145–179.

Cronbach, L. J., & Meehl, P. E. (1955). Construct validity in psychological tests. *Psychological Bulletin, 52*, 281–302.

Curry, L. A., Snyder, C. R., Cook, D. L., Ruby, B. C., & Rehm, M. (1997). Role of hope in academic and sport achievement. *Journal of Personality and Social Psychology, 73*, 1257–1267.

Dziewulski, H. (1996, October 6). *Morale as a bone of contention.* Paper presented at the European Research Group on Military and Society (ERGOMAS) Biannual Conference, Zurich, Switzerland.

Franke, V. C. (2003). The social identity of peacekeeping. In T. W. Britt and A. B. Adler (Eds.), *The psychology of the peacekeeper: Lessons from the field*. Westport, CT: Praeger.

Gal, R. (1986). Unit morale: From a theoretical puzzle to an empirical illustration: An Israeli example. *Journal of Applied Social Psychology, 16*, 549–564.

Gal, R., & Manning, F. J. (1987). Morale and its components: A cross-national comparison. *Journal of Applied Social Psychology, 17*, 369–391.

Gillham, J. E., Shatte, A. J., Reivich, K. J., & Seligman, M. E. P. (2001). Optimism, pessimism, and explanatory style In E. C. Chang (Ed.), *Optimism & pessimism: Implications for theory, research, and practice* (pp. 53–75). Washington, DC: American Psychological Association.

Grinker, R. R., & Spiegel, J. P. (1945). *Men under stress*. Philadelphia: Blakiston.

Halverson, R. R., & Bliese, P. D. (1996). Determinants of soldiers support for Operation Uphold Democracy. *Armed Forces & Society, 23*, 81–96.

Hart, P. M. (1994). Teacher quality of work life: Integrating work experiences, psychological distress, and morale. *Journal of Occupational and Organizational Psychology, 67*, 109–132.

Hart, P. M., & Cooper, C. L. (2001). Occupational stress: Toward a more integrated framework. In N. Anderson, D. S. Ones, H. K. Sinangil, and C. Viswesvaran (Eds.), *Handbook of industrial, work, and organizational psychology: Vol. 2. Organizational Psychology* (pp. 93–114). London: Sage.

Hart, P. M., Wearing, A. J., Conn, M., Carter, N. L., & Dingle, R. K. (2000). Development of the school organizational health questionnaire: A measure for assessing teacher morale and school organizational climate. *British Journal of Educational Psychology, 70*, 211–228.

Higgins, E. T., & Spiegel, S. (2004). Promotion and prevention strategies for self-regulation: A motivated cognition perspective. In R. F. Baumeister and K. Vohs (Eds.), *Handbook of self-regulation: Research, theory, and applications*. (pp. 171–187). New York: Guilford Press.

House, R. J. (1996). Path-goal theory of leadership: Lessons, legacy, and a reformulated theory. *Leadership Quarterly, 7*, 323–352.

Ingraham, L. H., & Manning, F. J. (1981). Cohesion: Who needs it, what is it, and how do we get it to them? *Military Review, 61*, 3–12.

Jex, S. M. (1998). *Stress and job performance: Theory, research, and implications for managerial practice.* Thousand Oaks, CA: Sage.

Jex, S. M., & Bliese, P. D. (1999). Efficacy beliefs as a moderator of the impact of work-related stressors: A multilevel study. *Journal of Applied Psychology, 84*, 349–361.

Kellett, J. (1982). *Combat motivation: The behavior of soldiers in battle.* Boston: Kluwer.

Kobasa, S.C. (1979). Stressful life events, personality, and health: An inquiry into hardiness. *Journal of Personality and Social Psychology, 37*, 1–11.

Leighton, A.H. (1943). A working concept of morale for flight surgeons. *Military Surgeon, 92*, 601–609.

Litz, B. T., King, L. A., King, D. W., Orsillo, S. M., & Friedman, M. J. (1997). Warriors as peacekeepers: Features of the Somalia experience and PTSD. *Journal of Consulting and Clinical Psychology, 65*, 6, 1001–1010.

Manning, F. J. (1991). Morale, unit cohesion, and esprit de corps. In R. Gal & D. Mangelsdorff (Eds.), *Handbook of military psychology* (pp. 453–470). New York: Wiley.

Manning, F. J., & Fullerton, T. D. (1988). Health and well-being in highly cohesive units of the U.S. Army. *Journal of Applied Social Psychology, 18*, 503–519.

Meyer, J. P., & Allen, N. J. (1991). A three-component conceptualization of organizational commitment. *Human Resource Management Review, 1*, 61–89.

Miller, L. L., & Moskos, C. C. (1995). Humanitarians or warriors? Race, gender, and combat status in Operation Restore Hope. *Armed Forces & Society, 21*, 615–637.

Mirowsky, J. (1996). Age and the gender gap in depression. *Journal of Health and Social Behavior, 37*, 363–380.

Motowidlo, S. J., & Borman, W. C. (1978). Relationships between military morale, motivation, satisfaction, and unit effectiveness. *Journal of Applied Psychology, 63*, 47–52.

Motowidlo, S. J., Dowell, B. E., Hop, M. A., Borman, W. C., Johnson, P. D., & Dunnette, M. D. (1976). *Motivation, satisfaction, and morale in Army careers: A review of theory and measurement* (ARI Technical Report No. TR-76-A7). Arlington, VA: U.S. Army Research Institute for the Behavioral and Social Sciences (NTIS No. AD A036390).

Motowidlo, S. J., & Van Scotter, J. R. (1994). Evidence that task performance should be distinguished from contextual performance. *Journal of Applied Psychology, 79*, 475–480.

Nelson, D. L., & Simmons, B. L. (2003). Health Psychology and work stress: A more positive approach. In J. C. Quick and L. E. Tetrick (Eds.), *Handbook of Occupational Health Psychology* (pp. 97–119). Washington, DC: American Psychological Association.

Nezlek, J. B. (2001). Multilevel random coefficient analyses of event- and interval-contingent data in social and personality psychology research. *Personality and Social Psychology Bulletin, 27*, 771–785.

Nezlek, J. B. (2003). Using multilevel random coefficient modeling to analyze social interaction diary data. *Journal of Social and Personal Relationships, 20*, 437–469.

Orsillo, S. M., Roemer, L., Litz, B. T., Ehlich, P., & Friedman, M. J. (1998). Psychiatric symptomatology associated with contemporary peacekeeping: An examination of post-mission functioning among peacekeepers in Somalia. *Journal of Traumatic Stress, 11*(4), 611–625.

Radloff, L. (1977). The CES-D Scale. A self-report depression scale for research in the general population. *Applied Psychological Measurement, 1*, 385–401.

Rosen, L. N., Moghadam, L. Z., & Vaitkus, M. A. (1989). The military family's influence on soldiers' personal morale: A path analytic model. *Military Psychology, 1,* 201–213.

Ryan, R. M., & Frederick, C. (1997). On energy, personality, and health: Subjective vitality as a dynamic reflection of well-being. *Journal of Personality, 65,* 529–565.

Schumm, W. R., Gade, P. A., & Bell, B. D. (2003). Dimensionality of military professional value items: An exploratory factor analysis of data from the spring 1996 Sample Survey of Military Personnel. *Psychological Reports, 92,* 831–841.

Segal, D., Rohall, D. E., Jones, J. C., & Manos, A. M. (1999). Meeting the missions of the 1990s with a downsized force: Human resource management lessons from the deployment of PATRIOT missile units to Korea. *Military Psychology, 11,* 149–167.

Seligman, M. E. P., & Csikszentmihalyi, M. (2000). Positive psychology: An introduction. *American Psychologist, 55,* 5–14.

Shamir, B., Brainin, E., Zakay, E., & Popper, M. (2000). Perceived combat readiness as collective efficacy: Individual- and group-level analysis. *Military Psychology, 12,* 105–119.

Shirom, A. (1976). On some correlates of combat performance. *Administrative Science Quarterly, 21,* 419–432.

Skinner, E. (1996). A guide to constructs of control. *Journal of Personality and Social Psychology, 71,* 549–570.

Smith, K. R. (1985). Understanding morale: With special reference to the morale of the Australian infantryman in Vietnam. *Defence Force Journal, 52,* 53–62.

Snyder, C. R., & Lopez, S. J. (Eds.) . (2002). *Handbook of positive psychology.* London: Oxford University Press.

Snyder, C. R., Sympson, S. C., Ybasco, F. C., Borders, T. F., Babyak, M. A., & Higgins, R. L. (1996). Development and validation of the State Hope Scale. *Journal of Personality and Social Psychology, 70,* 321–335.

Stouffer, S.A., Lumsdaine, A. A., Williams, R. B., Smith, M. B., Janis, I. L., Star, S. A., & Cottrell, L. S. (1949). *The American soldier: Vol. 2. Combat and its aftermath.* Princeton, NJ: Princeton University Press.

Thomas, J. L., & Castro, C. A. (2003). Organizational behavior and the U.S. peacekeeper. In T. W. Britt & A. B. Adler (Eds.), *The psychology of the peacekeeper: Lessons from the field* (pp. 127–146). Westport, CT: Praeger.

Wattendorf, J. M. (1992). The American soldier in a prewar desert environment: Observations from Desert Shield. *Social Science Quarterly, 73,* 276–295.

Weisaeth, L. (2003). The psychological challenge of peacekeeping operations. In T. W. Britt & A. B. Adler (Eds.), *The Psychology of the peacekeeper: Lessons from the field* (pp. 207–222). Westport, CT: Praeger.

CHAPTER 9

MILITARY GROUP COHESION

Guy L. Siebold

Group cohesion is a fundamental concept in the social and behavioral sciences. It is particularly basic to military psychology, where there has been a long-term focus by researchers and interest of military leaders in the dynamics needed to build and sustain cohesive and resilient military groups. As General Peter J. Schoomaker (2003) asked after being sworn in to his position as the Chief of Staff of the U.S. Army, "How do we man the Army in a way that provides cohesive, high performing units in this reality of continuous engagement?"

Military group cohesion is a special type of cohesion in that typically the group exists as part of a large, long-lived, somewhat isolated, highly regulated, hierarchical organization from which the group member cannot easily leave or travel about. Strong group leadership is expected. Members wear uniforms and usually are subject to control 24 hours per day. Further, there is a pervasive influence from life-endangering weapons and major combat systems, as well as the possible lethal threat from an external enemy force. Group members carry out multiple, mostly interdependent, real-world, ongoing tasks. These features of military groups make them different from many of the groups portrayed in the general behavioral and social science literature. Thus, the findings about group cohesion in the wider literature may not all transfer or be of concern to the military domain, and the findings about military group cohesion may not fully transfer to or be of concern in many nonmilitary groups. While the majority of the research on cohesion has been done with subjects from Western, individualistic cultures, the many common features of most

The views expressed in this chapter are those of the author and do not reflect the official policy or position of the U.S. Department of Defense or the U.S. Government.

military-organized small groups would suggest that cohesion and related variables would operate similarly, regardless of the culture of the wider societies from which the group members were drawn (e.g., see Henderson, 1985).

There are a number of related reasons for military interest in building cohesive units. First, there is the need for maintaining unit integrity in battle formations. The classic research on unit integrity was done by Shils and Janowitz (1948). They investigated why German soldiers at the end of World War II fought and held together in their small units, despite Allied propaganda and their understanding that the war effort around them was disintegrating. Underpinning the Shils and Janowitz analysis was their theoretical view that the small group provides for the support and basic needs of its members (Cooley, 1909/1962). One limitation of Shils and Jano-witz's work was that they used prisoners of war as their subjects; it has been suggested that the German prisoners told the researchers what they wanted to hear and deem-phasized their Nazi ideology. Nonetheless, concern about unit integrity is still relevant in light of the current employment of small units dispersed over wide areas and that can be rapidly moving. Those researchers who focus on unit integrity are frequently from the medical community and emphasize mental health, stress tolerance, and social support (e.g., Griffith & Vaitkus, 1999; Vaitkus, 1994).

A second reason for military interest in cohesion is that it is believed to enhance unit performance. While the cohesion–performance relation has been studied in a number of contexts, the relation has been a special focus of research on the military and sports (Carron, 1982, 1988). A meta-analysis of military research was carried out by Oliver, Harman, Hoover, Hayes, and Pandhi (1999), in which they estimated the correlation between cohesion and performance to be r = .40. Further, they found an inverse relation between cohesion and discipline problems. One typical example of cohesion–performance research was a project that measured cohesion in five light infantry companies prior to a 5-day 100-mile road march. Performance was measured by sets of independent raters, who scored tactical exercises at the end of each 20-mile segment of the march. The average overall cohesion in a company predicted well the overall performance score given to each company (Siebold & Kelly, 1987b). Summary results are displayed in Figure 9.1. Researchers who focus on unit performance are frequently from the military training community.

A third reason for military interest in unit cohesion is that it is believed to be integral to strong "we-are-all-in-it-together" mission motivation. As an historical example, Julius Caesar (51 B.C./1896) described how the Helvetii (from western - Switzerland) made preparations to conquer eastern Gaul (France). When ready to move, the Helvetii burned their own towns, villages, and crop fields so there would be no incentive to either remain or return home later. As another example, Pierre and his crew of seventeenth century Caribbean buccaneers attacked Spanish treasure ships from behind in small, fast boats. As the buccaneers reached a Spanish galleon, Pierre drilled holes in the bottom of his own boat so that the buccaneers' only chance of survival was to conquer their Spanish prey (Marrin, 1999). In more modern times, it is thought that mission motivation (or ideology) is vital to provide a foundation for cohesion and that cohesion is important to sustain commitment to the mission.

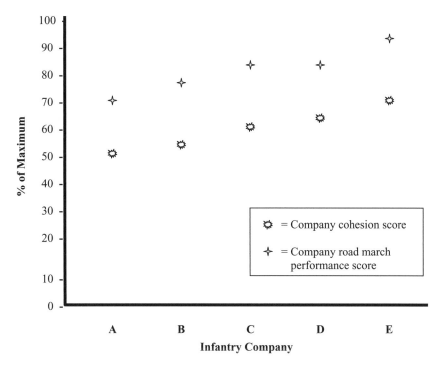

Figure 9.1
Cohesion and Road March Performance

Those researchers who focus on cohesion in relation to mission motivation are often from the leadership development and personnel policy communities (e.g., Henderson, 1985).

Thus, group cohesion is an abstract concept that has been treated in many different ways by researchers based on their different purposes and theoretical approaches. The initial sections of this chapter will address military group cohesion as a concept, its definition, other concepts closely related to cohesion, and theoretical treatments of group cohesion. The middle sections of this chapter will detail what has been found about the impact and outcome of different degrees of group cohesiveness. Attention will be paid to cohesion over time, cohesion in relation to joint lines of action, and the impact of leadership on cohesion. The last section will address the future of the concept of cohesion as it relates to unit-manning policies and the need for additional research.

Cohesion: The Concept

Group cohesion is an ambiguous and flexible concept. Therein lies some of its utility. Group cohesion can be loosely defined as a state where a group of relatively similar individuals holds together to accomplish its purpose, especially when the group is under stress. The term *cohesion* is used to describe a state in which the group is holding together; *cohesiveness* is used to describe the strength with which the group holds together (e.g., strong or high cohesiveness). *Adhesion* refers to the situation where relatively unlike groups coalesce for a period of time to accomplish a common purpose; such coalition processes are beyond the scope of this chapter.

Generally, cohesion is viewed as something good and desirable by the members of the group and by those who interact with the group to achieve common goals. This, of course, does not mean there is no downside to strong cohesion. Where group members are detached from higher leadership and group purpose, their strong cohesiveness might restrain innovation through an overemphasis on conformity of thought or deed; it might also support group deviancy. In any case, the ambiguity of the concept of cohesion can lead to problems in conceptualizing and designing research. As Mudrack (1989) noted, conceptualizing and defining cohesion have been *the problem* for many years, and they will be of concern here.

Some have tried to describe cohesion in a manner analogous to the physical sciences as the sum of forces acting on the group to hold it together (Lewin, 1935). Others have portrayed cohesion as member attraction to the group or perceptions of being part of the group (e.g., Hogg, 1992; Paxton & Moody, 2003). Still others have dealt well with the multidimensional nature of cohesion but primarily as a task-dependent construct affected by small-group processes found in temporary, randomly constructed groups in laboratory settings (e.g., Craig & Kelly, 1999). To address the concept holistically, one needs to set out the parameters that define the concept. Figure 9.2 is a heuristic tool for the reader to help put particular past studies in context and conceptualize and design future research and analyses. The figure is not meant to reflect how cohesion has been dealt with in the literature *per se* or to suggest boundaries or constraints for any particular academic discipline or researcher.

One particular difficulty with cohesion is its appropriate level of analysis. Some view it in terms of the individual level—feelings and perceptions about the group. Others see cohesion in terms of member interaction—how the individual behaves in interaction with group members and nonmembers. Still others focus on the group level of analysis, including group structure and networks (e.g., Moody & White, 2003). Generally, the dominant approach of a given researcher is a function of his/her training, academic discipline, and research objectives. Nonetheless, a study about the perceptions individuals have about a group and their feelings of cohesion with the group is quite different from a study examining the impact on cohesion of groups being structured in different ways or composed of members with different aggregate characteristics. The problem has not been coverage of the levels but rather that social and behavioral scientists have mixed inconsistent independent, causal, and outcome variables from different levels of analysis. Both the conceptualization of cohesion and the methodology to study it require a multilevel approach, multidisciplinary cooperation, a consistent attention to the level of analysis, and an explanation of how variables at one level of analysis are related to and transformed into variables at another level.

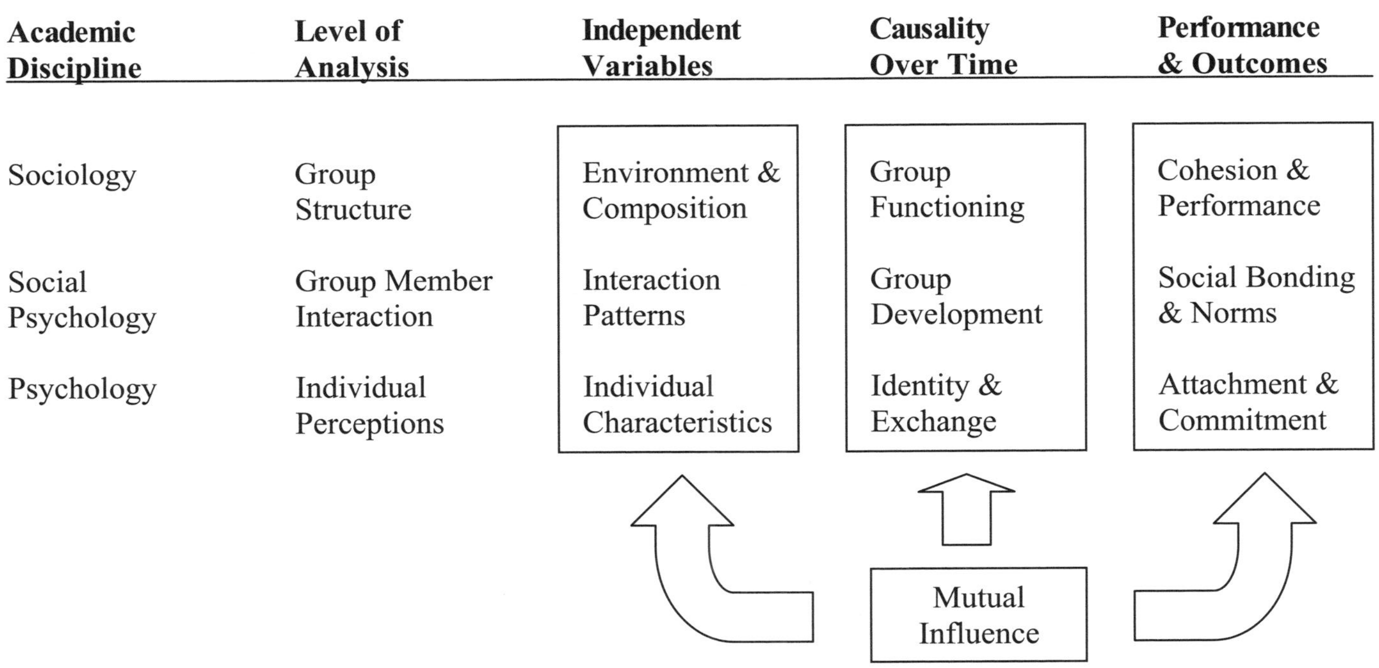

Academic Discipline	Level of Analysis	Independent Variables	Causality Over Time	Performance & Outcomes
Sociology	Group Structure	Environment & Composition	Group Functioning	Cohesion & Performance
Social Psychology	Group Member Interaction	Interaction Patterns	Group Development	Social Bonding & Norms
Psychology	Individual Perceptions	Individual Characteristics	Identity & Exchange	Attachment & Commitment

Mutual Influence

Figure 9.2
Simple Heuristic Model of Approaches to Cohesion

From the group-level perspective, cohesion can be looked at in terms of structures. Is the group organized as a hierarchical pyramid, circle, wheel with spokes, or inter-connected series of chains? To what extent are the structures or group boundaries open, permeable, or closed to new members or entities? Is the group structure con-stant or changing in patterned ways over time? At the group level, cohesiveness may be defined as the extent to which the group maintains its structure (pattern) or maintains an effective structure within its environment. In studying cohesion itself, one may look at the forces (internal and external) that created the group and how well each force operates to maintain the pattern. Henderson (1985), for example, compared the Vietnam War era personnel structures and policies of North Vietnam-ese, U.S., Soviet, and Israeli units as they affected cohesion and will to fight. On the other hand, one may be interested less in structure formation or maintenance (i.e., cohesion as a dependent variable) than in the impact of variations in structure or degree of cohesiveness on other dependent variables such as performance (i.e., cohe-sion as an independent variable). Likewise, cohesiveness can be treated as a suppres-sor or control variable.

From the perspective of interacting group members, cohesion can be looked at in terms of the patterns of the interaction as depicted by frequency, occurrence of rituals of integration and support (e.g., crisp saluting), and the following of norms and cus-toms. At the level of group member interaction, cohesiveness may be defined as the extent to which the members all pull together to accomplish their purpose or mis-sion. Note that a decline in group cohesion can occur at the group structure level, for example, when soldiers in a unit are separated due to a sandstorm or a number are lost as a result of combat. In comparison, a decline in group cohesion can occur at the interaction level if members of the unit no longer work together to accomplish the mission, due to the development of poor interpersonal relationships or other incapacity to work together. The result is the same—reduced cohesion—but based on different causal factors and processes at different levels of analysis.

From the individual-level perspective, cohesion can be looked at in terms of a per-son's perceptions of the group, such as one's strength of identification with the group, attachment to the group and its members, and perceptions of the group as a source of rewards. At the individual level, group cohesiveness may be defined as the extent to which members are attached to the group and committed to its purpose or mission. Note that a decline in cohesion can occur at the individual perception level if one or more individuals no longer care much about the group or its purpose. This decline can occur even though those individuals still remain as part of the group structure and pull together with others to accomplish the group mission, due to external norms or mechanisms of social control—that is, they are just going through the motions. In a sense then, cohesion (or cohesiveness) is a useful concept because it is ambiguous and flexible, partly as a result of being a multilevel concept.

Earlier definitions of cohesion reflected the behavioral science environment of their times (see Siebold & Lindsay, 1999). When psychology tried to present itself as a hard science, a *field-theory* definition was used—that is, cohesion was defined as the resultant of all forces holding the group together. Many have noted that this definition is a tautology. As a minimum, the definition should clarify that the forces holding the military group together are both internal (e.g., identity, socialization) and external (e.g., law, regulations, and norms). During the 1980s, military psychologists developed a more fine-grained and complex conceptual approach and pertinent measures (e.g., Marlowe, 1985; Siebold & Kelly, 1988a, 1988b) that took into account the nature of the military group, its leadership structure, and its being embedded in a larger organization.

This more complex conceptualization included components characterized as horizontal bonding, such as peer bonding at the service-member level and at the leader-team level. It also included bonding between the service members and their leaders, known as vertical bonding. These bonds were seen as having both an instrumental or active aspect, as well as an affective or emotional aspect. For example, service-member peer bonding was conceived as based on both pulling together to get the job done (instrumental aspect) and trust in each other (affective aspect). In addition, the conceptualization recognized bonding between the service members, leaders, and their unit and larger-higher units as a whole, which was labeled organizational bonding. The instrumental aspect of organizational bonding was conceptualized as providing an effective organizational environment and climate, such as clear and consistent rules. The affective aspect included unit member pride in being a member of the organization (e.g., see Siebold, 1996). Much of the military psychology research over the last two decades has used some version of this complex conceptualization. The importance of this complex conceptualization is that it allows for a structured analysis of unit cohesion to identify cohesive strength, weakness, or imbalance in specific areas that can be fixed and monitored—that is, the various horizontal, vertical, and organizational bonding components.

The concept of small-unit cohesion raises questions that are also applicable to many behavioral and social science concepts. What are the meaningful independent variables; what are the primary causal factors; what happens over time; and what are relevant criteria or performance outcomes to assess the impact of cohesion? These questions are addressed below. The actual measurement of military group cohesion has been addressed in detail elsewhere (e.g., Bartone & Adler, 1999; Marlowe, 1985; Siebold, 1996; Siebold, 1999; Siebold & Kelly, 1988a, 1988b).

Related Constructs

A number of variable constructs are related to cohesion but should be distinguished from cohesion itself. For example, *morale* can be conceptualized as the emotional reaction of service members to their view, positive or negative, of their immediate situation based on layers of both short-term and long-term influencing factors. This suggests that morale may change quickly if a major factor influencing morale changes (see Britt & Dickinson, this volume). *Esprit de corps* (Clausewitz, 1831/ 1943, Book III, Chapter 5) is a construct that describes the long-term pride and confidence that service members have in being a member of their larger-higher unit. As such, *esprit*, if positive, may maintain and increase the motivation, resilience, and persistence of service-member efforts to accomplish their tasks and mission. *Will-to-fight* (Griffith, 1985), close to *esprit*, is a construct indicating the willingness to fight and determination to win in combat or to achieve the mission. The mean (average) will to win as a variable at the unit level appears to be a good predictor of a unit's motivation to perform well and appears similar in behavior to other organizational bonding variables such as pride. However, it can be a volatile variable difficult to measure in a unit that is not actually knowledgeable about combat or battle-hardened. Some research suggests that will-to-fight may not be as useful a longitudinal measure as cohesion to predict performance or unit staying power over time (e.g., Siebold, 1989).

Teamwork is the coordinated working together by team members (usually to a performance standard) to accomplish their team tasks. *Team motivation* may be conceived of as the amount of effort team members are willing to put forth to accomplish their tasks. *Team cohesiveness* may be conceived of as the extent to which the members try to coordinate with, help out, and back up each other to carry out their combined actions. As such, team cohesiveness is bound up with team action. Success is dependent on members developing their individual skills and competencies, recognizing other members' skills and patterns of behavior (lines of action), and learning how to mesh their joint lines of action so that the performance of the whole team is greater than the sum of its parts. While members may achieve team cohesiveness quickly in the sense of trying to work together, teamwork may require a substantial amount of time and practice to be highly effective.

Theoretical Bases

There are several theoretical approaches to dealing with the development of cohesion and its continuance at the social psychology level of analysis. One approach is collective (public) goods. The theory is that all members of the unit recognize strong cohesion as in their best interest because it enhances their performance and chances of survival (Kviz, 1978). Thus unit members act in a manner to develop and sustain cohesion as a public good and to ostracize free riders who do not contribute to cohesion as a public good. Presumably, the more important the mission is perceived or the more danger there is to unit members, the more critical is the public good of cohesion. The more critical the public good of cohesion, the higher cohesion will tend to be and the stronger the group rules and norms to enforce it. This position is supported by findings by Bartone and Adler (1999) that the perceived unit's ability to perform the mission was consistently over time among the strongest correlates of cohesion. The position is also consistent with the pattern of correlations between squad member cohesion and mission motivation over time in infantry units rotating to the Sinai (Siebold, 1996).

Another approach is to view the development of cohesion in terms of social capital. For example, if an infantry squad is attacking a machine gun in a pill box, it is to the collective advantage of the squad to have the machine gun taken out. It is to the advantage of any given member of the squad, however, to let someone else destroy the pill box. If two or three squad members take the lead in destroying the machine gun in the pill box on this occasion, the squad, if it remains intact over time, can call on others to take the lead the next occasion extra risk is required. Further, if certain squad members take on more risk over many occasions, other squad members can reward this behavior with deference and increased status for those who assume greater reasonable risk for the benefit of the group. This increased status can be used to obtain general benefits for those squad members in other situations. Thus the existence of a cohesive group over time allows for social credits or capital to build up and be allocated to support norms and values that benefit the group (Coleman, 1988a, 1988b). With a stable network of group members over time, reciprocal exchanges and practices tend to become norms that are enforced by that network. Psychologically, the development of these norms transfers control over actions from individual members to the group as a whole and is experienced as an external group constraint on behavior. The service member does not want to let his/her buddies down, and further, can feel the strong social support of the group so as to elevate the service member to actions above and beyond the call of duty. The dense mutual obligations and high trustworthiness of the social network (i.e., with substantial social capital) in small units that have experienced combat may result in service members electing to reenlist or otherwise stay with their buddies and unit rather than leave them for the less dense, fragmented networks they find in other social groupings. Given the influence over its members of the strong closed network of the tight-knit military unit, it is not surprising that the unit adopts totemic symbols to stand for the group and imbue it with spiritual meaning.

A third theoretical approach to the development of unit cohesion is in terms of social function. A military unit is involved with the use of extreme lethal force. Therefore, there is a need for substantial social control over unit members so that lethal force is used safely and in accordance with the rules of engagement. This substantial social control structure (e.g., law, regulation, norms) with heavy penalties for failure to comply makes it necessary for service members to develop cohesiveness to act within the control structure and avoid penalties. Research results consistently show the strong correlations of rule clarity and leadership competency with horizontal peer cohesion that support this approach (e.g., Siebold, 1996).

Finally, there is an approach that looks at the development of cohesion in terms of the natural development of human social groups, in which the members look to the group to obtain basic needs such as help, support, sociability, and protection (Cooley, 1909/1962). Cohesion develops to enable the human group to serve the basic needs of its members through mutual give and take. Research on units over time (e.g., Bartone & Adler, 1999; Siebold, 1996) reports that leaders' concern for their soldiers and the learning climate in the unit are important to peer cohesion and appear to support the approach to cohesion in terms of group development. Nonetheless, whatever theoretical approach one might use, service members generally try to develop and maintain small-unit cohesion because it is to their individual and collective advantage. Cohesion leads to more efficient and effective performance, better use of resources, stronger social support and comfort, and greater chances of survival.

Cohesion over Time

It is important to view group cohesiveness as a property that varies over time rather than something a group possesses or does not. Data suggest that groups go through specific stages (e.g., forming, storming, norming, performing; Tuckman, 1965) and that many service members and groups, in which most members joined together, go through a U-shaped pattern of cohesion over time (e.g., Siebold, 1989, 1996). This pattern, similar to organizational socialization in industry, starts with cohesion being high at the start, in a sort of honeymoon period, then starting to decline after the first 60 to 90 days, and continuing to decline for about a year. After "hitting bottom," cohesion starts to increase to a sustainable level about halfway back to that at the initial honeymoon period (see Figure 9.3). While this U-shaped pattern seems to fit most manpower intensive units, such as light infantry, it appears to be muted in equipment-dominated units such as armor and in intense personal training situations such as learning a foreign language. In contrast, Bartone and Adler (1999) found an inverted U-shaped pattern in a medical task force where the task force members developed the highest cohesiveness when most involved in using their skills to help others. But the affective aspects of cohesion and service-member mission

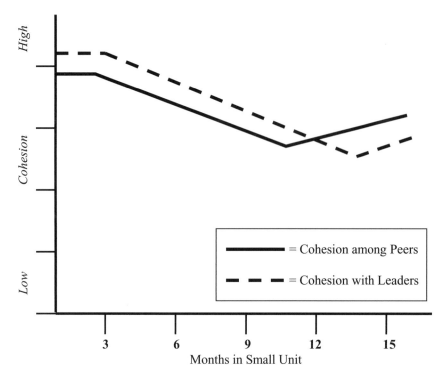

Figure 9.3
Perceived Cohesion Among Service Members Over Time

motivation are the most volatile variables with the biggest differences among small units. It is these variables that decrease the most over time to produce the typical U-shaped pattern (Siebold, 1989, 1996), most likely because service members increasingly perceive over time that they are not fully using their skills or accomplishing a mission as meaningful as they once saw it.

A frequently asked question is approximately how long it takes to develop cohesion in a unit. The answer is that there is already some cohesion in a unit at any given time. The question really being asked is, How long does it take high team cohesiveness to develop so that the group can exhibit highly coordinated teamwork and a strong ability to withstand stress? That answer is open ended, depending on difficulty of skill development to its standards and available training time and resources. As an anecdote, consider an Asian middle-aged man and a young black service member waiting at a bus stop near an Army post. An elderly white lady with a cane walks up to the bus stop but slips on some ice and falls down. Immediately, without talking, the Asian man and service member together help the elderly lady up, pick up her cane, and give it to her. The men ask if the lady is all right. She answers that she is and, although embarrassed, thanks the men. In the anecdote, the actors use cultural understandings to define the situation, their potential roles in it, and take immediate coordinated and cohesive action without the need for words or specialized training or skills and despite the lack of common demographic characteristics. Thus, the development of cohesion is only partially time-dependent and can result from cultural ritual interaction or joint action that is succeeding in a specific context.

Another question frequently asked is how long members, especially leaders, of a unit have to be stabilized to ensure the development of cohesion. The quick answer is that there is no fixed time requirement and that cohesiveness in a unit does not depend on any given member. Research data showed, for example, that the time a unit leader has spent in a unit has little relation to its cohesion. The rationale is that especially good leaders who can build strong cohesion are also more likely to be promoted quickly, thereby spending less time as the leader of a specific unit. This higher turnover limits the time these especially good leaders have to build cohesion in their unit; less exceptional leaders with more time may build an equally high level of cohesion in their units.

Leadership, Causality, and Cohesion

A cohesive unit is a resource leaders use to promote unit functioning and performance, but leaders are also responsible for developing cohesion as a resource in a number of ways. Leaders are directly responsible for building and monitoring the vertical cohesion between themselves and those above and below them in the organizational pyramid. Vertical bonding is thus a dimension of leadership. Leaders are responsible for facilitating cohesive interaction with leaders at their own level and among the soldiers, so that the soldiers can develop peer bonding and perform up to their capability. Leaders are responsible for fostering organizational cohesion—that is, integration between the service member and his/her larger unit—by building pride and support for the mission. Additionally, leaders must insure that there is rule clarity, that service members can achieve their goals, and that service-member needs are met. In doing this, leaders must manage the "commons" or cultural infrastructure and climate of their unit (Siebold, 1993; Siebold & Kelly, 1987a), which become a context for cohesion. In some cases, improving unit cohesion may be simply a matter of changing the subunit and individual reward structure in an area of endeavor, for example, to one of attaining standards rather than direct competition (e.g., Blades, 1986) or shortening the time between exemplary service-member action and reward for the action (Lindsay & Siebold, 1992). In any case, leadership is a key causal context in which military group cohesion is embedded. Leadership can act as an independent variable affecting a dimension of cohesion or as a conditional variable heightening or dampening the impact of cohesion on various dependent variables.

Some earlier studies of cohesion were designed to look at one or a few independent variables with cohesion as a dependent variable. Some of these independent variables were similarity of personal characteristics, degree of mutual interdependence, and length of time service members were together to share common experiences. Most of these independent variables had only modest or insignificant correlations with cohesion. For example, Siebold and Lindsay (1999) found that correlations of soldier racial-ethnic group proportions, marital status, and housing arrangements with perceived cohesion were neither significant nor sizeable.

Other earlier studies treated cohesion as an independent variable and looked at its impact on dependent variables such as service members' ability to withstand stress, reduction in discipline problems, unit performance, and other positive outcomes. With the exception of equipment-dominated units and groups focusing intensely on learning their separate individual skills and competencies (e.g., foreign language training), well-measured unit cohesion was usually moderately and significantly correlated with these outcome measures. The correlations were stronger when cohesion was matched up with the appropriate outcome measures, such as the preparation and execution phases of performance rather than the planning phase. The latter phase should be linked to leader team and/or staff cohesion rather than general unit cohesion.

Later studies and analyses were designed to go beyond the basic independent–dependent variable approach and look at cohesion as one of a system of interrelated, mutually influencing variables, or at least variables that are subject to conditional causality. For example, Blades (1986) found in a sample of 45 Army mess hall work groups that the correlation between cohesion and performance was $r = .69$; $n = 12$; $p < .05$ when the group members had high ability and motivation, but was $r = -.52$; $n = 10$; *nsf* when the group had low member ability and motivation, and was $r = .08$; $n = 23$; *nsf* when the group members were either low in ability or in motivation. Likewise, Sternberg and Siebold (1991) found in a sample of 75 infantry and armor platoons from three rotations through the U.S. Army National Training Center, Fort Irwin, CA, that the correlation between platoon mean Armed Forces Qualification Test (AFQT) ability scores and mission accomplishment, as measured by independent observer/controllers, was $r = .41$; $n = 35$; $p < .01$ where platoon member horizontal bonding was above average and r = −.23; n = 36; *nsf* where that bonding was below average. Similarly, Sternberg and Siebold found that where platoon members had low military skills but high platoon member cohesion, the relation between average AFQT level and mission accomplishment was r = .61, n = 18, $p < .01$. On the other hand, where platoon members had high skill level but low member cohesion, there was a negative correlation between average AFQT level and performance, r = −.45, n = 15, $p < .05$. In essence, these findings indicate that it is insufficient to look at how much variations in independent variables cause different degrees of cohesion or how much different degrees of cohesion cause variations in some desired outcome such as group performance, reenlistment rates, or group member average feelings of satisfaction or well-being. A more all-encompassing model or approach is needed that incorporates mutual and conditional influences.

Nevertheless, if cohesion, related variables, and performance are measured well and appropriately, one should expect to obtain a correlation of about r = .4 between the horizontal (peer) bonding components and subsequent unit performance (Oliver et al., 1999). Further, if units are divided between those with more effective leadership and those with less effective leadership, one should find the correlation between peer cohesion and performance to be about r = .6 in units with more effective leadership but much lower and not significant under less effective leadership. Two points are important to highlight here. One is that good leaders provide the context in which proactive (as opposed to defensive) peer bonding becomes more meaningful and likely to translate into performance. In contrast, less effective leaders seem less able to provide the context that makes cohesion meaningful. The second point, quite critical, is that the slope of the relation between peer cohesion and performance is so high that small increases in cohesion correspond to large differential increases in unit performance.

The Future of Cohesion

Personnel Policy

There has been substantial attention given to appropriate personnel policies designed to encourage unit cohesion and, thereby, performance. For example, Henderson (1985) presents many tables of unit personnel policies and associated features that he suggests, explicitly or implicitly, would result in high cohesion and good combat performance. The essence of these policies is a substantial increase in physical, social, and emotional control over the unit member by the unit leaders and other members. This includes control over rewards, punishment, on- and off-duty time, basic needs such as food and housing, and training and career development. The thrust is to greatly lessen the influence of the centralized bureaucracies that use universalistic criteria and highly rationalized procedures and to greatly increase the power of the unit leaders and small group to control the events, actions, and life situation of the service member through particularistic criteria useful to the unit.

A central theme of many proposals aimed at increasing cohesion is keeping service members or leadership teams together for longer periods of time so that they have the opportunity to build stronger, more adaptive joint lines of action. Such personnel stabilization requires system adjustments in terms of promotions, the scheduling of out-of-unit training, rotational assignments, change-of-station patterns, reenlistments, and schedules of end-of-term of service. Basically, it is cheaper to manage personnel and training by individuals and to maximize individual opportunity (individual equity) such as attending institutional training than to manage by blocks of people or units and to maximize unit concerns (unit equity) such as collective training preparation and execution. In the past, military systems have had difficulty providing trained leaders and training resources to the degree needed to help units with stabilized personnel reach their performance potential. Some problems that arose were friction between stabilized cohesive service members who "knew their stuff" and replacement NCOs who were unable to lead them to more advanced training levels. Further, where the personnel and training systems produce cohesive horizontal bonding among service members but poor vertical or organizational bonding, service members may generate group discipline problems or worse performance than if the service members had been less cohesive and motivated (Siebold, 1994). Because of the difficulties and costs of full, long-term stabilization, the services generally adopt the in-between position of freezing personnel turbulence for a number of months (especially before a major training event or deployment) and confining most turbulence to scheduled periods.

Needed Areas of Research

A significant amount of research on cohesion was conducted over the last two decades that improved conceptualization, measurement, and the clarification of causal relations. Yet there is still a major need for a crisp effort that collects longitudinal data on sufficient numbers of service members and units using fine-tuned measures to address more precisely the mutual causation among the more or less standard set of variables (e.g., job and mission motivation) shown in the past to be strong correlates with the various components of cohesion and unit performance and integrity. In essence, the interacting variables need to be modeled or put in an empirical, structured order for clearer theoretical interpretation that goes beyond recent efforts (Bartone & Adler, 1999; Siebold, 1994, 1996).

Another area of cohesion research that has received little public attention but needs further progress is that of social demolition. Most cohesion research has focused on describing cohesion processes and determining how to build cohesion in units. There are other cases, however, where it may be of interest to destroy cohesion, motivation, morale, group integrity, and performance. These cases include enemy formations, smugglers of illegal drugs and other contraband, and loosely connected terrorist groups. Research needs to identify the focal points to apply pressure to demolish or at least weaken these negative organizations and networks.

A third area needing more research on cohesion is that of ad hoc operator networks electronically linked through digital systems to conduct network-enabled warfare. Most operators are trained to operate their own digital equipment and to learn how to do their job using it. There is usually insufficient time, technology, or resources, however, to train with potential role partners at different nodes in a network, whether for staff planning or field operations, such as those using unmanned aerial vehicles. In war, digital equipment operators will be key to information dominance and getting ahead of the decision cycle of the enemy. The operators, however, must learn to work over a network with unfamiliar others without a common operator culture or vocabulary and without a track record of successful interactions that would form a foundation for trust. Much has been learned about the bases for cohesiveness and cohesion-enhanced performance in direct interpersonal groups. Now, research needs to address the bases for indirect, nonpersonal network cohesion.

Summary

For social psychology, cohesiveness can be defined as the extent to which group members maintain a pattern of relationships that allows them to pull together to accomplish their goals or mission, especially under stress. Members and leaders develop and sustain cohesion because it is in their best interest. While numerous principles of cohesion could be listed, cohesion will occur where leaders are skilled in their jobs, can operate well within their organizational systems, and function as good role models who train their subordinates well, treat them fairly, and take care of them within available resources. Cohesion is decreased when that pattern of social relationships is disturbed through excessive turbulence, when there is a change in organizational structure, or if that structure is made less meaningful due to lack of group success in achieving its goals or mission. Cohesion contributes to performance by enhancing efficiency, motivation, discipline, flexibility, and the establishment of joint lines of action among group members, including leaders. The cohesive structure in a unit is increased by skillful leadership, a learning climate, passion for the mission, the fulfillment of member goals and basic needs, and efforts to work well with one's peers. As long as the military carries out its affairs by structured and ad hoc small groups, cohesion will be a key factor, whether the interaction of the service members is carried out in person, electronically, or by other means.

References

Bartone, P. T., & Adler, A. B. (1999). Cohesion over time in a peacekeeping medical task force. *Military Psychology, 11*(1), 85–107.

Blades, J. W. (1986). *Rules for leadership: Improving unit performance.* Washington, DC: National Defense University Press.

Caesar, G. J. (1896). *Caesar's commentaries on the Gallic War* (L. Wallace, Trans.). Philadelphia: David McKay. (Original work published about 51 B.C.)

Carron, A. V. (1982). Cohesiveness in sport groups: Interpretation and considerations. *Journal of Sport Psychology, 4,* 123–138.

Carron, A. V. (1988). *Group dynamics in sport.* London, Canada: Spodym.

Clausewitz, K. von (1943). *On war* (O. J. M. Jolles, Trans.). New York: Modern Library. (Original work published 1831)

Coleman, J. S. (1988a, Spring). Free riders and zealots: The role of social networks. *Sociological Theory, 6*, 52–57.

Coleman, J. S. (1988b). Social capital in the creation of human capital. *American Journal of Sociology, 94*, S95–S120.

Cooley, C. H. (1962). *Social organization.* New York: Schocken. (Original work published 1909)

Craig, T. Y., & Kelly, J. R. (1999). Group cohesiveness and creative performance. *Group Dynamics: Theory, Research and Practice, 3*(4), 243–256.

Griffith, J. (1985). The measurement of "soldier will." In D. H. Marlowe (Ed.), *New Manning System Field Evaluation* (Technical Report No. 1). Washington, DC: Department of Military Psychiatry, Walter Reed Army Institute of Research.

Griffith, J., & Vaitkus, M. (1999). Relating cohesion to stress, strain, disintegration, and performance: An organizing framework. *Military Psychology, 11*(1), 27–55.

Henderson, W. D. (1985). *Cohesion: The human element in combat.* Washington, DC: National Defense University Press.

Hogg, M. A. (1992). *The social psychology of group cohesiveness: From attraction to social identity.* New York: New York University Press.

Kviz, F. J. (1978, Fall). Survival in combat as a collective exchange process. *Journal of Political and Military Sociology, 6*, 219–232.

Lewin, K. (1935). *A dynamic theory of personality* (D. K. Adams and K. E. Zener, Trans.). New York: McGraw Hill.

Lindsay, T. J., & Siebold, G. L. (1992). *The use of incentives in light infantry platoons* (Research Report 1611). Alexandria, VA: U.S. Army Research Institute for the Behavioral and Social Sciences. (DTIC No. AD A240425)

Marlowe, D. H. (Ed.)(1985). *New Manning System Field Evaluation* (Technical Report No. 1). Washington, DC: Department of Military Psychiatry, Walter Reed Army Institute of Research. (DTIC No. AD A162087)

Marrin, A. (1999). *Terror of the Spanish Main: Sir Henry Morgan and his buccaneers.* New York: Dutton.

Moody, J., & White, D. R. (2003). Structural cohesion and embeddedness: A hierarchical concept of social groups. *American Sociological Review, 68*(1), 103–127.

Mudrack, P. E. (1989). Defining group cohesiveness: A legacy of confusion? *Small Group Behavior, 20* , 37–49.

Oliver, L. W., Harman, J., Hoover, E., Hayes, S. M, & Pandhi, N. A. (1999). A quantitative integration of the military cohesion literature. *Military Psychology, 11*(1), 57–83.

Paxton, P., & Moody, J. (2003). Structure and sentiment: Explaining emotional attachment to group. *Social Psychology Quarterly, 66*, 1, 34–47.

Schoomaker, P. J. (2003). Arrival message on assuming the position of the 35th Chief of Staff of the Army, August 1.

Shils, E. A., & Janowitz, M. (1948). Cohesion and disintegration in the *Wehrmacht* in World War II. *Public Opinion Quarterly, 12*(2), 280–315.

Siebold, G. L. (1989, April). *Longitudinal patterns in combat platoon cohesion.* Paper presented at the 1989 Leadership Conference of the Center for Army Leadership, U.S. Army Command and General Staff College, Kansas City, MO.

Siebold, G. L. (1993). Leadership as the management of the commons. In *Proceedings of the 35th Annual Conference of the Military Testing Association* (pp. 667–673). Washington, DC: Office of Personnel and Training, U.S. Coast Guard.

Siebold, G. L. (1994). The relation between soldier motivation, leadership, and small unit performance. In H. F. O'Neil, Jr. & M. Drillings, (Eds.), *Motivation: Theory and research* (pp. 171–190). Hillsdale, NJ: Erlbaum.

Siebold, G. L. (1996). Small unit dynamics: Leadership, cohesion, motivation, and morale. In R. H. Phelps & B. J. Farr (Eds.), *Reserve component soldiers as peacekeepers* (pp. 237–286). Alexandria, VA: U.S. Army Research Institute for the Behavioral and Social Sciences. (DTIC No. ADA321857)

Siebold, G. L. (1999). The evolution of the measurement of cohesion. *Military Psychology, 11*(1), 5–26.

Siebold, G. L., & Kelly, D. R. (1987a). Cohesion as an indicator of command climate. *Proceedings of the Third Annual Leadership Research Conference, 1,* (pp. 19–46). Fort Leavenworth, KS: Center for Army Leadership, U.S. Army Command and General Staff College.

Siebold, G. L., & Kelly, D. R. (1987b). *The impact of unit cohesion on unit performance, morale, and ability to withstand stress: A field exercise example* (Leadership & Management Technical Area Working Paper 87–13). Alexandria, VA: U.S. Army Research Institute for the Behavioral and Social Sciences.

Siebold, G. L., & Kelly, D. R. (1988a). *Development of the Combat Platoon Cohesion Questionnaire* (Technical Report 817). Alexandria, VA: U.S. Army Research Institute for the Behavioral and Social Sciences. (DTIC No. AD A204917)

Siebold, G. L., & Kelly, D. R. (1988b). *Development of the Platoon Cohesion Index* (Technical Report 816). Alexandria, VA: U.S. Army Research Institute for the Behavioral and Social Sciences. (DTIC No. AD A205478)

Siebold, G. L., & Lindsay, T. J. (1999). The relation between demographic descriptors and soldier-perceived cohesion and motivation. *Military Psychology, 11*(1), 109–128.

Sternberg, J. J., & Siebold, G. L. (1991, April). *Relation of platoon AFQT scores to platoon performance at the National Training Center*. Unpublished manuscript.

Tuckman, B. W. (1965). Developmental sequence in small groups. *Psychological Bulletin, 63,* 384–399.

Vaitkus, M. A. (1994). *Unit Manning System: Human dimensions field evaluation of the COHORT company replacement model* (Walter Reed Army Institute of Research Technical Report 94–0017). Fort Detrick, MD: U.S. Army Medical Research and Materiel Command. (DTIC No. AD A285942)

CHAPTER 10

Stress-CARE: An Integrated Model of Individual Differences in Soldier Performance under Stress

Robert R. Sinclair and Jennifer S. Tucker[1]

Both researchers and military planners recognize that stress leads to detrimental effects on performance (cf. Jex, 1998) and that personality traits affect both job performance (e.g.,
Barrick & Ryan, 2003; Hough & Ones, 2001; Hough & Schneider, 1996; Mount & Barrick, 1995) and stress-response processes (Contrada & Guyll, 2001). Relatively little research, however, has considered the joint influence of personality and stress-related processes on soldiers' job performance. Our chapter fills this gap in the current literature by accomplishing four goals. First, we will define the general construct of personality and discuss two approaches to understanding the connection between personality, stress, and job performance. Second, we will describe three forms of individual performance and review empirical research concerning the relationship between personality traits and each of these performance dimensions. Third, we will discuss some of the unique aspects of military settings relevant to personality, stress, and performance research. Fourth, we will discuss several implications for future interventions and directions for future research concerning the application of this model to military settings.

Approaches to the Study of Personality and Job Performance

Funder (2001) defines personality as "an individual's characteristic patterns of thought, emotion, and behavior, together with the psychological mechanisms behind those patterns" (p. 2). As Saucier and Goldberg (2003) note, personality refers to psychological characteristics of individuals that are reasonably (i.e., not completely) stable over time. Thus, Funder's definition distinguishes personality traits from temporary mood states (e.g., angry versus happy), general evaluations (e.g., good versus bad), and physical attributes (e.g., tall versus short). Beyond this common ground, there are a wide variety of theories of personality and definitions of personality constructs. Our chapter describes two approaches to studying personality–performance relationships in military contexts. The personality literature includes a diverse array of theoretical perspectives, however, and we encourage readers to consult other in-depth reviews (e.g., Pervin & John, 1999; Roberts & Hogan, 2001) for literature falling outside the scope of this chapter.

The Five-Factor Model of Personality

Some theorists argue that a taxonomic structure of personality traits is a necessary precondition to establishing a science of personality (e.g., Eyesenck, 1991). One such taxonomy, the five-factor model (FFM, or Big 5 Model) dominates organizational psychology research on personality–performance relationships. The FFM was developed from the lexical research tradition, which suggests that traits are encoded in terms people use to describe themselves and others (Wiggins, 1996). Through many factor-analytic studies, lexical researchers converged on five broad trait dimensions: openness to experience, conscientiousness, extroversion, agreeableness, and neuroticism. FFM adherents view these traits as the highest-level taxonomic structure into which traits can be organized, with each dimension defined by several narrower facets (e.g., Costa & McRae, 1992a; McCrae & Costa, 1999).

Costa and McRae's (1992b) NEO-PI-R, one of the most widely used FFM questionnaires, defines each FFM dimension in terms of six facets. Neuroticism reflects emotional vulnerability, anxiety, angry hostility, depression, self-consciousness, and impulsiveness. Extroversion reflects interpersonal warmth, gregariousness, assertiveness, energy, excitement seeking, and positive emotionality. Agreeable people tend to be trusting, straightforward, altruistic, compliant, modest, and kind. Openness to experience is associated with imagination, humor, an interest in the arts and culture, and unconventional values and ideas. Finally, conscientious people typically are described as competent, orderly, dutiful, ambitious, disciplined, and careful.

For the most part, FFM-driven performance research tests behavioral-consistency hypotheses linking the behavioral content of FFM dimensions to the behavioral content of a particular job. Thus, because extroversion measures tap social behavior, a researcher might hypothesize that extroversion predicts leader effectiveness, because social interaction is an important component of leadership. Such relationships do not necessarily explain *how* personality traits affect performance. Nonetheless, researchers have accumulated a great deal of research linking FFM traits to performance in many occupational settings.

Despite this large body of empirical research, both personality theorists (Block, 1995; Eyesenck, 1991; Zuckerman, 1992) and industrial psychologists (Hough, 1992) have leveled many criticisms at the FFM. Some researchers contend that more narrow constructs, such as facets of the FFM dimensions, are better predictors of performance and may be more helpful for constructing theories about human behavior (Paunonen & Nicol, 2001). Others have proposed alternative trait classification schemes ranging from the three factors of Eyesenck's PEN model (cf. Eyesenck & Eyesenck, 1991) to the 16 factors of Catell's 16 PF (cf. Cattell, Eber, & Tatsuoka, 1970). Still others have debated whether personality traits need to be linked to physiological systems and whether factor analysis is an appropriate strategy for developing trait models. FFM proponents have vigorously responded to most of these criticisms (e.g., Costa & McRae, 1992b; 1995; Goldberg & Saucier, 1995), and it seems safe to conclude that, although the FFM may not be *the* model of personality, it provides a useful foundation for studies of individual differences in organizational behavior.

Some FFM-related research focuses on compound traits (sometimes referred to as syndromes) reflecting combinations of the FFM dimensions. For example, occupational personality scales assess personality constructs related to work performance in a specific setting. Ones and Viswesvaran (2001) distinguish job-focused occupational personality scales (JOPS) and criterion-focused occupational personality scales (COPS). JOPS capture traits necessary for success in a particular job, such as the Sales Potential and Managerial Potential scales of the Hogan Personality Inventory (Hogan & Hogan, 1995); COPS predict specific behaviors relevant to several occupations. Ones and Viswesvaran (2001) present validity evidence for four COPS (tests of integrity, drug and alcohol use, stress tolerance, and customer service) which appear to be compounds of conscientiousness, agreeableness, and neuroticism. One interesting direction for future research might be the development of COPS or JOPS specifically designed to predict performance in military settings.

The Stress-CARE Personality Process Model

A second personality approach focuses on identifying specific psychological processes that explain how personality traits affect job performance or how stress might change the nature of the personality–performance relationship. We call our version of this approach the stress-CARE personality process model (or simply, the stress-CARE model) as depicted in Figure 10.1. Whereas the FFM represents an empirically derived taxonomy of personality traits, the stress-CARE model is an amalgamation of several narrow traits, each with a well-developed theoretical foundation.[2] The stress-CARE model groups these constructs into cognitive, affective, and self-regulatory traits. Cognitive traits include externally directed cognitions such as hardiness and internally directed cognitions such as core self-evaluations. Affective dispositions refer to positive and negative affect. Self-regulatory traits refer to goal orientations and self-control. The stress-CARE model assumes all of these traits are somewhat plastic; they may develop, decline, or remain unchanged depending on the nature of an individual's interactions with the world.

The largest bolded arrows pointing from each trait cluster to the stages of the stress-response process in Figure 10.1 reflect primary propositions about trait–stress–performance relationships. The dashed and nonbolded arrows represent other direct effects of personality traits on the stress-response process, trait-stress

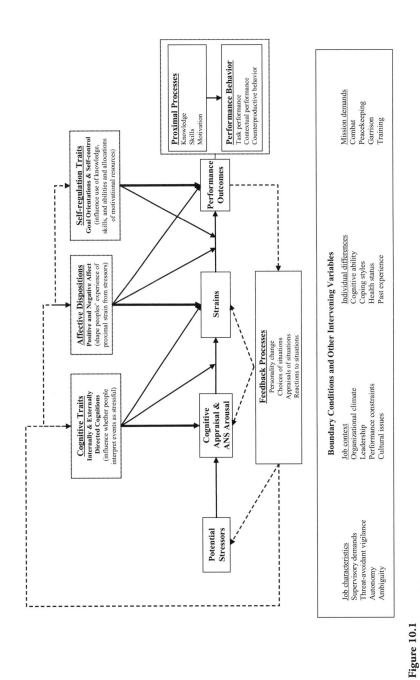

Figure 10.1
Stress-CARE Model

Self-regulation Traits
Goal Orientations & Self-control
(influence use of knowledge,
skills, and abilities and allocations
of motivational resources)

Affective Dispositions
Positive and Negative Affect
(shape peoples' experience of
proximal strain from stressors)

Cognitive Traits
Internally & Externally
Directed Cognitions
(influence whether people
interpret events as stressful)

Proximal Processes
Knowledge
Skills
Motivation

Performance Behavior
Task performance
Contextual performance
Counterproductive behavior

Performance
Outcomes

Strains

Cognitive
Appraisal &
ANS Arousal

Potential
Stressors

Feedback Processes
Personality change
Choices of situations
Appraisals of situations
Reactions to situations

Boundary Conditions and Other Intervening Variables

Job characteristics
Supervisory demands
Threat-avoidant vigilance
Autonomy
Ambiguity

Job context
Organizational climate
Leadership
Performance constraints
Cultural issues

Individual differences
Cognitive ability
Coping styles
Health status
Past experience

Mission demands
Combat
Peacekeeping
Garrison
Training

interactions, and feedback processes. Specifically, we propose that cognitive traits exert their strongest effects on how people appraise potentially stressful events and moderate the relationship between stress appraisals and strain. Affective dispositions should most strongly affect the strain associated with stressful events and should moderate the effects of strain on performance. Self-regulatory traits should influence performance under stress by facilitating task motivation and by enabling people to effectively use their knowledge, skills, and abilities. Finally, the model also recognizes that many other variables influence the stress-response process, including other individual differences, job and organizational characteristics, and mission demands. However, the main goals of the model are to link characteristic patterns of cognitive, affective, and self-regulatory processes with commonly studied elements of the stress-response process and to link these two theoretical traditions with research on the criterion domain of job performance.

Cognitive traits focus on characteristic ways people evaluate situations they find themselves in or characteristic ways people evaluate themselves. Judge and colleagues (e.g., Judge & Bono, 2001; Judge, Ere & Bono, 1998; Judge, Lock & Durham, 1997) describe *core self-evaluations* as one's general self-concept. Positive core self-evaluations include high levels of self-esteem, self-efficacy, and locus of control and low levels of neuroticism. Their research links core self-evaluations to performance (e.g., Judge et al., 1998). Other studies link specific concepts from their model to stress-strain relationships (e.g., Jex, Bliese, Buzzell & Primeau, 2001: self-efficacy and stress) and job performance (e.g., Jones & Wuebker, 1993: safety locus of control and safety performance).

Hardiness (often referred to as dispositional resilience), consists of three cognitive styles, which are ways people interpret potentially stressful events (cf. Maddi, 1990). *Commitment* reflects the ability to find meaning and purpose in potentially stressful events. *Control* refers to the belief that one is capable of effectively responding to a stressful event. *Challenge* describes the tendency to see potentially threatening events as opportunities for personal growth. Thus, hardy individuals see meaning in their lives, feel in control of events affecting them, and prefer challenging environments to safety and security. Several studies demonstrate the relevance of hardiness to military research. For instance, hardiness buffers the effects of army disaster assistance work on illness (Bartone, Ursano, Wright & Ingraham, 1989), buffers the relationship between stress and training performance for Israeli military cadets (Westman, 1990), and buffers the relationship between stress exposure and symptom reports for army reserve personnel mobilized for the Persian Gulf War (Bartone, 1999).

One way to integrate research on hardiness with research on core self-evaluations is to consider the nature of the cognitive processes involved. We regard hardiness as a set of externally oriented appraisal styles focusing on individuals' perceived ability to find meaning in, exert control over, and feel safe in potentially stressful situations. In contrast, core self-evaluations consist of a set of largely internally focused evaluations that people make of their general self-worth and their mastery over specific tasks. Incorporating both core self-evaluations and hardiness into the stress-CARE model yields a set of internally and externally directed cognitive styles that we view as important influences on the stress-response process.

Affective dispositions are among the most heavily studied personality constructs in the stress literature (cf. Contrada & Guyll, 2001). Many affect researchers believe two broad dispositions capture most affective traits: positive and negative affect. People high in positive affect (PA) experience many positive emotions and are described by others as outgoing, energetic, and cheerful. On the other hand, people high in negative affect (NA) experience many negative emotions and are often described as anxious, worrisome, or depressed. Past research demonstrates that PA and NA are distinct dimensions such that people can have high levels of both, either, or neither (cf. Watson, Clark & Tellegen, 1988).

PA and NA may be caused by different underlying biological systems with distinct influences on peoples' interpretations of and reactions to daily events (Gable, Reis & Elliot, 2000; Gray, 1987). Specifically, PA appears to be associated with behavioral activation systems that respond to positive events (e.g., rewards) whereas NA is associated with behavioral inhibition systems that respond to negative events (e.g., punishments). Researchers afford NA a critical role in the stress-response process. Although PA is associated with organizationally beneficial behavior (George, 1996), less research has examined the effects of PA on stress-response processes. However, because PA and NA have distinct biological bases, we expect them both to affect the strain people experience in response to stress, with higher PA being beneficial and higher NA being detrimental.

A third set of personality constructs focus on self-regulatory traits. Baumeister (2001) defines self-regulation as "the processes by which the self alters or preserves its inner states so as to achieve various goals and meet certain standards" (p. 299). He proposes that many of the contemporary problems that beset industrialized nations, such as crime, substance abuse, and sexually transmitted diseases, are at least in part related to failures of self-control. Baumeister's ego depletion model treats self-control as a limited but renewable resource. Thus, people expend self-regulatory resources to control their behavior (e.g., to suppress impulses). If they expend too many resources, they may exhaust their capacities for self-control. People also recover resources over time, however, and may even strengthen their self-regulatory ability. Thus, self-regulatory processes resemble human muscles in that people have a finite amount of self-regulatory capacity, which becomes exhausted through effort (e.g., similar to lifting heavy weights), may be recovered following use (similar to resting after physical activity), and develops through repeated use over time (e.g., similar to the benefits of physical exercise).

Baumeister's research demonstrates that, in the short term, effortful self-regulation is associated with several negative outcomes, including lowered physical stamina, less task persistence, weaker self-control, and tendencies to respond passively to unpleasant situations. However, little research has applied his model to work behavior. Cox (2000) described self-control as one aspect of leaders' moral development. She found that state government supervisors' ratings of self-control (e.g., impulsivity, unreliability) predicted their followers' ratings of how much they trusted their supervisor.

Interestingly, under more stressful conditions, leaders' self-control ratings were more strongly related to their followers' trust. Such findings suggest that self-regulatory processes are particularly important in demanding situations, such as those faced by military personnel on combat deployments. Moreover, because self-regulation consumes motivational resources, self-control may be more important for discretionary aspects of job performance and for controlling impulses. For example, when combat stress depletes soldiers' ego resources, they may be less willing to volunteer for extra assignments and may have difficulty controlling impulses (e.g., engaging an enemy when mission rules prohibit it).

A second approach to self-regulation focuses on the role of motivational traits in the goal orientation process (Kanfer & Heggestad, 1997). This research draws from goal theories of motivation to describe dispositional aspects of goal selection, goal commitment, and performance. Kanfer and Heggestad describe two central motivational processes that have dispositional elements and influence goal-related motivation. *Emotion-control* processes regulate individuals' experiences of performance anxiety, off-task distraction, and frustration while learning tasks. For example, general anxiety and fear of failure are traits indicating a lack of emotion control. *Motivation-control* processes regulate desires to perform well and to perform better than others. Examples of motivation-control traits include personal mastery (desire to perform at high levels) and competitive excellence (desire to outperform others). Kanfer and Heggestad review research linking goal orientations to stress resistance and to performance under different levels of task demands. Other research suggests that goal-related traits may influence performance in extreme environments. For instance, Sandal (1999) concluded that strong achievement orientation, a form of motivational control, helps people cope with the demands of extreme environments such as space, submarines, and polar expeditions.

Personality and Job Performance

Campbell and colleagues define job performance as "goal-relevant actions that are under the control of the individual, regardless of whether they are cognitive, motor, psychomotor, or interpersonal" (Campbell, McCloy, Oppler & Sager, 1993, pp. 40–41). Campbell et al. (1993) also suggested that the effects of distal individual differences (attitudes, values, traits, etc.) on performance are completely mediated by the proximal effects of job-related knowledge, skills, and motivation. Other researchers have elaborated on this proposition by describing additional mediators and moderators of the personality–performance relationship including situational demands, cognitive ability, and work attitudes (Barrick, Mitchell & Stewart, 2003; Johnson, 2003; Robertson & Callinan, 1998). Despite differences among these models, they all emphasize that personality influences performance by enhancing or undermining one's task motivation and by hindering or facilitating one's ability to gather and/or use performance-related knowledge, skills, and abilities.

Campbell et al.'s (1993) model assumes that one common set of proximal psychological processes accounts for job performance (i.e., motivation, knowledge, skills).

Each specific form of performance, however, should have a different profile of distal antecedents that affect those proximal processes. Thus, at least three broad dimensions—task performance, contextual performance, and counterproductive work behavior—may be distinguished in terms of their conceptual content and their relations with various FFM dimensions. Table 10.1 summarizes several meta-analyses concerning the relationship between the FFM and these performance dimensions. Meta-analyses combine the results of several different studies so that the figures in the table represent the best available estimates of the "true" relationship between each FFM trait and each performance outcome.[3] Most of these relationships are based on thousands of people, several different personality questionnaires and multiple sources of performance data, including both subjective ratings and objective indicators. In the sections below, we describe some of these findings for task performance, contextual performance, and counterproductive work behavior.

Task Performance

Task performance consists of behaviors involved in the production of goods and services or activities that sustain the technical core of the organization. The extensive criterion development and validation work of Project A, the Army Selection and Classification Project, suggested two distinct components of entry-level soldiers' task performance (Campbell, McHenry & Wise, 1990). *Core technical proficiency* concerns tasks central to soldiers' primary job duties, such as a mechanic's mechanical proficiencies. *General soldiering proficiency* reflects general soldiering tasks, such as wearing protective gear and reading grid coordinates on military maps. Also, at higher levels of the command hierarchy, task performance includes management and administration, as well as leadership and supervision (Campbell et al., 1993; Campbell, Gasser & Oswald, 1996).

Table 10.1 shows several meta-analyses focused on overall job performance,[4] task performance, and leadership. Performance modeling research usually assumes that task performance is more strongly related to individual knowledge and ability than to motivation (cf. Borman & Motowidlo, 1993). As our results show, however, most FFM traits predicted at least some task performance outcomes. In particular, conscientiousness predicted nearly all the criteria, usually with somewhat stronger relationships than other FFM traits. Given that conscientiousness reflects dutifulness, achievement striving, and organization, this is not surprising. Conscientious employees should be goal-oriented and organized in their approach to accomplishing work tasks. Most of the FFM dimensions predicted performance in occupations requiring more interpersonal interaction (e.g., performance on teams, ratings of interpersonal behavior), and all FFM traits, except agreeableness, predicted the leadership performance criteria. Finally, we also examined performance in specific occupations. These effects were fairly consistent with the rest of the analyses. Conscientiousness obtained the largest and most consistent effects across occupations, with more varied estimates for other traits.

Table 10.1
Selected Meta-Analyses of the Relationship Between Five-Factor Model (FFM) Traits and Job Performance

Criteria	True Score Correlations and Validities for the FFM				
	Conscientiousness	Emotional Stability	Extraversion	Agreeableness	Openness
Task Performance					
Overall and task performance					
Overall performance[1]	.20ρ_v[a]	.13ρ_v[a]	.09ρ_v	.11ρ_v	.06ρ_v
Overall performance[2]	.22ρ[a]	.08ρ	.13ρ	.07ρ	.04ρ
Overall performance (European samples)[3]	.15ρ[a]	.13ρ[a]	.08ρ	.01ρ_cv	.06ρ[a]
Overall job performance—Teams[4]	.21ρ[a]	.27ρ[a]	.22ρ[a]	.33ρ[a]	.16ρ[a]
Overall job performance—Dyadic[4]	.29ρ[a]	.12ρ[a]	.07ρ[a]	.13ρ[a]	.17ρ[a]
Job proficiency[1]	.22ρ_v[a]	.14ρ_v[a]	.09ρ_v	.10ρ_v	.05ρ_v
Job proficiency[2]	.23ρ[a]	.07ρ	.10ρ	.06ρ	-.03ρ
Task performance[1]	.15ρ_v	.13ρ_v[a]	.06ρ_v[a]	.07ρ_v	-.01ρ_v
Leadership criteria					
Overall leadership[5]	.28ρ[b,c]	.24ρ[b,c]	.31ρ[b,c]	.08ρ[b]	.24ρ[b,c]
Leader emergence[5]	.33ρ[b,c]	.24ρ[b]	.33ρ[b,c]	.05ρ	.24ρ[b,c]
Leader effectiveness[5]	.16ρ[b]	.22ρ[b,c]	.24ρ[b,c]	.21ρ[b]	.24ρ[b,c]
Performance in social settings					
Jobs requiring interpersonal interaction[4]	.26ρ[a]	.18ρ[a]	.14ρ[a]	.21ρ[a]	.17ρ[a]
Interacting with Others – Teams[4]	.17ρ[a]	.25ρ[a]	.16ρ[a]	.35ρ[a]	.07ρ[a]
Interacting with Others—Dyadic[4]	.23ρ[a]	.14ρ[a]	.13ρ[a]	.22ρ[a]	.12ρ[a]
Supervisor ratings of interactions[4]	.20ρ[a]	.19ρ[a]	.14ρ[a]	.27ρ[a]	.10ρ[a]
Interacting with others—dyadic[4]	.23ρ[a]	.14ρ[a]	.13ρ[a]	.22ρ[a]	.12ρ[a]

Table 10.1 Continued

Overall performance in specific occupations

Performance in civilian occupations[8]	.13ρ[a]	.11ρ[a]	.09ρ	.01ρ	.05ρ
Performance in military occupations[8]		.27ρv[a]	.10ρ		
Sales jobs[1]	.26ρv[a]	.13ρv[a]	.15ρv[a]	.05ρv	.04ρv[a]
Sales jobs[2]	.23ρv[a]	.07ρv	.15ρv	.00ρv	-.02ρv[a]
Customer service jobs[1]	.25ρv[a]	.12ρv[a]	.11ρv	.17ρv[a]	.15ρv[a]
Managerial jobs[1]	.17ρv	.12ρv[a]	.12ρv[a]	-.04ρv	-.03ρv
Managerial jobs[2]	.22ρv[a]	.08ρv	.18ρv[a]	.10ρv[a]	.08ρv
Skilled/Semiskilled jobs[1]	.15ρv	.08ρv	.01ρv	.10ρv	-.02ρv
Skilled/Semiskilled jobs[2]	.21ρv[a]	.12ρv	.01ρv	.06ρv	.01ρv
Professionals jobs[2]	.20ρv[a]	-.13ρv	-.09ρv	.02ρv[a]	-.08ρv
Police jobs[2]	.22ρv	.10ρv[a]	.09ρv[a]	.10ρv[a]	.00ρv

Contextual performance

Job dedication[1]	.18ρv	.13ρv[a]	.05ρv	.08ρv	.01ρv
Interpersonal facilitation[1]	.16ρv[a]	.16ρv[a]	.10ρv	.10ρv[a]	.05ρv
Altruism (self & other ratings)[6]	.22Mρ[b]			.13Mρ[b]	
Altruism (only other ratings)[6]	.04Mρ				
Generalized compliance (all rating sources)[6]	.30Mρ[b]			.11Mρ[b]	
Generalized compliance (only other ratings)[6]	.23Mρ[b]				

Counterproductive behaviors

Absenteeism (absence of)[7]	.06ρv	-.04ρv	-.08ρv	-.04ρv	-.00ρv
Deviant behavior (absence of)[7]	.26ρv[a]	.06ρv	-.01ρv	.20ρv[a]	-.14ρv

ρ = estimated corrected correlation (both predictor and criterion); ρv = true (operational) validity (criterion only); Mρ = mean population corrected correlations estimates. Superscripts denote original sources of the estimates: 1 = Hurtz & Donovan, 2000; 2 = Barrick & Mount, 1991; 3 = Salgado, 1997; 4 = Mount, Barrick, & Stewart, 1998; 5 = Judge, Bono, Ilies, & Gerhardt, 2002; 6 = Organ & Ryan, 1995; 7 = Salgado, 2002; 8 = Salgado, 1998.
Bolded correlations are meaningfully different from zero using the following criteria: a = 90 percent credibility value/interval excludes zero; b = 95 percent confidence interval excludes zero; c = 80 percent credibility interval excludes zero around the sample-weighted mean r.
excludes zero; c = 80 percent credibility interval excludes zero; d = 95 percent confidence interval excludes zero around the sample-weighted mean r.

We located only two meta-analyses that directly compared personality–performance relationships in army and civilian occupations. Salgado (1998) found that emotional stability and conscientiousness predicted performance across occupations and criteria in civil samples, but only emotional stability predicted performance in military samples. Salgado notes generalizability concerns with his findings because all of the military studies examined pilot training proficiency. The results from his study, therefore, may not apply to other military populations. Tett, Jackson, and Rothstein (1991) found that personality traits were stronger predictors of performance in military samples. They did not distinguish, however, among specific measures of personality within the military samples. Tett et al. cautioned that when a single large study (Project A) was removed from the analyses, there were no differences between military and civilian populations. These studies raise questions about whether civilian personality research generalizes to military samples. The unanswered questions from this research, however, prevent definitive conclusions about civilian–military differences.

Taken as a whole, we draw three general conclusions from the task performance findings: (a) conscientiousness consistently predicts performance across most occupations; (b) other personality traits predict performance in some, but not all occupations. and (c) personality matters more in jobs requiring interpersonal interaction or leadership. These findings establish the importance of understanding the demands of a particular job or occupational setting when conducting personality research. Future research should investigate whether specific trait–performance relationships differ across specific civilian and military settings. For example, the demands of infantry units in combat have few, if any, civilian analogues and also are quite different from other military jobs. The personality-based predictors of performance in combat infantry positions may be quite different from the predictors of performance in civilian settings or less demanding military settings. On the other hand, supply personnel in garrison settings may not differ from similar civilian jobs. We discuss some of these issues in the context of stress research later in this chapter. At the very least, we caution military readers to carefully consider the nature of the sample and the occupation being studied when evaluating the potential relevance of civilian performance research for military applications.

Contextual Performance

Contextual performance, also called organizational citizenship behavior (OCB; cf. Organ, 1997), supports the organizational, social, and psychological environment in which the technical core functions (e.g., Motowidlo, Borman & Schmit, 1997; Motowidlo & Van Scotter, 1994; Podsakoff, MacKenzie, Paine & Bachrach, 2000). Based on an in-depth literature review, Podsakoff et al. (2000) suggested seven distinct forms of OCB[5]: (a) *helping behavior* (altruism, interpersonal facilitation); (b) *sportsmanship* (tolerating inconveniences, maintaining a positive attitude); (c) *organizational loyalty* (loyal boosterism, spreading goodwill); (d) *organizational compliance* (internalized acceptance of organizational rules and procedures); (e) *individual initiative* (making innovative suggestions; volunteering for extra assignments); (f) *civic virtue* (participation in organizational governance; protecting the organization); and (g) *self-development* (voluntary efforts to improve knowledge, skills, and abilities).[6] Several entry-level soldier performance dimensions from Project A (e.g., Campbell et al. 1993; 1996) fit at least one of these seven OCB dimensions. *Personal discipline* requires adherence to army regulations and traditions, self-control, and a commitment to high standards of conduct and resembles Podsakoff et al.'s (2000) compliance. Similarly, *physical fitness and military bearing* involves maintaining an appropriate military appearance and bearing and staying in good physical condition, and resembles compliance. Finally, *effort and leadership* reflects effort to complete job tasks, perseverance under dangerous conditions, and leadership and support toward peers, and resembles a mix of helping and individual initiative. Thus, we use the term contextual performance as an all-inclusive label for both OCB and these Project A dimensions.

Most researchers describe contextual performance as largely voluntary extrarole behavior not typically found on job descriptions (e.g., Borman & Motowidlo, 1993, Organ, 1988; Organ & Ryan, 1995). Thus, researchers expect personality and attitudinal constructs to be more strongly related to contextual performance whereas they expect task performance to be more strongly related to training, abilities, and job experience (e.g., Borman & Motowidlo, 1993; Borman, Penner, Allen & Motowidlo, 2001). To date, research has generally supported this proposition with military samples (Hurtz & Donovan, 2000; McHenry, Hough, Toquam, Hanson & Ashworth, 1990; Motowidlo & Van Scotter, 1994). As with the task-performance dimensions, conscientiousness appears to be the strongest FFM correlate of contextual performance. Other reviews of personality-based predictors of OCB also support this conclusion (e.g., LePine et al., 2002). Interestingly, LePine et al. (2002) conclude that most forms of OCB have similar antecedents. Most past research on OCB, however, has focused on altruism and generalized compliance; relatively few studies have investigated FFM correlates of the wide range of OCBs identified by Podsakoff et al. (2000). Thus, previous literature indicates the importance of conscientiousness for contextual performance but also highlights the need for further research on FFM traits as predictors of alternate forms of contextual performance.

Counterproductive Workplace Behavior

Counterproductive workplace behavior (CWB) is defined as "any intentional behavior on the part of an organizational member viewed by the organization as contrary to its legitimate interests" (Sackett & DeVore, 2001, p. 145). Sackett and DeVore propose a hierarchical model in which a general CWB construct is organized into narrower constructs, which are subsequently organized into specific CWBs. Some examples of CWB constructs related to the military context include Campbell and colleagues' (1990, 1993) *Maintaining Personal Discipline* and *Physical Fitness/ Military Bearing*. Examples of specific behaviors include acts of insubordination, absences without leave (AWOL), violations of regulations (e.g., failing to maintain a proper appearance or physical fitness), failures to adhere to safety procedures, and criminal acts such as Uniform Code of Military Justice violations (MacDonough, 1991; Trlek, 2003).

As compared with task and contextual performance, far less research has focused on counterproductive behavior, and fewer meta-analyses have investigated the FFM correlates of CWB. The meta-analyses (Table 1) show that conscientiousness and agreeableness are negatively related to deviant behavior, but none of the FFM dimensions predict absenteeism.[7] Other literature also supports the focus on conscientiousness in relation to CWB (cf. Sackett & DeVore, 2001). Specifically, conscientiousness and/or facets of conscientiousness appear to effectively predict integrity-related counterproductive behavior (Hough, 1992; Ones, Viswesvaran & Schmidt, 1993) and maintaining discipline (Campbell et al., 1990). Moreover, the table does not include COPS of integrity, which as we noted earlier, represent a mix of conscientiousness, agreeableness, and neuroticism and predict several forms of counterproductive behavior (Ones & Viswesvaran, 2001).

The Stress-CARE Model and Job Performance

The stress-CARE model focuses on a set of theoretically derived stress-related antecedents of job performance. The Five Factor model develops hypotheses by linking the behavioral content of personality measures to the behavioral content of a job. Although direct studies of personality–performance correlations provide empirical data to guide other research, they do not address the explanatory mechanisms underlying personality–performance relationships. Moreover, although there are some conceptual similarities between the broad FFM dimensions and some of the traits in the stress-CARE model, the stress-CARE traits are narrower constructs, and the model makes relatively specific predictions about how they should be indirectly related to job performance through stress-response processes.

Consistent with Campbell and colleagues' model of job performance (Campbell et al., 1993; 1996), the stress-CARE model proposes that the effects of personality on performance are mediated by knowledge, skills, and motivation. We further assume that stress affects performance by hindering soldiers' use of their knowledge and by undermining their motivation. Thus, personality traits influence how people interpret and respond to potentially stressful events. Their responses either constrain or enhance their ability to use their knowledge and their allocations of motivational resources to task performance. The model depicts several personality effects including direct effects on soldiers' appraisals of potentially stressful events, experiences of strain once they have interpreted an event as stressful, and their performance-related behavior. Traits also may moderate the relationship between cognitive appraisal of stress and the strain associated with those appraisals or between strain and job performance.

The intense nature of many military stressors, coupled with the relative youth of many military personnel, suggests the potential for personality change following experiences of intense stress. Consequently, the stress-CARE model also includes several feedback loops intended to highlight the potential dynamic relationships between stressors, personality traits, and performance. Although some research has addressed the role of occupational experiences in personality development (e.g., Roberts, Caspi & Moffitt, 2003), little attention has been paid to how military experiences might lead to personality changes. Further, peoples' reactions under stress may play a role in later health and performance outcomes. For instance, one study found that although decorated Israeli war heroes experienced higher levels of battlefield stress than other groups, they also had among the highest levels of postwar functioning (Dekel, Solomon, Ginzburg & Neria, 2003). Further, Britt, Adler, and Bartone (2001) found that soldiers with higher levels of hardiness were more likely to believe they were engaged in meaningful work during a deployment and more likely to report long-term benefits from the experience.

Stress and Job Performance in Military Contexts

The forgoing review identified several personality traits that are likely to affect soldiers' performance. In this section, we turn to a discussion of how military stressors may influence readiness and describe a framework for studying the influence of personality variables on the stress-response process. We will identify dimensions of performance deserving of additional attention from personality and stress researchers and point out that personality–performance relationships may change in stressful military settings.

The Stress-Response Process

Bliese and Castro (2003) proposed the soldier adaptation model (SAM) as a research framework to study the effects of stressors on military personnel. They conceptualize the SAM as a meta-theory that may be used to construct specific hypotheses about the effects of stress on deployed soldiers. Drawing from this framework and past organizational psychology research on stress and job performance (cf. Jex, 1998), we distinguish three components of the stress-response process: potential stressors, strains, and performance outcomes.

Potential stressors are events requiring an adaptive response by a worker, including intense role demands, high workload, interpersonal conflict, situational constraints, and perceived control (cf. Jex, 1998). Theories of occupational stress describe several mechanisms through which potential stressors create strain, including (a) the coupling of high work demands with low control (Karasek & Theorell, 1990; Spector, 1998); (b) a lack of fit between one's personality and one's work environment (e.g., Edwards, Caplan & Van Harrison, 1998); and (c) an imbalance between perceived levels of effort and rewards (e.g., Siegrist, 1998). *Strains* are the set of negative responses to stressors. Strains may be cognitive (e.g., distractibility; memory impairment), affective (e.g., irritability, emotional exhaustion), or physical (e.g., fatigue, insomnia) in nature. Consistent with the SAM, we assume that cognitive appraisal processes mediate the stressor–strain relationship, such that events must be appraised as threatening to be experienced as stressful. Finally, *performance outcomes* refer to the consequences of strain for soldier readiness. We assume that strain affects performance by hindering an individual's ability to utilize knowledge, skills, and abilities and by depleting his/her motivational resources.

Stressors in Modern Military Settings

Military research has played a central role in the development of theories of job performance and the role of personality traits as predictors of performance. As we noted above, concerns must be raised about the extent to which research using civilian samples generalizes to the demands of contemporary military roles. Military researchers distinguish three occupational environments in which stressors might affect performance: garrison, training, and deployment (cf. Adler, McGurk, Stetz & Bliese, 2003). Deployment can be further divided into peacekeeping and combat missions. In this section, we describe each of these settings and identify performance issues we view as especially important in stressful military contexts.

Garrison and Training

The garrison setting is most analogous to traditional civilian contexts. Thus, stressors from this setting are most likely to resemble those in the civilian world. Even in garrison settings, however, soldiers may face stressors not commonly experienced by civilian workers. For example, Barrick and Mount (1991) found that openness to experience and agreeableness predicted training proficiency (in civilian and paramilitary occupations). There are several reasons to be cautious about the extent to which this finding generalizes across all military occupations. First, military training often serves as a form of personnel selection (e.g., Navy Seals, Army Rangers, and other Special Forces) in which relatively large attrition is expected. Second, military training can be quite dangerous and stressful, and proficiency in this context may be quite different than in other contexts. Given the size of the literature on personality and military training outcomes (e.g., proficiency, attrition) it seems clear that traits are important predictors of training success. It is unclear, however, to what extent these relationships are attributable to stress-related mechanisms or other issues. Although many military training contexts are presumed to be stressful, there is a need for further research investigating the intersection of stress and personality with training success.

Peacekeeping and Combat

One important issue in military research concerns whether research conducted in garrison and training settings generalizes to peacekeeping and combat deployments (cf. Vineberg & Joyner, 1989). Peacekeeping and combat deployments differ from training and garrison in several ways. Some deployments are characterized by long periods of boredom interrupted by explosive periods of intense stress. Others may be characterized by a need to be constantly vigilant for threats from an unseen (or difficult to recognize) enemy. The fatigue associated with such stressors may lead to substantial decrements in decision-making effectiveness (Cannon-Bowers & Salas, 1998). For example, Larsen (2001) found that the majority of a sample of sleep-deprived junior officers fired on human targets they had initially assumed to be dummies. Further, only one officer who did not fire attempted to warn others. Finally, even preparing for deployment can be quite stressful. Deployments typically involve tremendous logistical demands associated with moving personnel and equipment large distances in short periods of time coupled with family-related stress associated with the impending separation. U.S. military interventions following the September 11, 2001 terrorist attacks have also extensively used National Guard and reserve units, which may be less prepared to cope with the stress of deployments.

Three forms of combat stress have been heavily studied over the years: combat itself, witnessing death/handling bodies, and being a prisoner of war. Both combat and peacekeeping, however, present additional stress-related challenges that have not been widely recognized or studied. A sampling of these includes minefields, extreme poverty, substandard living conditions, lack of privacy, lack of entertainment, interaction with hostile civilian groups and corrupt organizations, terrorist assaults, and the threat of being taken hostage (cf. Adler, Litz & Bartone, 2003). Moreover, some traditional stressors may take on new forms, or be more intense. These include: extended separation from one's family; role ambiguity issues, such as having to learn the norms of a foreign culture; predictability concerns related to being uncertain about the length of one's deployment; self-control demands, such as having to refrain from an aggressive response to confrontations; and workload demands from long shifts, continuous physical work, and so on. The stress associated with these demands may undermine effective performance or stimulate increased counterproductive behavior. Personality-related processes may influence solders' reactions to these stressors even as the experiences shape their personality development.

Adaptive Performance

Effective performance often requires soldiers to function effectively in the "the fog of war," with incomplete or inaccurate information, the need to improvise solutions to unanticipated problems, or both. Accordingly, researchers have become interested in adaptability as a unique form of performance. Pulakos, Arad, Donovan, and Plamondon (2000) describe six components of adaptive performance: (a) solving problems creatively; (b) dealing with uncertain and unpredictable work situations; (c) learning new work tasks, technologies, and procedures; (d) interpersonal adaptability (e.g., flexibility); (e) cultural adaptability (e.g., learning the norms, values, language demands of a new culture), and (f) physical adaptability (e.g., contending with challenging environments). Some research suggests that adaptive performance may be linked to the FFM. For example, LePine, Colquitt, and Erez (2000) found that students with higher levels of openness and lower levels of conscientiousness (i.e., dependability) appeared to be more adaptable to changing task requirements for decision making. This research is compelling, but there is a clear need for studies examining specific dimensions of adaptive performance in more depth. For example, whereas highly conscientious people might perform quite well in relatively structured situations, they might have trouble making decisions during combat missions that may take unpredictable turns and involve difficult to anticipate situations.

Transformational Leadership

The research reviewed above suggests that the effects of personality on performance may differ in jobs that require leadership. Bass's seminal work on transformational leadership is particularly relevant to the study of stress in military contexts (e.g., Bass, 1996; 1998). Bass (1998) describes four characteristics of transformational leadership: idealized influence (e.g., providing an appropriate role model); inspirational motivation (e.g., articulating a vision, challenging subordinates); intellectual stimulation (e.g., creative and novel problem solving); and individualized consideration (e.g., taking a personal interest in subordinates). Judge and Bono (2000) demonstrated that both extraversion and agreeableness are related to transformational leadership. Interestingly, they also concluded that specific facets of openness, extraversion, and agreeableness were better predictors than the respective broad dimensions of these personality constructs.

Much of Bass's work on transformational leadership was conducted in military settings. He and other researchers have shown that transformational leadership predicts performance in stressful circumstances such as combat (cf. Bass, 1996; 1998). However, the personality–leader–behavior relationship also may change under stress. For example, Ployhart, Lim, and Chan (2001) found that openness to experience was a better predictor of transformational leadership ratings under conditions requiring maximum performance (i.e., more demanding conditions), whereas neuroticism predicted performance under typical conditions. Further, Cox (2000) found that leaders' self-regulatory traits more strongly influenced follower trust when leaders reported higher levels of stress. Such findings imply that leaders' personalities either help or hinder their ability to function under stress and that followers are sensitive to these effects. We view the self-regulatory traits as particularly important for leaders under stress and believe that further attention needs to be devoted to exploring the extent to which such traits can be developed.

Military Discipline

Donohue (1993) proposed a model of military discipline that implies that some distinctions between task performance, contextual performance, and counterproductive work behavior may be blurred in military settings. Donohue describes two forms of discipline necessary for a truly committed, excellently performing soldier. Discipline B(ehavior) reflects externally enforced or learned behavioral responses typically referred to as *compliance,* such as obedience, attention to detail, working together, restraint, and stress resistance, which are taught and enforced throughout basic training. Donohue proposes that leaders elicit these behaviors by relying on position power, rewards, and punishments. On the other hand, Discipline A(ttitude) reflects voluntary and self-sustaining behaviors such as courage and initiative. Donohue contends that leaders elicit Discipline A behaviors through visionary and inspiration-al leadership, which stimulates follower identification and internalization of unit goals. One of his key points is that the functions of Discipline A are insufficient (but necessary) for unit effectiveness. That is, soldiers must not only be courageous and demonstrate initiative, they must be willing to engage in behaviors that reflect obedience, self-control, and attention to detail.

Disciplines A and B resemble task and contextual performance but also parallel distinctions between different types of OCB, such as organizational compliance and individual initiative. In either case, understanding distinctions between Disci-pline A and B may be particularly important for military stress and personality research. For example, because Discipline A is more discretionary and more influ-enced by leadership, stress may undermine leaders' ability to encourage Discipline A. Moreover, because leaders need to create meaning for their followers, cognitive styles such as hardiness may be especially relevant to encouraging Disipline A. Disci-pline B behaviors could be more resistant to stress because they are the primary focus of military training. Thus, stress may initially affect courage and initiative and then eventually undermine compliance and self-discipline. Moreover, because Discipline B involves self-control, teamwork, and restraint, it might be more strongly related to self-regulatory processes.

Safety Performance

There has been a surge of interest in psychosocial aspects of safety behavior (e.g., Barling & Frone, 2004; Hofmann & Tetrick, 2003). Given that accidents cause many military casualties, understanding and promoting safety is of obvious impor-tance. Several studies link conscientiousness to safety performance (e.g., Cellar, Nel-son, Yorke & Bauer, 2001; Wallace & Vodanovich, 2003) and link managers' consci-entiousness to accident rates in their units (Thoms & Venkataraman, 2002). Some research, however, suggests conscientiousness may be negatively related to safety behavior under some conditions. For example, aviation research suggests that pilots with higher levels of conscientiousness may be more likely to have accidents (e.g., King, Retzlaff & Orme, 2001; Lardent, 1991). King et al. suggested that the rigidity or inflexibility associated with some facets of conscientiousness hinders pilots' abil-ities to deal with the demands of novel situations, such as in-flight emergencies. Thus, stress and conscientiousness may interact to influence safety performance.

Interventions and Directions

Personality-Oriented Interventions

Personnel selection and classification are the most common trait-based interven-tions. These models attempt to screen personnel during the selection process or match people to jobs based on personality traits. Personality issues receive less attention once soldiers have been screened and placed. Two broad categories of personality-oriented interventions, however, are worthy of future attention.

First, *developmental trait training* consists of an intentional focus on developing a particular personality trait. Although few training programs explicitly state such a focus, such developmental processes are critical to military training. For example, hardiness researchers have made some progress in developmental trait training (cf. Maddi, Kahn & Maddi, 1998), but this area generally has great, relatively untapped, potential.

The second intervention, *compensatory trait training*, involves teaching people requisite sets of skills to compensate for maladaptive aspects of their personalities or to capitalize on their existing personal strengths. Stress management programs that incorporate individual differences are perhaps the best example of such interventions (e.g., Quick, Quick, Nelson & Hurrell, 1997). Further, like many civilian organizations, the U.S. military uses the Myers Briggs Type Inventory (MBTI) and related tools in team building and leader development programs. Such programs provide individuals with personality-related feedback to enhance their effectiveness through personal insight. Although these programs may not be explicitly focused on stress and performance issues, they may reduce stress and enhance performance by increasing peoples' awareness of personal strengths and weaknesses.

One issue with present stress management programs concerns the use of the MBTI in personal development interventions. Gardner and Martinko's (1996) review of empirical research on the MBTI (using managerial samples) suggested that "the low quality of much of this research has undoubtedly undermined the MBTI's reputation and created skepticism about its utility" (p. 58). Consistent with other MBTI literature reviews (e.g., Carlson, 1985), however, they conclude that the reliability and validity evidence is promising enough to warrant further investigation of the MBTI. Thus, we echo Gardner and Martinko's call for more rigorous research on the MBTI. One of the most important directions for such research regards stress management, as very few studies have investigated the MBTI in this specific context (exceptions include Elliot & Maples, 1991; Goodspeed & DeLucia, 1990).

Research Directions

Validating the Stress-CARE Model

The stress-CARE model integrates several distinct lines of prior research. Thus, several construct validation questions need to be examined in future research. First, multivariate studies are needed to examine the complete set of stress-CARE propositions in relation to the components of the stress-response process. Although many studies have focused on subsets of the stress-CARE traits, few (if any) have investigated all the traits in a single study. Second, research should compare the stress-CARE model to the FFM to determine which model provides a better accounting of stress–performance relationships. Third, several of the traits we described in the stress-CARE model cover similar conceptual ground; research should examine whether a more parsimonious list of traits could be identified.

Research on the stress-CARE model also could examine whether other traits play distinct roles in the stress-response process. For instance, self-monitoring refers to the extent to which people observe and control how they appear to other people in social/interpersonal contexts (Snyder, 1987). A meta-analysis by Day, Schleicher, Unckless, and Hiller (2002) showed that self-monitoring is related to several constructs in our model, including perceptions of job stressors (e.g., role ambiguity and conflict), ratings of job performance, and leadership emergence. Self-monitoring might play an important role in individuals' abilities to respond to the shifting demands of garrison, training, peacekeeping, and combat settings.

Applied research has investigated two elements of risktaking that might be related to personality processes: risk perceptions (judgments of the level of risk associated with a situation) and risk proneness or tolerance (usually defined as a tendency or willingness to engage in risky behavior). Risk researchers frequently study the personality trait of sensation-seeking in order to understand risk perceptions and proneness. According to Zuckerman (1979) high-sensation seekers seek thrilling and novel experiences and, as a result, are more likely to engage in risky behavior. Thus, high-sensation seekers should be more likely to choose risky occupations and less likely to perceive potentially dangerous events as risky, but may potentially be better able to withstand stress in dangerous situations. Some research has investigated these issues in applied settings. For example, Hunter (2002) found that risk perceptions, but not risk tolerances, were associated with involvement in dangerous aviation events. Others have shown that pilots are more risk prone when under stress (Sicard, Jouve & Blin, 2001). Finally, younger workers are more likely to engage in risk-taking behaviors that contribute to accidents (cf., Loughlin & Frone, 2004). Thus, young sensation-seekers under stress (a description characterizing many military personnel) may be particularly likely to engage in high-risk behavior. Therefore, they represent an important target for safety–performance interventions. Our discussion of sensation- seeking implies that interventions should address how soldiers assess risk, as well as their willingness to engage in risky behavior. Feedback from sensation-seeking assessments may help stimulate perceptual and behavioral change.

Situational Constraints

One important direction for future research will be to understand how personality characteristics interact with psychosocial demands of a particular situation to influence job performance. For instance, Tett and Burnett (2003) propose a trait-activation model in which organizational, social, and task cues influence which traits are relevant in a situation. One important set of cues concerns the extent to which the situation contains clear expectations about appropriate behavior. Personality traits should have stronger effects in situations containing fewer cues about desired behavior (Beaty, Cleveland & Murphy, 2001), and traits may be more strongly related to contextual performance in jobs with more autonomy (Gellatly & Irving, 2001). These findings imply that traits should have stronger effects on performance for soldiers in ambiguous and/or uncontrollable situations, such as peacekeeping or combat deployments. Traits also should have stronger effects for military personnel who have more autonomy because of their rank (e.g., officers) or because of the nature of their jobs (e.g., snipers). For example, high conscientiousness might be desirable in highly structured settings (such as classroom training), but less desirable in unstructured situations (such as combat).

New Research Methods and Designs

Emerging statistical techniques and research designs create interesting opportunities for further research. For example, multilevel modeling of stress effects (cf. Bliese & Jex, 2002) permits researchers to investigate stressors at multiple levels of analysis (e.g., person, group) as well as across levels (e.g., person X group interactions). Some research has investigated group-level personality processes in relation to performance (e.g., George, 1990) but not clearly in relation to stress. Other studies are needed to investigate whether certain traits exacerbate or intensify the effects of group-level stressors.

Several other statistical models and research designs could be given more attention in future studies. First, researchers may use repeated measures designs to track health or performance effects over several days or weeks. For example, such designs sometimes show that personality traits exhibit different effects within one person over time than they do between people at one time (Gable et al., 2000). Second, researchers may employ nonlinear analyses to investigate issues such as the inverted-U relationship between conscientiousness and safety described earlier. Similarly, some models of self-control suggest that overcontrol of one's anxiety, behavior, or impulses may be as undesirable as a lack of control (e.g., Block, 2002; Clark & Watson, 1999). Third, researchers might consider various profile approaches to personality–stress–performance relationships. These could include cluster-oriented approaches to identify stress-related personality profiles or tests of interactions among multiple traits. Although all of these topics are potentially interesting, quantitatively oriented psychologists interested in military settings need to conduct their research with an eye toward generating useful applications and interventions. More elegant analyses and designs are useful to the extent that their findings help generate applications that enable soldiers to be effective and remain healthy under stress.

Exploring the Role of Culture

Although the research we reviewed focuses mostly on U.S. military units, the issues discussed in this chapter clearly pertain to military members from most countries. Consequently, applied personality research needs to consider how cultural differences might influence the personality-related processes we described. Cultural issues intersect with individual differences in stress and performance on several levels. Cultures differ in their conceptions of personality and may differ in the effects of stress and personality constructs on individual behavior. For example, people from collectivist cultures have self-concepts that are more strongly shaped by the social networks in which they reside, and effective behavior is more likely to be defined in terms of identifying and adapting to group norms (Cross & Markus, 1999). These differences suggest the possibility of cultural differences in whether certain performance behaviors are viewed as discretionary or in the sanctions associated with various forms of counterproductive behavior. For example, a country with strong individualistic values might have weaker sanctions for minor violations of compliance with policies and procedures, whereas heavy sanctions might be imposed on soldiers from collectivist cultures. However, we also caution against overestimating the role of culture. Military units typically have strong collectivist organizational cultures. Thus, military personnel from different cultures may resemble one another more in some respects than they do civilians from their own cultures (see Soeters et al., Volume 4 of this set).

Cultural differences between occupying forces and members of the local civilian population or differences among members of multinational forces also raise the possibility of cultural conflicts in how to respond to the stressful demands of military missions. For example, in Operation Iraqi Freedom (OIF), the U.S. military faces daily interactions with civilians from multiple religious traditions (e.g., Kurds, Shiites, and Sunni Muslims). Such culture differences heighten the possibility of interpersonal or intergroup conflicts based on intercultural misunderstandings (or actual conflicts). In these circumstances, soldiers need to exert considerable self-restraint, as poorly chosen responses may lead to unexpected or uncontrollable escalation of a situation. The stress-CARE model highlights three important points about such conflicts. First, soldiers differ in their self-regulatory capacities; some soldiers may be especially apt to react negatively to such conflicts. Second, stress undermines self-regulatory capacity, and dangerous escalations are particularly likely when soldiers are under stress. Third, the assumption that self-restraint may be trainable suggests the value of training programs aimed at minimizing culture-based conflicts with local populations or other military personnel.

Moreover, cultural differences might influence the relationship between some aspects of the stress-CARE model and individual job performance. For example, members of collectivist cultures might be less sensitive to variations in their own stress levels and much more sensitive to stressors in their groups as an integrated whole. Similarly, certain forms of stress, such as interpersonal conflict, may be more stressful for soldiers from collectivist cultures. At the same time, the personality–performance relationship might be weaker in military units from collectivist nations where soldiers face strong organizational and cultural norms about appropriate behavior.

Health, Personality, and Performance

Finally, although health issues were not an explicit focus of this chapter, personality traits also may influence individual performance through their impact on health outcomes. Past research shows that personality traits are associated with a wide array of health outcomes ranging from immune system functioning to health maintenance behaviors (cf. Contrada & Guyll, 2001; Smith & Gallo, 2001). Our model suggests that poor health influences performance by weakening one's motivation and by hindering one's ability to make full use of knowledge, skills, and abilities. In addition to direct effects on health, personality traits also might moderate the health–performance relationship. For example, individuals with strong ego resources may be better able to sustain performance when they are sick or injured. Thus, we encourage readers to be mindful of the idea that actions, interventions, or situations that affect health also are likely to directly or indirectly affect performance, and that soldiers most likely differ in the strength of these connections.

Conclusion

There is little doubt that soldiers vary considerably in their reactions to stressful events and that their reactions have significant implications for individual and unit effectiveness. As demonstrated in this chapter, personality and health psychologists can draw from a large body of empirical research and prior theory to explain such individual differences. A similarly large body of industrial/organizational psychology has focused on the relationship between personality traits and job performance. Relatively few studies, however, have explored how personality factors might influence the relationship between stress and job performance. In this chapter, we proposed a theoretical model integrating disparate streams of personality, performance, and stress research. We also identified several promising directions for future personality research in military settings. This research should extend current personality theories in organizational psychology and help develop interventions that protect soldiers' health while improving their effectiveness. We are excited about the future of this domain of military psychology and look forward to other researchers' contributions to these understudied but critical challenges.

Notes

1. The authors gratefully acknowledge Amy Adler, Carl Castro, Jennifer Cullen, Alison Dezsofi, Cynthia Mohr, Celina Oliver, and Ellen Skinner for their assistance with issues related to the preparation of this chapter.
2. We regard the Stress-CARE model as a midlevel theory of job stress, rather than a comprehensive theoretical model. Other personality traits clearly affect stress-response processes (some of which we mention in this chapter). Moreover, we generally avoid issues related to exposure to stressors (such as people's decisions to place themselves in stressful situations), because most self-selection processes presumably occur prior to enlistment in the military.
3. Although there is considerable overlap between some of the meta-analyses, more recent meta-analyses do not necessarily include all of the studies from prior meta-analyses of the same topic.
4. For the purpose of our paper, we equated overall performance with task performance. It is important to recognize, however, that both contextual and task performance contribute to overall job performance (Johnson, 2001). Moreover, relationships between personality traits and overall performance could be attributed to the contextual elements of overall performance rather than to task performance.
5. We use the terms OCB and contextual performance interchangeably.

6. LePine, Erez, and Johnson (2002) found that the relationship between OCB and several attitudinal and dispositional variables was similar across OCB dimensions. They propose that the dimensions be considered as equivalent indicators of a latent construct defined as "a general tendency to be cooperative and helpful in organizational settings" (p. 61).

7. Salgado (1998) also conducted analyses for accidents (no FFM correlates) and absenteeism (all five FFM traits predicted turnover). We omitted accidents from our table because they less clearly fit the intentional aspect of our definition of counterproductive behavior. We felt that turnover overlapped with contextual performance and that, because of the fixed length of military contracts, that civilian turnover research was less relevant to military settings.

References

Adler, A. B., McGurk, D. M., Stetz, M. C., & Bliese, P. D. (2003). Military occupational stressors in garrison, training, and deployed environments. *Work, stress, & health: New challenges for a changing workplace.* Conference sponsored by the National Institute of Occupational Safety and Health and the American Psychological Association, Toronto, Canada.

Adler, A. B., Litz, B. T., & Bartone, P. T. (2003). The nature or peacekeeping stressors. In T. W. Britt & A. B. Adler (Eds.), *The psychology of the peacekeeper: Lessons from the field* (pp. 149–167). Westport, CT: Praeger.

Barling, J., & Frone, M. R. (Eds.). (2004). *The psychology of workplace safety.* Washington, DC: APA Books.

Barrick, M. R., Mitchell, T. R., & Stewart, G. L. (2003). Situational and motivational influences on trait-behavior relationships. In M. R. Barrick & A. M. Ryan (Eds.), *Personality and work: Reconsidering the role of personality in organizations* (pp. 60–82). San Francisco: Jossey-Bass.

Barrick, M. R., & Mount, M. K. (1991). The Big Five personality dimensions and job performance: A meta-analysis. *Personnel Psychology, 44,* 1–26.

Barrick, M. R., & Ryan, A. M. (Eds.). (2003). *Personality and work: Reconsidering the role of personality in organizations.* San Francisco: Jossey-Bass.

Bartone, P. T. (1999). Hardiness protects against war-related stress in Army reserve forces. *Consulting Psychology Journal: Practice and Research, 51,* 72–82.

Bartone, P. T., Ursano, R. J., Wright, K. M., & Ingraham, L. H. (1989). The impact of a military air disaster on the health of assistance workers: A prospective study. *The Journal of Nervous and Mental Disease, 177,* 317–328.

Bass, B. M. (1996). *A new paradigm of leadership: An inquiry into transformational leadership.* Alexandria, VA: U.S. Army Research Institute for the Behavioral & Social Sciences.

Bass, B. M. (1998). *Transformational leadership: Industry, military, and educational impact.* Mahwah, NJ: Erlbaum.

Baumeister, R. F. (2001). Ego depletion, the executive function, and self-control. In B. W. Roberts and R. Hogan (Eds.), *Personality psychology in the workplace* (pp. 299–316). Washington, DC: APA Books.

Beaty, J. C., Cleveland, J. N., & Murphy, K. R. (2001). The relation between personality and contextual performance in "strong" versus "weak" situations. *Human Performance, 14,* 125–148.

Bliese, P. D., & Castro, C. A. (2003). The soldier adaptation model (SAM): Applications to behavioral science peacekeeping research. In T. W. Britt & A. B. Adler (Eds.), *The psychology of the peacekeeper: A multinational perspective* (pp. 185–203). Westport, CT: Praeger.

Bliese, P. D., & Jex, S. M. (2002). Incorporating a multilevel perspective into occupational stress research: Theoretical, methodological, and practical implications. *Journal of Occupational Health Psychology, 7,* 265–276.

Block, J. (1995). A contrarian view of the five-factor approach to personality description. *Psychological Bulletin, 117,* 187–215.

Block, J. (2002). *Personality as an affect-processing system: Toward an integrative theory.* Mahwah, NJ: Erlbaum.

Borman, W. C., & Motowidlo, S. J. (1993). Expanding the criterion domain to include elements of contextual performance. In N. Schmitt, W. F. Borman, & associates (Eds.), *Personnel selection in organizations* (pp. 71–98). San Francisco: Jossey-Bass.

Borman, W. C., Penner, L. A., Allen, T. D., & Motowidlo, S. J. (2001). Personality predictors of citizenship performance. *International Journal of Selection and Assessment, 9,* 52–69.

Britt, T. W., Adler, A. B., & Bartone, P. T. (2001). Deriving benefits from stressful events: The role of engagement in meaningful work and hardiness. *Journal of Occupational Health Psychology, 6,* 53–63.

Campbell, J. P., Gasser, M. B., & Oswald, F. L. (1996). The substantive nature job performance variability. In K. R. Murphy (Ed.), *Individual differences and behavior in organizations* (pp. 258–299). San Francisco: Jossey-Bass.

Campbell, J. P., McCloy, R. A., Oppler, S. H., & Sager, C. E. (1993). A theory of performance. In N. Schmitt, W. F. Borman, & associates (Eds.), *Personnel selection in organizations* (pp. 35–70). San Francisco: Jossey-Bass.

Campbell, J. P., McHenry, J. J., & Wise, L. L. (1990). Modeling job performance in a population of jobs. *Personnel Psychology, 43,* 313–333.

Cannon-Bowers, J. A., & Salas, E. (Eds.). (1998). *Making decisions under stress: Implications for individual and team training.* Washington, DC: APA Books.

Carlson, J. G. (1985). Recent assessments of the Myers-Briggs Type Indicator. *Journal of Personality Assessment, 49,* 356–365.

Cattell, R. B., Eber, H. J., & Tatsuoka, M. M. (1970). *Handbook for the Sixteen Personality Factor Questionnaire (16 PF).* Champaign, IL: Institute for Personality and Ability Testing.

Cellar, D. F., Nelson, Z. C., Yorke, C. M., & Bauer, C. (2001). The five-factor model and safety in the workplace. Investigating the relationships between personality and accident involvement. *Journal of Prevention and Intervention in the Community, 22,* 43–52.

Clark, L., & Watson, D. (1999). Temperament: A new paradigm for trait psychology. In L. A. Pervin & O. P. John (Eds.). *Handbook of personality: Theory and research* (2nd ed., pp. 399–423). New York: Guilford.

Contrada, R. J., & Guyll, M. (2001). On who gets sick and why: The role of personality and stress. In A. Baum, T. A. Revenson, & J. E. Singer (Eds.). *Handbook of health psychology* (pp. 59–84). Mahwah, NJ: Erlbaum.

Costa, P. T., & McRae, R. R. (1992a). Four ways five factors are basic. *Personality and Individual Differences, 13,* 653–665.

Costa, P. T., & McRae, R. R. (1992b). *Revised NEO Personality Inventory (NEO-PI-R) and NEO Five-factor Inventory (NEO-FFI) professional manual.* Odessa, FL: Psychological Assessment Resources.

Costa, P. T., Jr., & McCrae, R. R. (1995). Solid ground in the wetlands of personality: A reply to Block. *Psychological Bulletin, 117,* 216–220.

Cox, S. (2000). *Leader character: A model of personality and moral development.* Unpublished doctoral dissertation, University of Tulsa.

Cross, S. E., & Markus, H. R. (1999). The cultural constitution of personality. In L. Pervin & O. John (Eds.). *Handbook of personality theory and research* (2nd ed., pp. 378–396). New York: Guilford.

Day, D. V., Schleicher, D. J., Unckless, A. L., Hiller, N. J. (2002). Self-monitoring personality at work: A meta-analytic investigation of construct validity. *Journal of Applied Psychology, 87*, 390–401.

Dekel, R., Solomon, Z., Ginzburg, K., & Neria, Y. (2003). Combat exposure, wartime performance, and long-term adjustment among combatants. *Military Psychology, 15*, 117–131.

Donohue, K. S. (1993). *The anatomy of discipline* (School of Advanced Military Studies Monograph). Fort Leavenworth, KS: United States Army Command and General Staff College.

Edwards, J. R., Caplan, R. D., & Van Harrison, R. (1998). Person-environment fit theory. In C. Cooper (Ed.), *Theories of organizational stress.* (pp. 26–67). New York: Oxford University Press.

Elliot, T. R., & Maples, S. (1991). Stress management training for employees experiencing corporate acquisition. *Journal of Employment Counseling, 28*, 107–114.

Eyesenck, H. (1991). Dimensions of personality: 16, 5 or 3?—Criteria for a taxonometric paradigm. *Personality and Individual Differences, 12*, 773–790.

Eyesenck, H. J., & Eyesenck, S. B. G. (1991). *Manual of the Eyesenck Personality Scales (EPS Adult)*. London: Hodder & Stoughton.

Funder, D. C. (2001). *The personality puzzle* (2nd ed.). New York: Norton.

Gable, S. L., Reis, H. T., & Elliot, A. J. (2000). Behavioral activation and inhibition in everyday life. *Journal of Personality and Social Psychology, 78*, 1135–1149.

Gardner, W. L., & Martinko, M. J. (1996). Using the Myers-Briggs Type Indicator to study managers: A literature review and research agenda. *Journal of Management, 22*, 45–83.

Gellatly, I. R., & Irving, P. G. (2001). Personality, autonomy, and contextual performance of managers. *Human Performance, 14*, 231–245.

George, J. M. (1990). Personality, affect, and behavior in groups. *Journal of Applied Psychology, 75*, 107–116.

George, J. A. (1996). Trait and state affect. In K. R. Murphy (Ed.), *Individual differences and behavior in organizations* (pp. 145–171). San Francisco: Jossey-Bass.

Goldberg, L. R., & Saucier, G., (1995). So what do you propose we use instead? A reply to Block. *Psychological Bulletin, 117*, 221–225.

Goodspeed, R. B., & DeLucia, A. G. (1990). Stress reduction at the worksite: An evaluation of two methods. *American Journal of Health Promotion, 4*, 333–337.

Gray, J. A. (1987). *The psychology of fear and stress* (2nd ed.). New York: Cambridge University Press.

Hofmann, D. A., & Tetrick, L. E. (2003). *Health and safety in organizations: A multilevel perspective*. San Francisco: Jossey-Bass.

Hogan, R., & Hogan, J. (1995). *Hogan personality inventory manual*. Tulsa, OK: Hogan Assessment Systems.

Hough, L. M. (1992). The "Big Five" personality variables-construct confusion: Description versus prediction. *Human Performance, 5*, 139–155.

Hough, L. M., & Ones, D. S. (2001). The structure, measurement, validity, and use of personality variables in industrial, work, and organizational psychology. In N. Anderson, D. S. Ones, H. K. Sinangil, & C. Viswesvaran (Eds.), *Handbook of industrial, work, and organizational psychology* (Vol. 1, pp. 233–277). London: Sage.

Hough, L. M., & Schneider, R. (1996). Personality traits, taxonomies, and applications in organizations. In K. R. Murphy (Ed.), *Individual differences in behavior in organizations* (pp. 31–88). San Francisco: Jossey-Bass.

Hunter, D. R. (2002). Risk perception and risk tolerance in aircraft pilots. *Federal Aviation Administration Final Report.* Report No. PB2003-100818 DOT/FAA/AM-2/17.

Hurtz, G. M., & Donovan, J. J. (2000). Personality and job performance: The Big Five revisited. *Journal of Applied Psychology, 85,* 869–879.

Jex, S. M. (1998). *Stress and job performance: Theory, research, and implications for managerial practice.* London: Sage.

Jex, S. M., Bliese, P. D., Buzzell, S., & Primeau, J. (2001). The impact of self-efficacy on stressor-strain relations: Coping style as an explanatory mechanism. *Journal of Applied Psychology, 86,* 401–409.

Johnson, J. W. (2001). The relative importance of task and contextual performance to supervisor judgments of overall performance. *Journal of Applied Psychology, 86,* 984–996.

Johnson, J. W. (2003). Toward a better understanding of the relationship between personality and individual job performance. In M. R. Barrick & A. M. Ryan (Eds.), *Personality and work: Reconsidering the role of personality in organizations* (pp. 83–149). San Francisco: Jossey-Bass.

Jones, J. W., & Wuebker, L. J. (1993). Safety locus of control and employees' accidents. *Journal of Business & Psychology, 7,* 449–457.

Judge, T. A., & Bono, J. E. (2000). Five-factor model of personality and transformational leadership. *Journal of Applied Psychology, 85,* 751–765.

Judge, T. A., & Bono, J. E. (2001). Relationship of core self-evaluations traits—self-esteem, generalized self-efficacy, locus of control, and emotional stability—with job satisfaction and job performance: A meta-analysis. *Journal of Applied Psychology, 86,* 80–92.

Judge, T. A., Bono, J. E., Ilies, R., Gerhardt, M. W. (2002). Personality and leadership: A qualitative and quantitative review. *Journal of Applied Psychology, 87,* 765–780.

Judge, T. A., Erez, A., & Bono, J. E. (1998). The power of being positive: The relation between positive self-concept and job performance. *Human Performance, 11,* 167–187.

Judge, T. A., Locke, E. A., & Durham, C. C. (1997). The dispositional causes of job satisfaction: A core evaluations approach. *Research in Organizational Behavior, 19,* 151–188.

Kanfer, R., & Heggestad, E. D. (1997). Motivational traits and skills: A person-centered approach to work motivation. In B. M. Staw & L. L. Cummings (Eds.), *Research in organizational behavior* (Vol. 19, pp. 1–56). Greenwich, CT: JAI Press.

Karasek, R., & Theorell, T. (1990). *Healthy work: Stress, productivity, and the reconstruction of working life.* New York: Basic Books.

King, R. E., Retzlaff, P. D., & Orme, D. R. (2001). A comparison of U.S. Air Force pilot psychological baseline information to safety outcomes. *AFSC-TR-2001-0001.* Kirtland AFB: Air Force Safety Center.

Lardent, C. L. (1991). Pilots who crash: Personality constructs underlying accident-prone behavior of fighter pilots. *Multivariate Experimental Clinical Research, 10,* 1–25.

Larsen, R. P. (2001). Decision making by military students under severe stress. *Military Psychology, 13,* 89–98.

LePine, J. A., Colquitt, J. A., & Erez, A. (2000). Adaptability to changing task contexts: Effects of general cognitive ability, conscientiousness, and openness to experience, *Personnel Psychology, 53,* 563–593.

LePine, J. A., Erez, A., & Johnson, D. E. (2002). The nature and dimensionality of organizational citizenship behavior: A critical review and analysis. *Journal of Applied Psychology, 87,* 52–65.

Loughlin, C., & Frone, M. R. (2004). Young workers' occupational safety. In J. Barling & M. R. Frone (Eds.), *The psychology of workplace safety* (pp. 107–125). Washington, DC: APA Books.

MacDonough, T. S. (1991). Noncombat stress in soldiers: How it is manifested, how to measure it, and how to cope with it. In R. Gal & A. D. Mangelsdorff (Eds.), *Handbook of Military Psychology* (pp. 531–558). New York: Wiley.

Maddi, S. R. (1990). Issues and interventions in stress mastery. In H.S. Friedman (Ed.), *Personality and disease* (pp. 121–154). New York: Wiley.

Maddi, S. R., Kahn, S., Maddi, K. L. (1998). The effectiveness of hardiness training. *Consulting Psychology Journal: Practice and Research, 50,* 78–86.

McCrae, R. R., & Costa, P. T. (1999). A five-factor theory of personality. In L. R. Pervin and O. P. John (Eds.). *The handbook of personality* (2nd ed., pp. 139–153). New York: Guilford.

McHenry, J. J., Hough, L. M., Toquam, J. L., Hanson, M. A., & Ashworth, S. (1990). Project A validity results: The relationship between predictor and criterion domains. *Personnel Psychology, 43,* 335–354.

Motowidlo, S. J., Borman, W. C., & Schmit, M. J. (1997). A theory of individual differences in task and contextual performance. *Human Performance, 10,* 71–83.

Motowidlo, S. J., & Van Scotter, J. R. (1994). Evidence that task performance should be distinguished from contextual performance. *Journal of Applied Psychology, 79,* 475–480.

Mount, M. K., & Barrick, M. R. (1995). The Big Five personality dimensions: Implications for research and practice in human resources management. In G. R. Ferris (Ed.), *Research in personnel and human resources management* (Vol. 13, pp. 153–200). Greenwich, CT: JAI Press.

Mount, M. K., Barrick, M. R., & Stewart, G. L. (1998). Five-factor model of personality in jobs involving interpersonal interactions. *Human Performance, 11,* 145–165.

Ones, D. S., & Viswesvaran, C. (2001). Personality at work: Criterion-focused occupational personality scales used in personnel selection. In B. W. Roberts & R. Hogan (Eds.), *Personality psychology in the workplace* (pp. 63–92). Washington, DC: APA Books.

Ones, D. S., Viswesvaran, C., & Schmidt, F. L. (1993). Comprehensive meta-analysis of integrity test validities: Findings and implications for personnel selection and theories of job performance [Monograph]. *Journal of Applied Psychology, 78,* 679–703.

Organ, D. W. (1988). *Organizational citizenship behavior: The good soldier syndrome.* Lexington, MA: Lexington Books.

Organ, D. W. (1997). Organizational citizenship behavior: It's construct cleanup time. *Human Performance, 10,* 85–97.

Organ, D. W., & Ryan, K. (1995). A meta-analytic review of attitudinal and dispositional predictors of organizational citizenship behavior. *Personnel Psychology, 48,* 775–802.

Paunonen, S. V., & Nicol, A.A.A.M. (2001). The personality hierarchy and the prediction of work behaviors. In B. W. Roberts & R. Hogan (Eds.), *Personality psychology in the workplace* (pp. 161–191). Washington, DC: APA Books.

Pervin, L. A., & John, O. P. (Ed.). (1999). *Handbook of personality: Theory and research* (2nd ed.). New York: Guilford.

Ployhart, R. E., Lim, B. C., & Chan, K. Y. (2001). Exploring relations between typical and maximum performance ratings and the five-factor model of personality. *Personnel Psychology, 54*, 809–843.

Podsakoff, P. M., MacKenzie, S. B., Paine, J. B., & Bachrach, D. G. (2000). Organizational citizenship behaviors: A critical review of the theoretical and empirical literature and suggestions for future research. *Journal of Management, 26*, 513–563.

Pulakos, E. D., Arad, S., Donovan, M. A., & Plamondon, K. E. (2000). Adaptability in the workplace: Development of a taxonomy of adaptive performance. *Journal of Applied Psychology, 85*, 612–624.

Quick, J. C., Quick, J. D., Nelson, D. L., & Hurrell, J. J., Jr. (1997). *Preventative stress management in organizations*. Washington, DC: APA Books.

Roberts, B. W., Caspi, A., & Moffitt, T. E. (2003). Work experiences and personality development in young adulthood. *Journal of Personality and Social Psychology, 84*, 582–593.

Roberts, B. W., & Hogan, R. T. (2001). *Personality psychology in the workplace*. Washington, DC: American Psychological Association.

Robertson, I., & Callinan, M. (1998). Personality and work behaviour. *European Journal of Work and Organizational Psychology, 7*, 321–340.

Sackett, P. R., & DeVore, C. J. (2001). Counterproductive behaviors at work. In N. Anderson, D. S. Ones, H. K. Sinangil, & C. Viswesvaran (Eds.), *Handbook of industrial, work, and organizational psychology* (Vol. 1, pp. 145–164). London: Sage.

Salgado, J. F. (1997). The five-factor model of personality and job performance in the European Community. *Journal of Applied Psychology, 82*, 30–43.

Salgado, J. F. (1998). Big Five personality dimensions and job performance in army and civil occupations: A European perspective. *Human Performance, 11*, 271–288.

Salgado, J. F. (2002). The Big Five personality dimensions and counterproductive behaviors. *International Journal of Selection and Assessment, 10*, 117–125.

Sandal, G. M. (1999). The effects of personality and interpersonal relations on crew performance during space simulation studies. *Human Performance in Extreme Environments, 4*, 43–50.

Saucier, G., & Goldberg, L. R. (2003). The structure of personality attributes. In M.R. Barrick & A. M. Ryan (Eds.), *Personality and work: Reconsidering the role of personality in organizations* (pp. 1–29). San Francisco: Jossey-Bass.

Sicard, B., Jouve, E., & Blin, O. (2001). Risk propensity assessment in military special operations. *Military Medicine, 166*, 871–874.

Siegrist, J. (1998). Adverse health effects of effort-reward imbalance at work. In C. Cooper (Ed), *Theories of organizational stress* (pp. 190–204). New York: Oxford University Press.

Smith, T. W., & Gallo, L. C. (2001). Personality traits as risk factors for physical illness. In A. Baum, T. A. Revenson, & J. E. Singer (Eds.), *Handbook of Health Psychology* (pp. 139–173). Mahwah, NJ: Erlbaum.

Snyder, M. (1987). *Public appearances/private realities: The psychology of self-monitoring*. New York: Freeman.

Spector, P. E. (1998). A control theory of the job stress process. In C. Cooper (Ed.), *Theories of organizational stress* (pp. 153–169). New York: Oxford.

Tett, R. P., & Burnett, D. D. (2003). A personality trait-based interactionist model of job performance. *Journal of Applied Psychology, 88*, 500–517.

Tett, R. P., Jackson, D. N., & Rothstein, M. (1991). Personality measures as predictors of job performance: A meta-analytic review. *Personnel Psychology, 44*, 703–742.

Thoms, P., & Venkataraman, R. R. (2002). Relations of managers' personality to accident and injury rates. *Psychological Reports, 91*, 1107–1115.

Trlek, M. (2003). *Risk factors of military discipline violation.* Paper presented at the annual meeting of the International Applied Military Psychology Symposium, Brussels, Belgium.

Vineberg, R., & Joyner, J. N. (1989). Evaluation of individual enlisted performance. In M. F. Wiskoff & G. M. Rampton (Eds.), *Military personnel measurement: Testing, assignment, evaluation* (pp. 169–200). New York: Praeger.

Wallace, J. C., & Vodanovich, S. J. (2003). Workplace safety performance: Conscientiousness, cognitive failure and their interaction. *Journal of Occupational Health Psychology, 8*, 316–327.

Watson, D., Clark, L. A., & Tellegen, A. (1988). Development and validation of brief measures of positive and negative affect: The PANAS scales. *Journal of Personality and Social Psychology, 54*, 1063–1070.

Westman, M. (1990). The relationship between stress and performance: The moderating effect of hardiness. *Human Performance, 3*, 141–155.

Wiggins, J. S. (1996). *The five-factor model of personality: Theoretical perspectives.* New York: Guilford Press.

Zuckerman, M. (1979). *Sensation seeking: Beyond the optimal level of arousal.* Hillsdale, NJ: Erlbaum.

Zuckerman, M. (1992). What is a basic factor and which factors are basic? Turtles all the way down. *Personality and Individual Differences, 13*, 675–681.

PART V

FUTURE DIRECTIONS

CHAPTER 11

MILITARY PERFORMANCE: COMMON THEMES AND FUTURE DIRECTIONS

Thomas W. Britt, Carl Andrew Castro, and Amy B. Adler

Spencer Campbell, a veteran of three wars, begins this volume with "What Has Befallen Me?", a searing account of the long-term impact his experiences as a marine in combat had on his development, health, and life perspective. In his struggle to place his Vietnam experiences into context, he acknowledges the gritty reality that combat soldiers encounter: the death, the exhaustion, the courage inherent in the act of surviving, and in returning to the front line. His account crosses many boundaries and serves as a cornerstone not only for this volume but the entire book set. Campbell addresses the different levels of stress, and the different kinds of individual, group, and cultural experiences that affect a veteran's adjustment to the demands of combat and its aftermath. In "What Has Befallen Me?" Campbell asks a fundamental question facing all service members: How does one come to terms with the psychological changes that result from confronting war?

The chapters in Volume 1 echo many of these profound themes. In his chapter, Gifford details how military personnel function in combat and describes the potential psychological effects of killing. By raising compelling arguments, Gifford sets the stage for researchers to examine the impact the act of killing has on service members, a topic that Campbell confronted head-on in the jungles of Vietnam.

The chapters on the physiological and cognitive dimensions of military operations review the impact of sleep deprivation and high-intensity environmental stressors on cognitive functioning and performance. In their chapter on sleep loss, Wesensten, Belenky, and Balkin detail the extended impact of sleep deprivation and sleep restriction on military performance, which has profound implications for conducting continuous military operations. In their chapter on stress and decision making, Driskell, Salas, and Johnston emphasize the negative performance consequences of operational stressors such as noise, high workload, and time pressure. Campbell describes the personal impact of these kinds of real-world stressors in his first-person account of war more than 30 years ago. These same demands are present today. Modern military operations, in particular, require immense cognitive resources, and Muth, Kruse, Hoover, and Schmorrow describe cutting-edge methods of enhancing cognitive adaptation to high-intensity environments.

The section on social and personality dimensions of military operations describes the context in which operational performance occurs. The social milieu of military operations includes the dimension of cohesion, a vital component of unit functioning, as analyzed by Siebold in his chapter on group cohesion. The importance of cohesion in military operations is exemplified by Campbell's earlier discussion of what military personnel fight for—their buddies. Campbell's account also reveals the difficulty in maintaining morale under difficult operational conditions. The determinants of positive morale are modeled by Britt and Dickinson in their chapter on military morale.

While the group exercises an impact on individual motivation and morale, individual differences also play a key role in military performance. The complexity of understanding the role of individual difference variables is illustrated by Sinclair and Tucker in their chapter on personality. Campbell's first-person account reveals that adaptation to the demands of military operations is a deeply individual process.

Although not specifically mentioned by Campbell, the conduct of military operations is affected by the judicious use of psychological operations. Collins discusses the history and importance of alternative methods to combat in influencing the outcome of military operations. The very nature of military operations has shifted as current conflicts are complicated by the threat of terrorism. The psychological consequences of dealing with the fear of terrorism are outlined by Bobo, Keller, Greenberg, Alfonzo, Pastor, and Grieger.

Taken together, these chapters address the key psychological dimensions of performance during different types of military operations. From these chapters, we can derive fundamental principles that can inform the development of strategies for enhancing performance under stressful military operations.

Core Principles for Military Performance

1. Combat forces service members to deal with their own mortality. The reality of combat challenges service members to live with the fear of being killed and to perform effectively despite this fear.

2. Military operations can push service members to the limits of their endurance. Complex decision making and performance of military tasks can be affected by lack of sleep and information overload. Training technology and pharmacological interventions can offset these combat-related performance decrements.

3. Morale and cohesion sustain individual and unit performance during military operations. These psychological elements are powerful and positive forces in optimizing military

performance. Leaders play a primary role in establishing the level of morale and cohesion in their units.

4. Personality differences contribute importantly to how service members perform during military operations. Through training and awareness, individuals can maximize their ability to cope with the challenges of deployment by adapting strategies to complement their personality.

5. Terrorism represents a type of combat stress that adversely affects the health and well-being of service members. Training can be adapted to help service members be prepared to deal with the psychological threat of terrorism.

Future Directions

Although researchers in military psychology have made a great deal of progress in understanding the human dimension of performance in various deployments, there is a need for additional research in many areas. As Gifford articulates, little empirical attention has been devoted to the psychological impact of killing and the various factors that may moderate its impact. For example, what is the psychological impact of killing on the well-being of military personnel, the functioning of their units, the performance of those who return to battle, and their families? Furthermore, what impact does the mission's meaning and purpose have on the psychological effects of killing? These research questions regarding the impact of killing are directly relevant to the functioning of individuals, units, and military families.

Another area in need of further research is the possible benefits of successfully performing in difficult military operations, and the consequences of deriving benefits for psychological health and future performance. As Britt and Dickinson note in their chapter, much more research has been conducted on what causes a minority of service members to develop mental illnesses following military operations than on what causes service members to grow and strengthen as a result of their deployment. We do not mean to suggest that the study of psychological problems following military operations is unimportant. Rather, we are calling for additional research on the benefits accrued from successful performance, and how these benefits may protect service members from the adverse consequences of high-intensity stressors.

Finally, little research has been conducted on the role of personality variables in the performance of military personnel during different types of military operations. The resurgence of interest in personality discussed by Sinclair and Tucker needs to be harnessed and applied to military performance in operational environments. It may be the case that different personality variables predict performance in different operational environments (e.g., combat, peacekeeping, fighting terrorism). An understanding of these differences will guide training and professional development programs.

Ultimately, our understanding of the role of psychological factors on military operations will depend on the development of new measures of performance during such operations. Researchers examining the role of psychological variables in a military setting have employed discrete proxies of military performance as outcome measures, since the means for assessing actual battlefield performance has not been developed. Despite this limitation in operational research, understanding the relationships between the demands of military operations and performance is necessary for providing specific recommendations that can improve service member performance across the deployment spectrum.

Success on the battlefield is the ultimate outcome relevant to military psychology. Research in military psychology has shown that the demands of military operations affect sleep and cognitive functioning, both of which are linked to operational performance. Factors such as morale, cohesion, and personality have the capacity to promote successful performance under stress. The strategic enhancement of these factors will optimize the performance of military personnel as they confront the reality of military operations.

Index

About the Contributors

AMY B. ADLER is a research psychologist with the U.S. Army Medical Research Unit–Europe, Walter Reed Army Institute of Research (WRAIR), in Heidelberg, Germany. She is science coordinator at the unit, has deployed in support of peacekeeping operations, and is interested in deployment-related stress and early interventions. She and Thomas Britt edited a book published by Praeger Press in 2003, *The Psychology of the Peacekeeper: Lessons from the Field*.

CHRISTOPHER A. ALFONZO is a lieutenant in the U.S. Navy. He is a former flight surgeon and is now engaged in postgraduate training in psychiatry. His academic interests include military operational psychiatry and mental health consequences of terrorism and disaster.

THOMAS J. BALKIN is a research psychologist and chief of the Department of Behavioral Biology at the Walter Reed Army Institute of Research. He is also codirector of the Howard County General Hospital Sleep Disorders Center. His research interests include the neurophysiology of alertness and performance deficits during sleep deprivation and development of fatigue countermeasures for the operational environment.

GREGORY BELENKY is a physician, psychiatrist and research professor and director, Sleep and Performance Research Center, Washington State University Spokane. He is a retired U.S. Army colonel and was formerly director, Division of Neuropsychiatry, WRAIR. From 1984 to 2004, he directed the U.S. Army's research program in sleep and performance. He deployed to the 1990–91 Gulf War and served as chief of the mental health team of the U.S. Army Second Armored Cavalry Regiment.

WILLIAM V. BOBO is a lieutenant commander in the U.S. Navy Reserves and an assistant professor in the Department of Psychiatry at the Uniformed Services University of the Health Sciences in Bethesda, Maryland. He is also the assistant program director for the National Capital Consortium Military Psychiatry Residency Program headquartered at the Walter Reed Army Medical Center, the National Naval Medical Center and Malcolm-Grow U.S. Air Force Medical Center (Andrews Air Force Base). Included among his research interests are the psychological consequences of mass disasters and body handling duty.

THOMAS W. BRITT is an associate professor in the Department of Psychology at Clemson University. He was a uniformed research psychologist in the U.S. Army from 1994 to 1999 and deployed in support of peacekeeping, humanitarian, and contingency operations. His research interests include the search for factors that enhance resiliency and morale among soldiers serving on different types of military operations. Together with Amy Adler, he edited the book, *The Psychology of the Peacekeeper: Lessons from the Field* (Praeger Press, 2003).

SPENCER J. CAMPBELL retired after 38 years of military service with the Marines and the Army. He is a combat veteran of Vietnam, Desert Shield/Storm, Bosnia, Operation Enduring Freedom, and Operation Iraqi Freedom. During his military career Dr. Campbell progressed from the rank of Marine Corps private to the retirement rank of Army lieutenant colonel. Dr. Campbell's significant military awards include the Combat Medical Badge, Silver Star, Legion of Merit, Purple Heart, four Meritorious Service Medals, Combat Action Ribbon, the Republic of Vietnam Gallantry Cross, and the Republic of Vietnam Civil Actions Service Medal. In 1991 he received the Chief, Medical Service Corps Award of Excellence for Health Sciences. He has a Ph.D. in social work and is a board-certified diplomate by the National Association of Forensic Counselors and National Board of Addiction Examiners, is a board-certified diplomate in clinical social work, a board-certified expert in traumatic stress, and a diplomate of the American Academy of Experts in Traumatic Stress. He is the author of *LEADERSHIP! A Comprehensive Guide to Understanding and Development* (2000) and *Reflections of a Vietnam Veteran* (1983).

CARL ANDREW CASTRO is a lieutenant colonel and research psychologist in the U.S. Army. He is chief of the Department of Military Psychiatry at the WRAIR. He has served tours of duty in Bosnia, Kosovo, and Iraq. His research interests include understanding the impact of deployments on the health and well-being of soldiers and families and how values improve individual performance.

STEVEN COLLINS is a lieutenant colonel in the U.S. Army and currently the deputy chief of staff for operations at the Defense Language Institute Foreign Language Center. Previously, he was the chief of psychological operations at NATO's Supreme Headquarters Allied Powers Europe. A career psychological operations officer, he has deployed numerous times in support of U.S. and NATO military operations, particularly in the Balkans. A graduate of the U.S. Military Academy (West Point) and Yale University, he is a frequent writer and speaker on the topics of military psychological operations, information operations, public diplomacy, and perception management.

JAMES M. DICKINSON is an industrial/organizational psychologist and consultant for nonprofit organizations. His research interests include morale in military operations, the unique contributions of positive psychology constructs in the workplace, and volunteerism. He also focuses on relating I/O psychology theory and practice to nonprofit settings.

JAMES E. DRISKELL is president of Florida Maxima Corporation and adjunct professor of psychology at Rollins College, Winter Park, Florida. At Florida Maxima, he has conducted research on team performance, human performance under stress, and training for the U.S. Army, Navy, Air Force, NASA, FAA, National Science Foundation, Department of Homeland Security, and others. He previously worked as a research psychologist at a Naval research laboratory.

ROBERT K. GIFFORD is a senior scientist in the Center for the Study of Traumatic Stress at the Uniformed Services University of the Health Sciences, specializing in the study of traumatic stress, particularly combat stress, operational stress, and the aftermath of workplace incidents. Dr. Gifford served as a research psychologist in the U.S. Army for 30 years, retiring as a colonel. While in the Army, he conducted psychological research in the field in the Persian Gulf War (Operation Desert Shield/ Storm), in Somalia, and in Bosnia, as well as at field sites in Germany and the United States.

NEIL GREENBERG is a surgeon lieutenant commander and a military psychiatrist who works in the United Kingdom in a split post between Portsmouth and London. In addition to working in the Royal Navy managing military personnel with mental health needs he is also the military liaison officer to the King's Centre for Military Health Research in London. His research interests include traumatic stress in the military, in particular U.K. military peacekeeping personnel and organizational responses to traumatic stress. He sits on national and international committees which are concerned with traumatic stress in the military.

THOMAS A. GRIEGER is a captain in the U.S. Navy and an associate professor in the Department of Psychiatry at the Uniformed Services University of the Health Sciences in Bethesda, Maryland. Dr. Grieger has published extensively in the areas of trauma and disaster psychiatry, including the psychiatric consequences of the recent terrorist attack on the Pentagon, as well as traumatic stress in the military.

ADAM HOOVER is an associate professor in the Electrical and Computer Engineering Department at Clemson University. His research interests include tracking systems, embedded computing, and machine vision. His research has been funded by the U.S. Army, Navy, and Department of Defense.

JOAN H. JOHNSTON is an industrial/organizational psychologist and senior research psychologist working at NAVAIR Orlando Training Systems Division. She is responsible for managing military training systems research programs that address tactical decision making under stress and team performance assessment and training.

RICHARD T. KELLER is a retired major who served in the Nursing Corps in the U.S. Army. He has over 25 years of experience in mental health and 15 years of experience in disaster mental health and combat stress operations. He is considered a subject matter expert on the psychological consequences of exposure to human remains and establishing and maintaining peer support programs for organizations working in hostile or harsh environments. He served on two U.S. Army Surgeon General task forces to assess behavioral heath issues and develop programs for soldiers serving in Operation Iraqi Freedom and Operation Enduring Freedom.

AMY A. KRUSE is a program manager in the Defense Sciences Office at the Defense Advanced Research Projects Agency (DARPA) in Arlington, Virginia. Prior to her work at DARPA, she conducted NIH funded research at the Beckman Institute for Advanced Science and Technology. Dr. Kruse is a neuroscientist, and her research interests include the newly emerging area of operational neuroscience. Her areas of expertise include learning and memory, neurophysiology, and noninvasive sensor technologies.

ERIC R. MUTH is an associate professor in the department of psychology at Clemson University. He was a uniformed aerospace experimental psychologist in the U.S. Navy from 1997–2000, completing studies of naval significance related to night vision, motion sickness and the use of flight simulators in the shipboard environment. His research focuses on the effects of stress in high workload environments (e.g., performing tasks while in moving vehicles and military operations in urban terrain) on the autonomic and gastrointestinal systems.

LARRY H. PASTOR is clinical assistant professor of psychiatry at the George Washington University Medical Center, Washington, DC; adjunct assistant professor of psychiatry at the Uniformed Services University of the Health Sciences in Bethesda, Maryland; and adjunct professor of social, cultural and behavioral studies (psychology) at the American Military University, Charles Town, West Virginia. He is also a major in the U.S. Army Reserves. Dr. Pastor has more than 17 years of experience providing medical support for military operations and has provided expert testimony to federal courts concerning mental health consequences of terrorism. His academic interests include psychiatric effects of state-sponsored terrorism, risk factors for suicidal and assaultive behavior, and disaster and trauma psychiatry.

EDUARDO SALAS is trustee chair and professor of psychology in the Department of Psychology and the Institute for Simulation & Training at the University of Central Florida. He has over 20 years of research experience on team training, simulation-based training, and training effectiveness, and he has published over 300 articles, chapters, and papers on those topics.

DYLAN SCHMORROW is a U.S. Naval commander and is an aerospace experimental psychologist in the Navy's Medical Service Corps. He is a program manager serving at the Defense Advanced Research Projects Agency (DARPA) where he is responsible for executing cutting-edge basic science and technology development. In this role, he supports DARPA's mission to create and foster imaginative, innovative, and often high-risk research ideas yielding revolutionary technological advances in science and technology in support of the U.S. military.

GUY L. SIEBOLD is a research psychologist in the Force Stabilization Research Unit, U.S. Army Research Institute for the Behavioral & Social Sciences, with three decades of experience conducting psychological and sociological research on military issues. His publications focus on training, unit dynamics, and personnel matters with special emphasis on training as a military advantage, language training, cohesion, motivation, leadership, and morale. Dr. Siebold completed four years in the Air Force, including a tour in Vietnam. He holds both a law degree and a doctoral degree in social psychology.

ROBERT R. SINCLAIR is an assistant professor of industrial/organizational psychology and assistant director of the occupational health psychology program in the Department of Psychology at Portland State University. His research examines personal and contextual factors that influence the employee–employer relationship and individual and group differences in how people respond to stressful events. Prior to entering academia he was a member of the U.S. Marine Corps. Currently, he provides consultation to the WRAIR on the design and analysis of occupational health and organizational climate assessments.

JENNIFER S. TUCKER is a Ph.D. candidate in industrial/organizational psychology at Portland State University. She is employed as a research psychologist at the U.S. Army Research Institute, Infantry Forces Unit, Fort Benning, Georgia. Her research interests include the multilevel effects of stress on employees' health and performance. Prior to entering graduate school she served in the U.S. Air Force.

NANCY J. WESENSTEN is a research psychologist in the Department of Behavioral Biology, Division of Psychiatry and Neuroscience, WRAIR. Her most recent publications have focused on stimulant countermeasures for improving alertness and operationally relevant aspects of cognitive performance during continuous operations.